D1353707

British Superbikes

British Superbikes

The story and spectacle of BSB

By **Gary Pinchin** Foreword by **Niall Mackenzie**

Haynes Publishing
www.haynes.co.uk

Published in March 2006

A catalogue record for this book is available from the British Library

ISBN 1 84425 211 6

Library of Congress catalog card no. 9004117163

Haynes Publishing, Sparkford, Yeovil, Somerset BA22 7JJ, UK
Tel: +44 (0) 1963 442030
Fax: +44 (0) 1963 440001
E-mail: sales@haynes.co.uk
Website: www.haynes.co.uk

Haynes North America, Inc.,
861 Lawrence Drive, Newbury Park, California 91320, USA

Designed by Richard Parsons

Printed and bound by J.H.Haynes & Co Ltd, Sparkford, Yeovil, Somerset BA22 7JJ, UK

CONTENTS

RIGHT 2004 BSB Champion John Reynolds hard at work on the Rizla Suzuki GSX-R1000 during the early part of the 2005 season

ABOVE Niall Mackenzie spent 11 years in GPs before returning to BSB in 1996. It showed

ACKNOWLEDGEMENTS

One way or another I've followed British Superbike racing since the seventies when it was known as the *Motor Cycle News* Superbike Championship.

Back then I was part of a small group of bikers from a Wiltshire village who used to ride all over the country following the series.

Little did I realise I'd still be doing the same thing almost 30 years later – albeit on a slightly different level.

Since the series underwent a massive revamp in 1996, BSB has enjoyed incredible growth to become the world's premier superbike championship.

After each season it's almost unbelievable the racing can get any better, but it always does and that's a testament to the people driving the series and the teams and riders who put so much effort into producing this world-class show. I'm just proud to be part of it.

Covering the championship over the past five years for *Motor Cycle News* has given me unrivalled access to the sport's biggest names, but I've met so many wonderful people over the years and would like to say a big thank you to everyone: the riders and their wives or girlfriends, mechanics, team bosses, sponsors, and series organisers who have all given me the time of day to stop and talk racing. Guys, you've not only made my job a lot easier over the years, you've also made it fun.

I've known James Wright of Double Red ever since 1992 when we worked together on a Yamaha publicity magazine supplement for a small, independent racing mag I edited called *RPM*. I can't thank him enough for access to their huge library – or for their hospitality every race weekend. Keep the Rolo biscuits coming Sue!

Thanks also to Dave Fern, BSB Press Officer, and the only person I could trust to proof-read this book. Dave is a top journalist cranking out copy for the nationals each week and has been around BSB almost as long as I have. I can't think of anyone who has helped me more, week in, week out, to make sure I hit the *MCN* deadlines on a Sunday night. He's also a key figure in Lullington Cricket Club and a lifelong Burton Albion footy fan!

Finally, the biggest thanks of all have to go to my wife Angela and our four boys Joseph, Tyler, Zak and Kelly, for putting up with my crazy lifestyle that has taken me away for so many weekends every year.

GARY PINCHIN
MARCH, 2006

FOREWORD

By the autumn of 1995 I had spent eleven years in Grand Prix racing. Around the same time my second son was born so I knew I should stay at home and take care of my family.

I had always hoped to finish my career with one season in Britain, mainly because I really enjoyed my early years of racing in the UK and wanted to revisit the tracks one last time.

It turned out to be perfect timing for me as Robert Fearnall was aiming to re-launch the British Superbike Championship to create the series as we know it today.

Five years later it really was time to hang up my leathers, but bagging three titles along the way with the superb Cadbury's Boost Yamaha team gave my career the perfect Indian summer.

I am very grateful for what BSB has given me and I'm delighted to see it still going from strength to strength.

NIALL MACKENZIE
BSB CHAMPION 1996, 1997, 1998

BELOW After the toughest scrap yet, title number three

97
9
Silkolene
MICHELIN
SHARPLES
Arai
FM

INTRO

The early days of British Superbikes

Superbike racing began in Britain in 1971 when Motor Circuit Developments (MCD) and the weekly newspaper *Motor Cycle News* joined forces to promote the first-ever *MCN* Superbike Championship.

MCD owned four of the major tracks in the UK at the time and with the power of *MCN* they formed a powerful promotional partnership to help develop a whole new brand of bike sport.

In 34 seasons of racing since then the regulations governing the series might have changed radically but the British Superbike Championship (these days known simply as BSB by the cognoscenti) has never been more popular, or prestigious, than in recent years.

In the past eleven seasons of BSB the class has enjoyed real stability and direction that has allowed it to grow into the massive televised road show that everyone knows and loves. The reason for the success can largely be put down to a change of management. More precisely, promotion of the series was taken out of the hands of the old-school, conservative committee-led Auto Cycle Union (the ACU is the governing body of motorcycle sport in the UK) by the circuit promoters and subsequently has flourished in a way very few thought possible.

Ironically for many years the development of British Superbike racing followed American trends but recent times have seen the series grow in stature to the point where it is Britain setting the direction with some manufacturers preferring to race on UK circuits rather than in a turbulent World Superbike Championship that was crippled by the promoters adopting regulations contrary to the ideals of those manufacturers.

AMERICAN INFLUENCE

Back in 1971 the inaugural six-round *MCN* Superbike series was for Formula 750-type machines, a new category of racing devised by the Americans in 1969.

At that time the American Motorcyclists Association (AMA) was not part of the international bike racing

PREVIOUS PAGE Carl Fogarty (No.9) raced a Honda RC30 in BSB. He takes the inside line on Ray Stringer and Kawasaki's John Reynolds at the Mallory Hairpin during the non-BSB Transatlantic Match Races. Stringer is using an FZR1000 engine in his OWO1 for this meeting instead of his usual 750 (Photo courtesy *MCN* Archive)

ABOVE Origins of the superbike species. Formula 750-style line-up at Brands Hatch with Peter Williams sat on the original lowboy Norton he designed and developed. Sat next to him is Paul Smart on a works Triumph Trident (Photo courtesy *MCN* Archive)

governing body, the Federation Internationale de Motorcyclisme (FIM), and their sport had developed in a totally different direction to that in Europe.

While World Championship racing was separated into different disciplines with Grand Prix road racing regarded as the blue riband category of the sport, the Americans predominately raced on the plentiful supply of dirt track ovals at county fairgrounds all over the country. What little road racing there was took place on some very make-shift road courses that sometimes did not even include metalled surfaces and the bikes used were often high-barred dirt trackers bearing little resemblance to the highly-specialised, fully-faired GP exotica raced in Europe!

Road racing formed a minority part of the AMA Grand National series and even the course used for the championship's most prestigious event, the Daytona 200, incorporated a large section of the beach until 1960 when it moved to Daytona International Speedway and ran on a two mile road course. It was not until 1964 that the race was switched to the high-banked 3.81 mile circuit at a two and a half mile oval 'superspeedway' built primarily to host the jewel in the NASCAR stock car schedule, the Daytona 500. The motorcycle racing course incorporated part of the oval but also included a tighter infield section.

In addition to road racing, the AMA Grand National Championship covered four other disciplines of bike sport – mile and half-mile flat track (on dirt ovals), short track (on quarter-mile dirt ovals), Tourist Trophy (dubbed TT and based on dirt ovals but with infield corners and usually incorporating a jump) so the American racers were all-rounders with an ability to drift a motorcycle at high speed. Prior to 1969 AMA regulations, known as Class C, dictated that the bikes have production-based power units but limited overhead valve (ohv) engines to 500cc and permitted side-valve (ie Harley-Davidson) engines a top limit of 750cc. But from 1969 they opened up the dirt track class to 750cc across the board regardless of whether it was ohv, side-valve and didn't even make any distinction between four-strokes or two-strokes.

Their road racing rules weren't changed until the 1970 season but what a difference it made to motorcycle racing when they did – not just in the States but worldwide.

Even though the AMA was formed in 1924 it was not until 1970 that they finally became affiliated to the FIM. It was this move – and the new-look AMA rules – that gave motorcycle racing a bigger opportunity to expand across the globe.

GRAND PRIX DECLINE

At that time World Championship Grand Prix racing – much more a European-based series than the global circus it is now – was at a low ebb after the Japanese manufacturers, led by Honda, had withdrawn their factory support.

The European economy was being ravaged by sky-rocketing inflation, which meant new pure-bred road racing machines, and the spares to run them, were becoming prohibitively expensive.

By the turn of the decade the small Italian MV Agusta factory dominated 500 GPs with their exotic multis against a grid of enthusiastic privateers on predominantly British single-cylinder machines and a few two-stroke specials.

America, on the other hand, was experiencing a massive boom in motorcycling. The bikes raced there were very different – all based on a plentiful supply of production machinery. It was relatively easy and affordable for anyone to have a go at racing. Also there was a massive incentive for manufacturers and dealerships to compete in bike sport because it was a good way of promoting their business to the fans. 'Win on Sunday, sell on Monday' was the catch-phrase of US racing.

The AMA rule changes prompted Harley to develop a new ohv V-twin engine, known as the XR750 (initially with iron cylinder heads and later with aluminium ones), but also encouraged other manufacturers into the sport.

On the dirt track ovals it meant the Harleys faced much stiffer opposition from Triumph with their T120 Bonneville-based twin, BSA with the A65 Lightning twin, Norton's 750cc Commando and even Yamaha used the series to promote their first-ever four-stroke road bike, the XS650 twin.

However when the road racing regulations changed a year later it paved the way for even more diversification of machinery and a flood of interest from manufacturers.

Harley's Cal Rayborn won the 1969 Daytona 200 on an old KRTT side-valve with Ron Grant second on a 500cc Suzuki two-stroke twin and former GP star Mike Duff (who later became Michelle after his racing career ended) on a 350cc Yamaha, another two-stroke twin. That year there were just five road races in the Grand National series but already the Japanese two-stroke manufacturers were fielding factory-backed riders to promote their products.

FORMULA 750 LAUNCHED

The world's first real superbike road machines came in 1970 – a dramatic period in motorcycling evolution when the established manufacturers, particularly the British industry, suddenly woke up to the fact that the might of the Far East was a very serious threat to their business.

The Japanese had already begun infiltrating the bike industry with small capacity machines but their complacent rivals received a massive shock when Honda launched their incredibly complex overhead cam CB750 four at the Tokyo Show in the autumn of 1968. This was the first machine that really warranted the 'superbike' tag.

By contrast Britain's responses were the Triumph Trident and BSA's similar Rocket 3 triple (Triumph and BSA were part of the same company by then) – based on old pushrod twin designs and completely blown into insignificance by the new Honda.

To hammer home the message even harder, Honda built a brace of very special factory-kitted CB750s for the 1970 Daytona 200 where Dick Mann gave the Japanese a dream winning debut – beating a pair of Tridents ridden by Gene Romero and Don Castro.

BELOW Americans brought F750 to Europe. This is Cal Rayborn (right) on the grid at the Mallory Race of the Year with his factory Harley-Davidson XR750 V-twin four-stroke. To his left is Flying Finn Jarno Saarinen on a 350 Yamaha two-stroke twin (Photo courtesy *MCN* Archive)

The first race to similar F-750 rules in the UK was the end of season Race of the South at Brands Hatch won by Paul Smart from Ray Pickrell and Percy Tait, all three of them Triumph factory riders.

The following year saw the launch of the Anglo-American series, backed by Triumph/BSA to promote the triples and run by the enthusiastic MCD management who saw the potential to draw crowds to their circuits. A team of Americans brought their factory bikes to the UK to race the British works riders over the Easter weekend at Brands Hatch, Mallory Park and Oulton Park. No one gave the Americans much of a chance since they had little experience of road racing and had not even raced in the wet, yet riders like Mann (back on a BSA), Don Emde, David Aldana, Jim Rice and Don Castro gave a good account of themselves (even though the latter three had less than two dozen road races between them). Over 60,000 fans cheered a British victory and it kick-started an annual battle that would endure until the Eighties.

By 1971 the AMA road racing portion of their national series had grown to seven races. Mann won Daytona this time on a BSA triple and also took Kent, and Pocono. Brit John Cooper won the end of season Ontario, California race also on a BSA – but Harley, Kawasaki with their old 500cc triple and Yamaha (Kel Carruthers on a 350 twin) also scored wins to illustrate the amount of diverse machinery F-750 attracted. Other manufacturers represented in the series included Triumph (with twins as well as triples), Norton, BMW with their old flat-twin, and Suzuki with their 500 twin two-stroke.

In his book *Racing Motor Cycles*, published in 1973, Mick Woollett opened a chapter called 'The American Scene' by saying: "Undoubtedly the most significant development in motorcycle sport in the early 1970s was the progress that road racing made in the United States, and the effects that this had on European racing."

BRITISH SUPERBIKES

The growth of the US racing scene was not going unnoticed in Britain. Chris Lowe, then the Motorcycle Racing Director of MCD was poised and ready to seize on a golden opportunity to adopt the new, less expensive, vibrant brand of bike racing. It also had more in common with the type of motorcycles people were riding on the street. It was the very ethos that is still the cornerstone of modern superbike racing.

The howl of the triples from the 1971 Match Races could still be heard echoing as Lowe announced the brand new British Superbike series in *MCN*.

At the time MCD owned the most prestigious tracks in the UK and was desperately looking for a vibrant new product to encourage race-fans through the turnstiles at Brands Hatch in Kent; Mallory Park in Leicestershire; Oulton Park in Cheshire and Snetterton in Norfolk.

The story of the new British Superbike Championship made the 14 April front page lead of the then sports-orientated *MCN* – the week following the Anglo American Races. Lowe, discussing the exciting new concept of F-750 told the readers: "This is the best thing we have had in motorcycle racing for years. After what

BELOW Early F750 racing pitted 350 Yamaha two-stroke twins against the 750 four-strokes. This is Yamaha's Daytona line-up from 1972 Number 60 is a very young Kenny Roberts. Full works line-up (left to right): 73 Kel Carruthers, 60 Kenny Roberts, 21 Pat Evans, 19 Keith Mashburn, 18 Jim Odom and 7 unknown junior rider (Photo courtesy *MCN* Archive)

ABOVE Peter Williams on the John Player Norton. The 750cc four-stroke twin Commando-based racer remained competitive against the onslaught of more powerful Japanese two-strokes thanks to Williams' genius chassis and aerodynamics design ideas (Photo courtesy *MCN* Archive)

LEFT John Cooper – first-ever *MCN* Superbike Champion in 1973 on a BSA Rocket III (Photo courtesy *MCN* Archive)

we have seen this weekend (in the Match races) I can be sure that we will have some terrific racing."

Robin Miller was the Editor of *MCN* at that time and he added his vote of confidence for the class in his weekly 'Opinion' column: "This is an attempt to boost the new Formula 750 which we believe is a great step forward (for motorcycle racing worldwide). The championship will give manufacturers and constructors a chance to take part in big bike racing at big meetings as an introduction to the stricter rules of F-750 next year.

"We hope it will provide something even better with a challenge to Triumph and BSA from other manufacturers, including Norton Villiers (Norvil). There is over £2,000 to be won in this series. It should be quite a fight."

The series prize fund might not sound a lot now but was the equivalent of £25,000 then and certainly captured the imagination of riders, teams, manufacturers and, probably most important of all, the fans.

Historically most domestic racing in Europe followed GP trends so that meant the British Championship concentrated on the traditional classes: 125cc (Ultra-Lightweight), 250cc (Lightweight), 350cc (Junior), and 500cc (Senior). There was also a healthy interest in the bigger bikes too. This was not just for pure production racing but also for open class 1,000cc race bikes developed from the 'proddie' machines available from the established British bike manufacturers like Triumph, BSA, and Norton and also from major dealerships wanting to promote their names.

ABOVE Percy Tait on the works Triumph Trident. The British company was at the forefront of the original superbike movement (Photo courtesy *MCN* Archive)

The one encouragement for prospective entrants was that the full F-750 regulations would not be implemented until 1972 because the promoters felt no one had enough time to prepare new bikes to suit them. Instead the series would run to a much looser 501–750cc format with stricter homologation rules waived.

The *MCN* series captured everyone's imagination and the paper's preview in their 21 April issue said it all in quotes from leading industry figures. The Engineering Director of BSA Triumph commented: "The series can do nothing but help the breed. For the best development is that carried out under proper racing conditions."

Norvil Managing Director Peter Inchley agreed and was itching to show how competitive their new twin-cylinder Commando-based racer could be against the Triumph/BSA triples. He said: "I'm sure we'd be a match for the three-cylinders bikes." At that time no one knew that their rider Peter Williams – a gifted engineer in his own right – was busy building a new low-boy framed Commando specifically for the series.

London-based Norton dealers Gus Kuhn planned to run Charlie Sanby on one of their Commandos in the series. Managing Director Vincent Davey said: "We'll contest all the rounds. Considering the money spent by Triumph BSA on their Daytona threes it is like us sprinting in bare feet. None the less we do not feel overwhelmed and expect to do battle against tremendous odds."

Boyers was a Triumph dealer in Bromley, Kent and their director Stan Shenton added: "This series is a splendid idea and should help expand the 750cc racing class. I shall be pleased to enter two bikes, one of which will be a new three cylinder (Triumph)." Dave Nixon and Paul Butler rode for the Boyers Team.

The British *MCN* series was a huge success, although Triumph/BSA triples won every single race. Percy Tait clinched the title for Triumph from BSA's Ray Pickrell by just three points.

BSA's John Cooper also won the Mallory Race of the Year – a non-championship race run outside F-750 rules. But the fact that he managed to defeat World Champion Giacomo Agostini and the legendary 500cc MV Agusta triple showed just how competitive the production-based pushrod 750s had become when compared to the far more exotic GP multis.

But already the tide was turning for the four-strokes. Triumph/BSA were in financial difficulty and if their future looked bleak according to the balance sheets – it was even bleaker on the race track.

Former BSA factory rider Don Emde won the 1972 Daytona 200 as a privateer; Yamaha 350 twin two-strokes filled the top three places. But it was the arrival of two new 750cc two-strokes from their Japanese rivals that would ultimately sound the death-knell for the four-strokes.

Kawasaki's wild new 750 air-cooled triple and Suzuki's GT750 water-cooled three-cylinder tourer both provided good starting points for race-based projects. Neither had remarkably impressive chassis, in fact the early versions became known as flexi flyers because they handled so badly, but the power delivery, particularly that of the Kawasaki, was simply awesome. That they didn't win the 1972 Daytona was irrelevant. Their time would come.

Tobacco company John Player backed the new Norton team for the 1972 British series with an even more advanced version of the low-boy Commando designed by racer Peter Williams. Despite a lack of top end power the bike was kept competitive with some innovative Williams' ideas that produced a very small, well-packaged, aerodynamically-efficient machine.

Former World Champion Phil Read finished fourth at Daytona on the bike's debut – an impressive performance considering how much down on top speed the bike actually was against the new breed of Japanese superbikes. Williams finished third in the *MCN* Superbike series beaten by Triumph/BSA factory riders Cooper and Ray Pickrell.

WORLD SERIES

In 1973 the FIM finally acknowledged the growing class by establishing the FIM Formula 750 Championship and Barry Sheene won the title on a 750cc Suzuki triple from Yamaha TZ350 privateer John Dodds. The very same year saw the first US event billed as Superbike at Laguna Seca, promoted by Gavin Trippe and Bruce Cox.

Many thought the World F-750 series would bring the factories flooding back in 1974 but Yamaha decided to go the GP route the same year, with Jarno Saarinen and Tuevo 'Tepi' Lansivouri competing against the might of MV Agusta with a pair of very special OW19 four-cylinder 500cc two-strokes.

LEFT Freddie Spencer at Daytona on a CB750-based Honda superbike. The sit-up and beg production-based bikes were a thrilling antidote to a F750 formula stagnated by the dominance of the TZ750 Yamahas. (Photo courtesy *MCN* Archive)

Suzuki followed a year later with their RG500 square-four two-stroke so instead of taking over as the blue riband series, F-750 continued as an alternative championship with only limited factory support.

Where F-750 really scored was at domestic level because the production-based bikes were readily available and relatively affordable.

The undoing of the class was that FIM regulations required only 200 machines be produced to meet homologation. It was what the Brits wanted when the series began, a formula to work to with their four-strokes, but as soon as there is a rule-book, there will be engineers and tuners trying to figure loopholes to get the edge on their rivals.

BELOW One of the great rivalries in early *MCN* superbike days: Mick Grant (750cc Kawasaki two-stroke triple) leads Barry Sheene's square-four two-stroke Suzuki at Mallory in 1978 (Photo courtesy *MCN* Archive)

While Kawasaki and Suzuki used the rules to develop highly-competitive racers from their three-cylinder two-stroke road bikes, Yamaha came at it from a different angle. They created the TZ750 – a brand new bike with no conceivable link to any road bike in their range but produced 200 models to meet homologation. It was a fearsomely powerful, 700cc (which later grew to a full 750cc) four-cylinder, two-stroke, and developed specifically with F-750 in mind.

The 100bhp monster changed the face of F-750 overnight when it made a racing debut in 1974 and Giacomo Agostini won the Daytona 200 (decided over 180 miles that year in compliance with the government's request to economise due to a national fuel crisis).

The bike was fast, tractable and reliable – and quickly became the cornerstone of large capacity racing throughout the world. It offered pure privateers an opportunity to be seriously competitive with all but the very best of the factory versions of the same model.

The TZ750 was so good that Yamaha won the world series every year until it's demise in 1979, by which time rival manufacturer interest had virtually disappeared. In their Autumn Congress of 1978, the FIM announced that the series would no longer enjoy World Championship status from 1980 and that was the death-knell.

In the 1978 *Motocourse* F-750 season review Editor Barry Coleman sneered: "The FIM were sold the idea of 750 racing by the ACU who were enchanted by Doug Hele's (Triumph/BSA's) multi-purpose three – a good road bike and a really fruity racer. A world series for 750s. What a wonderful idea – and so much better if it were run to a formula connecting road to track. It would make manufacturers take it seriously.

"Suzuki did join in (and so terminated the career of Hele's threes) and because it suited them they stuck to the rules.

"Yamaha, like Suzuki love rules because they see it as a kind of challenge. Suzuki saw it as a way to make their road bike faster. Yamaha, with greater production resources, saw it as a way of leap-frogging the homologation requirements. They simply made more racers than the coy rule-makers anticipated. It was easy to see how, by the beginning of 1978 we were looking at a field composed entirely of Yamahas."

The Americans saw the demise of F-750 coming. Like the world series, their national road races had effectively become a one-make TZ750 event so in 1976 they created a new superbike championship, totally separate from their national road racing class, which continued to run to F-750 rules. Superbike was based solely on four-stroke production machines and can be seen as the forerunner to today's successful category bearing the same name.

MCLAUGHLIN'S SUPERBIKE CONCEPT

Professional racer Steve McLaughlin drafted the regulations with help from his race tuner Jerry Branch. McLaughlin, whose outspoken character earned him the nickname 'Motormouth', is probably the most important figure in the history of superbike racing. He had served for eight years as the AMA rider's representative and formed the basic concept of the superbike class after meeting Aussie racer Warren Willing in the States. He told McLaughlin about the production-based superbike class that had run in Australia until 1971.

The difference with McLaughlin's new format compared to the old F-750 rules was, instead of being the fully faired racers, the majority of the production superbikes then had high-bars and limited, or sometimes, no bodywork (bikes like the Z1000 Kawasaki or Suzuki GS1000) so that's how they had to be raced.

It was fitting that McLaughlin won the Daytona round riding a BMW, a flat-twin BMW R90S. He beat his team-mate and ex-pat Brit Reg Pridmore in a photo-finish on the banking that day, but 'Reggo' won the inaugural four-race series after taking wins at Laguna Seca and Riverside in California. Mike Baldwin won the Loudon, New Hampshire race on a Moto Guzzi. But the Japanese fours would soon come to dominate.

The AMA continued to run races for F-750 bikes but the class had now become Formula One catering for GP500 as well as the 'dinosaur' 750 machines. Then they began allowing ridiculously-expensive four-strokes like Honda's V-four FWS1000 – but incorporating all sorts of hard to implement restrictor rules to handicap these new, more powerful bikes.

At the end of 1986 the AMA finally dumped F1 and made Superbike their sole premier class.

British superbike racing was also seriously affected by the fate of the F-750 world series but did not react quite like the Americans. The writing was on the wall however in 1976 when Sheene ditched his 750 Suzuki mid-term to clinch the title on a more competitive 540cc square four – a bigger capacity version of his factory GP500 that he won the World title on.

The *MCN* British Superbike Championship continued to run on a bastardised set of F-750 rules (simply 351–1,300cc with three or more cylinders) until 1982 and the following year was renamed the *MCN* Masters (but largely ran to the same rules).

In the 1979 review of the *MCN* Superbike Championship Editor Bob Berry said: "There will be interest in the 750 class for some time to come yet, and enough competitive 750 machines to maintain the expected high level of the championship. The series was started for superbikes and that's what we intend for the future.

"We are confident the superbikes will be able to continue with a similar format for some time to come, although we shall always be on the lookout for alternatives if the need to make changes becomes a necessity."

Berry was said to be vehemently against big-capacity four-strokes but he was right about the quantity of 750

ABOVE The 1988 British title went to Darren Dixon on the Padgetts Suzuki RG500. Here he leads the works Suzuki GSX-R750s of James Whitham and Phil Mellor at Thruxton (Photo courtesy *MCN* Archive)

OPPOSITE Roger Hurst on the factory Kawasaki 750 in 1988. At that time British Championship racing ran to TT Formula One rules – loosely based on production engines but pretty much a free for all in chassis design (Photo courtesy *MCN* Archive)

machines available to fill the grid. What he and the ACU overlooked was the way British racing had diversified – to the detriment of the domestic sport in general. There were so many classes that no one really knew which one was the premier. Was it the *MCN* series by whatever name, TT Formula One (yet another production-based four-stroke formula initially launched in 1977 to boost flagging interest in the Isle of Man TT races), the ACU British Championship or even the ITV *World of Sport* Challenge?

In 1986 *MCN* put their name to an exciting new concept – Superstock, a Bruce Cox innovation. It was another production-based four-stroke series but tuning was limited and the idea was to feature the new breed of 750cc sportsbikes – the Honda VFR, Kawasaki GPZ, Suzuki GSX-R and Yamaha FZ.

The problem was that while the rules were pitched to keep tuning costs down, they were actually too restrictive and favoured the best bike to come out of the box.

Whichever manufacturer got it right when they first produced the bike tended to dominate the championship to the point of turning it into a one-make series. In 1998 Honda's RC30 V-four won every single round, with Brian Morrison taking all but two of them to clinch the title well before the end of the season. It spelled the end.

WSB ECLIPSES TTF1

A better working model was the FIM World Superbike rule package, based loosely on a mix of the AMA Superbike and British Superstock rules, with a selection of homologated machines, more liberal tuning, and a 1,000cc top limit for twin-cylinder machines to entice Italian manufacturer Ducati into the series although the fours were still restricted to 750cc.

The series began in 1988 and once again it was largely the brainchild of Steve McLaughlin. He saw the class building in America and spun in a few ideas of his own to create a series that rapidly became the world's premier production-based four-stroke racing series totally eclipsing the World TTF1 series, which was run primarily on public roads.

BELOW Rob McElnea did not just race in BSB on a Loctite Yamaha. He also managed the team

The reasons were obvious. TTF1 regulations covered not only the sprint race World Championship but also the World Endurance series that had become dominated by factory bikes like Honda's RVF750. However bikes like this had become too far removed for any production motorcycle. It was the demise of F-750 revisited.

Secondly, WSB was a massive promotional vehicle for the manufacturers. It had rules designed to make it attractive for the smaller firms as well as the Japanese giants. And thanks to the rules there was an intoxicating mix of twin-cylinder and four-cylinder machinery in the field.

To ensure the twins were competitive, McLaughlin's regulations set an upper limit for four-cylinder engines at 750cc but 1,000cc for twins. The twins also got a lower minimum weight limit of 140kg, as opposed to 165kg. The sole reason for this was to encourage Ducati into the championship with their new fuel-injected, four-valve-head, liquid-cooled 851.

Smaller volume manufacturers like them and Bimota, another Italian company, were also given much lower production numbers for homologation with just 200 units required while the large-volume companies such as the big four Japanese firms had to produce 1,000 examples to qualify for the series.

ABOVE Steve Spray became a British hero when he won British titles riding the rotary-engined JPS Norton

Thirdly, the big attraction of WSB was that it was run on FIM-sanctioned short circuits offering much greater circuit safety compared to the road courses favoured by the TTF1 series. Only a few die-hard TT racers complained.

The ACU had invented TTF1 in the first place to inject some World Championship interest back into the annual Isle of Man TT races so it was no surprise they did not embrace WSB rules for some time. Instead it suited them to retain the essence of TTF1 to allow the new Norton rotary into the series. Very much like the later stages of the original F-750-based *MCN* Superbike Championship or the AMA's F1 series, the British Championship became a hot-potch of different types of machinery, which at least presented a technically diverse and therefore interesting array of bikes.

For the '88 season Roger Hurst had a factory F1 Kawasaki, there were GSX-R750 Suzukis for James Whitham and Phil Mellor, exotic, but unreliable fuel-injected Bimota YB4ei's of 'Captain' Mark Phillips and Paul Iddon. Roger Marshall had a ride on the 825cc Quantel Cosworth twin that he had used to win that year's Daytona Pro Twins Grand Prix race. There were countless RC30s.

But the 1988 ACU Shell Oils TTF1 British Championship was won by Darren Dixon on a supposedly obsolete Suzuki RG500 square-four two-stroke. The light, nimble GP bike was more than a match for the heavier four-strokes, though by the end of the year Brian Crighton had developed the Norton rotary from an also-ran to race winner. Trevor Nation won at Cadwell Park and Steve Spray easily beat Dixon in the final round of the year at Brands Hatch.

The trouble was that while the F1 title did enjoy something of a revival it was lost in a morass of different

ABOVE John Reynolds won the British title in 1992 on a Kawasaki

championships with seemingly no structure. Among this wide ranging array of titles to be won, there was the TTF1, Superstock, Junior (250GP bikes), Production, Juniorstock, Seniorstock, Open sidecars, F2 sidecars. No less than eight British crowns to be won over 98 races – little wonder the ACU did not even manage to release the full fixture list until the season had started.

As John Cutts so rightly said in his review of British national racing in the 1988/89 *Motocourse*, "There was a time, many years ago, when the British Championship actually used to mean something. The sad fact is that it has come to count for less and less, a situation not helped by the fact that they change so dramatically with every new season."

For 1989 there was a multi-round British Championship and a five-round Shell Oils Supercup. The *MCN*-backed ACU British Championship featured TTF1, the Supercup had one race for 750cc TTF1 and another for Superbikes, which didn't allow the Nortons. More change – more confusion.

NORTON ROTARY SAVIOUR

The saving grace for the fans was the fact that the Nortons, now resplendent in black and gold livery thanks to JPS tobacco money, were totally dominant in the races they were eligible to race in!

Roland Brown, writing the 'British National Racing Review' in that year's *Motocourse* said: "Norton's success, coupled with some very exciting racing and a healthy dose of television exposure, gave domestic racing an invaluable shot in the arm. Crowds were up almost everywhere. With the Nortons to cheer it seemed to matter less that (Niall) Mackenzie and our other Grand Prix stars were rarely, if ever, seen on home circuits again."

For the following season the two major championships were amalgamated to form the seven-round Shell Supercup for the ACU British Championship and the majority of races were aired on BBC *Grandstand*. The rest of the season was padded out with an 11-round national series.

The JPS Norton team, now managed by former Rothmans Honda boss Barry Symmons, were not as dominant as the previous year but Nation finished third in the championship and Spray fourth to keep the fans entertained. For his efforts Nation topped the annual *MCN* Man of the Year readers' poll.

But it was Terry Rymer riding a Loctite Yamaha OW01 who won the title from Brian Morrison's Honda.

ACU Road Race Chairman Jim Parker admitted in *Motocourse*: "This is the first time for many, many years that the British Championship has really meant something. We've now got riders who are not going abroad to race but are preferring to stay at home and do our British Championship – and that's absolutely marvellous."

For 1991 the Supercup was still the predominant series but reduced to six rounds. Instead of concentrating every ounce of promotional energy on the series for maximum exploitation, the ACU scrapped the lesser national series and brought back a nine-round TT/Superbike Challenge, backed by *MCN*!

Despite the utter confusion of having two major titles again, the field was getting stronger. As well as the Loctite squad of Rymer and Rob McElnea, James Whitham was back with Suzuki on a very trick F1-spec GSX-R750, John Reynolds and King of Brands Tim Bourne were on Kawasakis, plus Silkolene Honda men Niall Mackenzie, Roger Burnett and occasionally Carl Fogarty when his WSB commitments allowed. Norton continued with their infamous rotary engine but had a new rolling chassis, designed by Symmons' former Rothmans Honda sidekick Ron Williams. He was better known as the boss of Maxton, a company renowned in the racing paddock for their race suspension service. Norton brought 'Rocket' Ron Haslam back from World Championship Grand Prix action to lead the team. This was a massive coup for the series.

As Nation struggled with injuries, Haslam reaffirmed the hero status with British race fans he enjoyed as a Grand Prix star by battling his way to runner-up place in the Supercup championship. Another ex-GP man Rob McElnea won the title on the Loctite Yamaha OW01.

Sadly, Haslam was unable to build on his successful return to the UK in the following season. Three rounds into the series he smashed his leg at Snetterton and was sidelined for six months. The blow was offset briefly when Terry Rymer stepped in to replace him with a winning double at Donington Park but endurance commitments kept the Londoner from making any real title challenge.

John Reynolds took both titles in 1992 for Kawasaki but he went GP500 racing with a Padgetts Yamaha in 1993. James Whitham won both British Championships on a Fast Orange-backed Yamaha YZF750, although Jim Moodie showed there was still plenty of fire left in the Norton rotary, albeit a totally different machine to the final Ron Williams-inspired version.

Moodie's Duckham's-backed bike was an update of the Roton originally built for the 1991 season by Brian Crighton – the original Norton rotary race engineer. The quirky bike featured an old-fashioned and unfashionable twin-shock, twin-spar aluminium frame fabricated by Spondon but it handled like a dream and was as fast as any of the more conventional superbikes.

The team was run by Colin Seeley who failed to get any real support from the ailing Norton factory so was forced to call in favours from old friends in the industry to finance the season's racing.

BRITISH RACING RATIONALISED

To bring some semblance of order and rationality into the British racing scene, the people at the financial sharp end, the circuit owners, through their 'Motorcycle Racing Promoters Committee (MRPC)' finally pressured the ACU to sort the mess out for the 1994 season.

The result was one 11-round Supercup Championship headlined by the TT Superbike class. The number

BELOW James Whitham – forever spectacular. This is 1993 on a Fast Orange Yamaha

ABOVE The final Duckhams Norton team line-up (left to right) with Colin Seeley (Team Manager), Dave Hickman (Technician), Jim Moodie (Rider), Brian Crighton (Chief Engineer) and Craig Webb (Technician). Crighton was the gifted engineer who turned the police bike into a title-winning superbike and Seeley brought a new professionalism to the series

BELOW Ian Simpson – BSB champion in 1994 on the Duckhams Norton

of races however created problems with television coverage. The BBC preferred to show an entire championship and 11 rounds was simply too much for their schedule at that time. They screened just four races and the series backers, Heat Electric Advisory Service (HEAT), opted to put money into the televised rounds only – even though they had backed the entire Supercup the previous year.

The Norton was now the bike to beat. Moodie had gone to ride for the revamped Loctite Yamaha team (which had worn Fast Orange livery the previous year) so Seeley signed Phil Borley and Ian Simpson – both well respected supersport 600 riders (Borley was the 1992 British Champion) but both under-rated on superbikes.

But by the end of the year, Simpson had won the title from Moodie, with Borley third after a clutch problem robbed him of the runner-up spot in the final round at Brands. The Norton duo scored no less than 31 podiums between them, including 14 race wins and they finished first and second no less than 11 times in the 11 round, 22 race series.

Despite the unparalleled success of the British bike it did little to encourage fans to the meetings. There were around 12,500 at Cadwell on August Bank Holiday Monday but most of the meetings never broke into five figures – in fact 4–5,000 crowds were the norm.

What British racing needed was vibrant new promotion, former GP heroes, and factory bikes to really give the championship a kick up the backside. And that was just around the corner.

POLITICAL CHANGE

On March 20, 1995 the Motorcycle Circuit Control Board took over major bike racing in the United Kingdom from the Auto Cycle Union.

It was a move that helped reshape the entire face of road racing in this country and is largely responsible for the massively successful, high-profile British Superbike Championship we now enjoy.

The MCRCB assumed control of the '95 Supercup series (which included British Superbike), the BBC-televised International Superbike series, and the National Cup. The MCRCB secretariat was also employed to plan the British Grand Prix, and both British rounds of the World Superbike Championships, although these races remained under the auspices of the ACU.

The MCRCB was run from an office at Donington Park, managed by Doug Barnfield (a former ACU man) with secretary Claire Fennell.

A limited company, the MCRCB consisted of four directors: John Quemby of the RACMSA who was the chairman of the MCRB Board, Robert Fearnall representing ARMCO (Association of Circuit Owners), Nicola Foulston representing the MRPC (Motorcycle Race Promoters Committee) and Bill Rawlinson representing the ACU (he was the ACU Chairman). ACU Road Racing Committee Chairman Jim Parker was appointed Clerk of the Course for all meetings run by the MCRCB.

The MCRB was forced into taking over British Championship motorcycle racing on the country's permanent circuits by the lack of commercial and promotional drive coupled with a blinkered 'racing for all' attitude shown by the ACU. Rather than create one well-defined, high profile superbike class they seemed to prefer to organise as many classes as possible and award them British title status.

Their last-minute announcements of race calendars and constant meddling with championship formats had also undermined the sport and left the circuits' owners concerned about their future livelihood. Fearnall, then the entrepreneurial boss of Donington Park, told *RPM* magazine in April '95: "The owners of permanent circuits need stability for motorcycle racing and to safeguard their investment. In 1995 they have committed £370,000 in prize money for the three major championships. No longer is it possible to be left in the hands of a committee whose membership and chairmanship can be changed every year at the whim of n[illegible]y politics."

By the time the MCRCB had assumed control of the series, it was too late to have any major effect on the 1995 British Superbike Championship except to add the new Triumph Speed Triple Challenge with its lucrative £75,000 prize fund to the programme.

In fact, Barnfield admitted at the time that it was unlikely anyone would see major changes in British racing for at least three years, though the MCRCB planned to announce their 1996 plans mid-way through the middle of the 1995 season. That, in itself, was a major step forward in planning compared to the pedestrian methods of the ACU.

There were fears that one-make racing, with the corresponding big bucks from the relevant manufacturer would come to dominate British racing but the MCRCB pledged to maintain the traditional racing classes: Superbikes, Supersport, GP250, GP125, with the smaller classes seen as vital feeders to BSB. However they also admitted that certain one-make championships might be viewed by paying customers as good entertainment value.

Entertainment was a keyword in the MCRCB's new initiative. They followed the guidelines of 'Racing Ahead', a document drawn up by the RACMSA (the governing body for car motorsport in the UK), the ACU, circuits and organisers to improve presentation and promotion of race meetings for cars and bikes. The aim at Supercup events was to offer more racing with the 125s and 250s given two races, instead of one, to fall into line with Superbikes. The MCRCB also pledged more professionally run meetings – and more variety at some of the lesser National Cup meetings.

Many industry people (and fans) wanted to see the British Superbike Championship develop in the same way as the then highly successful British Touring Car Championship – with its slickly-run meetings, high-profile teams, massive hospitality village, and captivating TV highlights programme.

The MCRCB voiced optimism that the amount of TV coverage for BSB would increase, once the series found stability and the levels of presentation were improved to match that of Touring Cars.

Fearnall added: "The circuit promoters have sat back long enough and let their investment be directed and run by whoever was 'in' at the ACU Road Race Committee at the time. The permanent circuit owners are committed and recognise that motorcycle racing can have a bright future indeed, but only by being in [illegible]rge of our own theatres."

Arai
LOOKWELL
11
2

1995

Hislop's title heralds new era

There may have been a radical shake up in the behind-the-scenes politics for 1995 but the attention paid to the series by the people who mattered most – the paying public – showed just how much of an uphill battle the promoters faced to take British superbike racing to the next level.

In the same season that a record 45,000 fans flocked to Brands Hatch in August to savour Carl Fogarty's double win in the World Superbike Championship round, just 4,000 people bothered to go to the last round of the British series at the same venue one month later.

That was pretty much the best turn-out for the majority of the rounds, although Cadwell Park continued to be the best attended British national meeting of the year with 10,000 spectators although even that figure was some 2,500 down on the previous year's estimates.

One problem was lack of focus. There was not one major British Superbike series, but two separate championships, each catering for superbikes, in 1995. The British Supercup was run over seven rounds and featured five different classes headlined by two British Superbike races. The programme also included two races each for the 125cc, 250cc, Supersport 600, and Sidecar classes. Then there was the separate Shell Advance Superbike Trophy run over just three rounds each with two races, starting at Brands Hatch in May, Oulton Park in June and climaxing at Donington Park in September.

The Shell Advance series was run to appease the BBC. They were keen to cover bike racing but the seven-round SuperCup series was too much for them because their scheduling meant they could only show selected races, thus a shorter series, which they could show in its entirety, suited their needs. It meant plenty of action. British race fans were spoilt for choice. They had two lots of British Championship racing (in one form or another) plus two World Superbike Championship races at Donington Park and Brands Hatch, plus the British Grand Prix at Donington Park, not forgetting another second-division National Cup series.

PREVIOUS PAGE Hizzy leads Jim Moodie, James Whitham, Matt Lewellyn, Michael Rutter and Dean Ashton

ABOVE Whitham pushed Hislop all year and was a definite title contender until he fell ill

The SuperCup was heading for a showdown between Steve Hislop and James Whitham – both on Ducati 916s. All year they had been virtually inseparable – even dead-heating at Snetterton but the title fight didn't go to the wire like everyone had hoped. Even though Whitham won the second race at Knockhill on July 9 to close within two points of Hislop in the points chase he complained of feeling tired and listless, something that had affected him for several weeks.

Whitham, given a 'wild-card' entry into the 500cc British Grand Prix, crashed the ROC he was riding during practice and medical tests soon afterwards revealed the worst. He was diagnosed with Hodgkin's disease, cancer of the lymphatic system.

It meant debilitating chemotherapy treatment, but incredibly Whitham attempted to ride at Cadwell in the next SuperCup round. His bravery and determination was beaten by sheer exhaustion and he had to withdraw from the meeting.

That left Hislop clear to take his first British Superbike title but it was not the way the Scot wanted to win it.

In *RPM*, a specialist road racing magazine at that time, Hizzy said: "When I was told Whit had cancer I was gutted. Obviously I felt bad for him. But suddenly I had no one to race either. Winning the championship meant nothing to me."

Ironically, privateer Matt Llewellyn clinched the Shell Advance title in similar fashion when Hislop, the leader in the points, was not able to compete in the final round The Scot complained of numbness in his right hand during the final SuperCup round at Brands Hatch and was diagnosed with a trapped nerve in his neck. That forced him to sit out the third and final Shell Advance round at Donington Park.

SEELEY'S WORKS HONDA BID

Although the politics changed the way the championship was run, there was not any immediate effect on the racing. The front end of the field was impressively strong but there was still no depth to the series and by the time the series ventured north of the border to Knockhill in July there were only 17 riders making the trip.

Pre-season though the top end of the entry list was looking good.

With the demise of the Norton enterprise Colin Seeley's 1994 title-winning Duckhams Norton team moved to Castrol Honda en masse. For this Honda Britain-backed effort Seeley retained the services of 1994 title-winner Ian Simpson and the man who ran him close to the title, Phil Borley. Somehow though, the Honda effort did not spark the same level of interest as the sweet-sounding Nortons had over the previous handful of years.

Chief engineer was again Brian Crighton who had earned an envious reputation as the man who turned a relatively docile police bike into a fire-breathing race winner with the Norton rotary engine.

Now he faced a big challenge with the RC45. Steve Hislop had campaigned the official Castrol-backed bike in 1994 but it was slow and didn't handle. It was only after changing to the Ohlins suspension he had begged for from the start of the year, and switched to engine tuner Tony Scott, that the bike became anything like competitive.

One of the limiting factors of the RC45 engine performance in '94 was its non-programmable injection system – the other was a lack of technical information being fed back from the factory effort in WSB (run by Neil Tuxworth who still manages all of Honda Racing's efforts – including BSB – in the UK).

They fielded Aaron Slight and Doug Polen but struggled all year with a lack of acceleration and massive understeer problems. Some said that the privateer Rumi bike ridden by Simon Crafar, which went to Ohlins suspension, handled better than the Showa-suspended HRC bikes.

Crighton opted to fit a French-made programmable Sodemo unit to his bikes and initiated his own engine development programme.

Stuart Medd's privateer team scored the only Honda RC45 BSB win of 1994, when James Haydon rode an inspired, yet typically aggressive race in appalling wet conditions to finish miles ahead of the competition at Snetterton.

Medd stuck with the Hondas for 1995 but, with 21-year-old Haydon off racing a Harris Yamaha YZR500 in 500cc Grand Prix, they hired 1994 SuperCup runner-up Jim Moodie from Loctite Yamaha and former 250cc British Champion Paul Brown. Medd also employed former Rothmans Honda technician Nick Goodison as crew chief and, like Crighton, he fitted a Sodemo system but turned to Cosworth for help to develop new engine parts.

DEVIMEAD SNAP UP HIZZY

After a difficult first half of the 1994 season with Medd Hondas and then switching to an 888 Ducati with Midlands-based bike shop Devimead, Ray Stringer worked hard all winter with them to build a new two-man team, managed by former touring car team boss Steve Horton.

They signed former Castrol Honda rider Steve Hislop to partner Stringer on brand new 916 Ducatis with Martin Bennett (who later worked in Suzuki's MotoGP team) heading up the team's impressive technical crew.

Hizzy's bike was a 916 Corsa, one of 60 customer races bikes (Matt Llewellyn, Michael Rutter and Dean Ashton had similar bikes) whereas Stringer had a modified 916SP road bike.

The Corsas were delivered with 955cc fully race-tuned engine with racing-spec valve gear, titanium rods, balanced cranks and race cams. The SPs had steel rods and Stringer had to modify his internals to match the spec of the Corsa to go racing. He also fitted a close-ratio gearbox, which was standard on a Corsa.

The frame geometry of the bikes was identical but the Corsa frames were different spec tubing and were TIG welded while the SP's were MIG. The Corsa also came with a lightweight magnesium swing-arm compared to the 20mm longer aluminium one fitted to the SP.

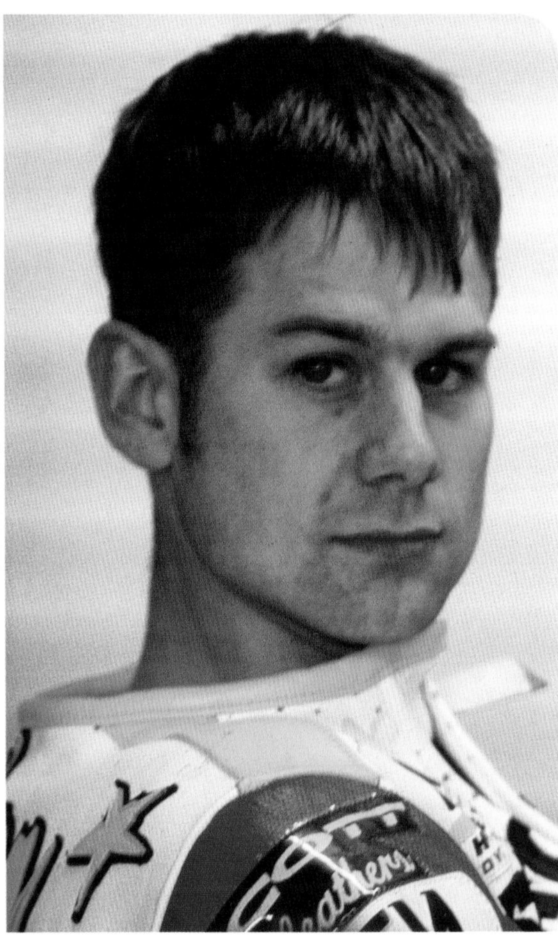

LEFT Whitham in a rare serious moment

BELOW Whitham (leading) raced an ex-WSB 1994 for Moto Cinelli Ducati while Hislop had a 1995 customer 916 Corsa in Devimead colours

The Corsas also came with Ohlins suspension front and rear but Stringer had to swap the stock SP Showa forks for the 46mm Ohlins customer forks (which were one mm longer than those on the Corsa) and ran an EMC shock and made his own Corsa-spec linkage because the stock SP was 20mm further forward than the Corsa's.

The deal was a 'get out of jail' card for Hizzy who had endured a difficult '94 season with the RC45. He had some impressive rides but the critical fuel-injection settings meant that even though Tony Scott had extracted some serious horsepower from the motor, there were days when the bike simply ran flat.

According to the *Motocourse* 1995/96 review of the season Hislop was, "washed up with no offers on the table and a career apparently in tatters. The Devimead deal threw him a lifeline and he grabbed it with both hands."

Hizzy and Stringer were not the only ones on Ducati machinery. In fact the Italian V-twins looked to have the upper hand in numbers before the season even started.

Hizzy's biggest rival looked to be James Whitham on the Rob McElnea-managed Moto Cinelli Ducati. Hoss Elm's Moto Cinelli shop was one of the major Ducati importers and Whitham brought with him the factory 916 he had raced to seventh place overall, including a victory at Sentul, Indonesia in August in the 1994 WSB series.

Michael Rutter, the 24-year-old son of former international racing star Tony, had a pair of privateer Ducatis for the 1995 season, the 926 on which he finished fifth in the SuperCup in '94 which he wanted to keep as a back-up bike, and a brand new 916 – both of them decked out in the bright yellow livery of McCulloch (a chainsaw manufacturer).

Matt Llewellyn was another privateer who had shown his potential on a Ducati 926 in 1994, finishing fourth in the SuperCup on a bike he maintained himself, although he had help from his dad and former racer Mark Phillips's father Derek. Llewellyn's philosophy was to stick rigidly to the manufacturer's specs and service limits and he had one of the most reliable Italian bikes in the series.

For 1995 he switched to one of the new 916s with backing from builder Joe Meakin and Saber, an office furniture company. Llewellyn was also one of the few riders opting to use Dunlop rubber. All his main Ducati rivals and the two Honda teams ran Michelins.

Other Ducati privateers included Baxi Heating-backed Dean Ashton, Andy Hatton riding East Midlands Superbikes and Scot Iain Duffus on an Akito-liveried machine.

Former 500GP privateer Peter Graves finished eighth in the '94 series but ditched his Italian 888 at the end of the year and opted to run a pair of ex-Loctite Yamaha YZF750s instead for himself and Dave Heal with backing from Cadbury's Boost.

Hizzy's new bike arrived late and he missed all the pre-season testing but the sweet-handling 916 suited his 250, high corner speed riding style perfectly and it only took him one round before he was into his rhythm.

BELOW The ill-handling Castrol Honda RC45 bit riders badly in 1995. When Ian Simpson was sidelined by injury Terry Rymer was drafted into the team at Cadwell and then finished second in both races of the final Brands round

ABOVE Matt Llewellyn won the three-round televised series and was a major player in BSB even though he had to maintain his own privately-run Ducati

RUTTER'S WINNING START

The series kicked off on the 2.5mile Donington Grand Prix circuit and Rutter grabbed the initiative, winning the first race and then taking fourth place in the second to lead the series.

Instead of racing the razor-sharp 916 in the treacherous damp conditions Rutter opted to use his old 926 with it's more forgiving handling and softer power delivery and cleared off into the distance in the first race.

Simpson gave the Castrol Honda team plenty to cheer about, finishing second in the first race with John Reynolds third on the Reve Kawasaki.

JR, as Reynolds is known throughout the Paddock, and his new team-mate David Jefferies had only raced the opening round of the series as a warm-up to their forthcoming WSB campaign with the Ben Atkins' owned, Stuart Hicken-managed team.

In the dry second race Whitham bounced back from a low-side at the Esses in race one to win from Reynolds and Hislop, who had finished fourth in the opener.

Rutter's fourth in race two though, gave him the series lead with 23 points, one point ahead of Reynolds, and five ahead of Hizzy. Whitham was fifth overall on 15 points, two behind Simpson (the scoring was the old GP method of 15 for a win, 12 for second, 10 for third down to one for 15th).

Whitham smashed Jim Moodie's long-standing Mallory record (set in September 1993 on the Duckhams Norton) and won both superbike races of the second round on the factory 916 to take a three-point lead in the series.

DUCATI STRANGLEHOLD

Ducati established a stranglehold on the series with the Italian bikes filling the first six grid places and the top four in both races.

Moodie put the Medd Honda up front at the start of race one but it was short-lived as Whitham took control to win from Hislop, Rutter – on his 916 now – and Llewellyn. The latter had opted for a too-soft Dunlop rear tyre that went off, losing him a shot at second place. Simpson was the top Honda in fifth from Moodie.

Privateer Shaun Muir entertained the crowd on the Colchester Kawasaki with some aggressive late braking antics at the Hairpin in the first race to move into third – but it was always bound to end in tears and he eventually lost the front going into the tight right-hander.

Between races Rutter crashed his 600 and broke a toe but that did not stop him taking part in the second Superbike clash. He eventually finished fourth.

Whitham did not have things his own way with Llewellyn and Hislop both pushing him hard. Whitham charged on, hard enough to establish a new lap record and to break clear, taking the win by over five seconds from Hislop and Llewellyn who was struggling for grip in the closing stages.

Whitham took a three-point lead over Hislop with him to Oulton Park. They shared race wins but Hizzy took the upper hand in the points chase after Whitham had a puncture in race two.

The Hizzy/Whitham scraps provided a great spectacle with their different riding styles – especially at Lodge

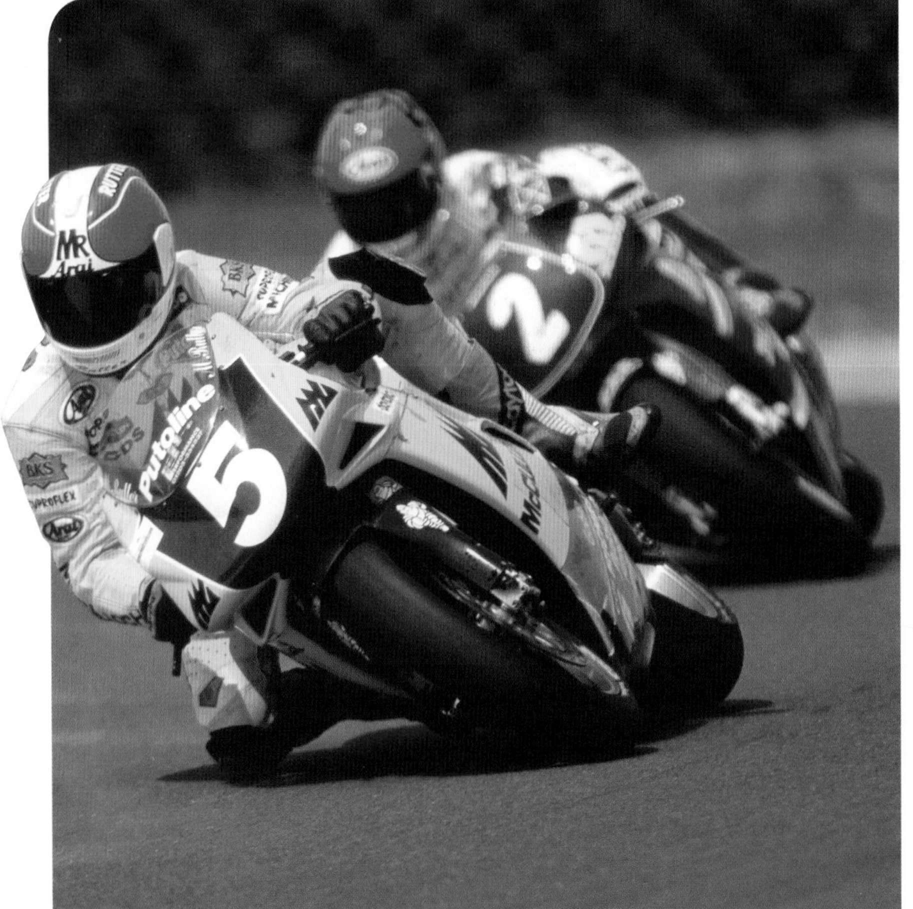

ABOVE Michael Rutter riding a Ducati backed by chainsaw manufacturer McCulloch leads Jim Moodie on the Medd Honda

OTHER HIGHLIGHTS OF '95

- Mick Doohan wins his second successive 500cc World Championship riding a Repsol Honda fettled by Jerry Burgess
- 1993 500cc World Champion Kevin Schwantz bids a sentimental farewell to Grand Prix racing in a party at the Assen GP. At the age of 30, his stellar career is cut short by a wrist injury
- At 29 years of age Carl Fogarty wins his second World Superbike title riding a Ducati 916
- In addition to Steve Hislop, Mike Edwards (Supersport 600), Jamie Robinson (250cc) and Darren Barton (125cc) are crowned Supercup champions
- Shell Advance International Superbike champion Matt Llewellyn misses out on the Triumph Speed Triple Challenge title by a solitary point to Mark 'Captain' Phillips

corner, the all-important final turn before the finish line. Whitham would come in absolutely on the limit of the braking efficiency of his bike, rear tyre hovering in the air and wagging from side to side. Then he would flop it on its side and pick it up as soon as possible to fire it out of the corner. Hislop would be much more controlled on the brakes – out wide to the left side of the track then let go of the lever and arc the machine down to the apex and out to the left side of the track on the exit, using the torque of the big V-twin to drive smoothly off the turn. And for many laps their paths would intercept somewhere on the way to, or from the apex. Advantage Hislop, 69 points to Whitham's 60.

If Oulton had produced close racing then the fans had not seen anything because the second Snetterton race was something else. For the first time in the history of SuperCup, sophisticated timing equipment, video evidence and certainly not the naked eye could tell who out of Hislop and Whitham crossed the line first in the second race. Whitham had already won the first one from Rutter, Llewellyn and Hislop. The Scot had been on pole but his rear tyre started squirming around after only six laps but he had no grip problems in race two.

He set the initial pace but Whitham fought back and took the lead on the second lap and the pair clocked a 14s lead over Llewellyn as they slugged out their own personal battle.

Hizzy looked home and dry on the last lap but missed a gear out of the final Russell's chicane and Whitham managed to draw level with the Devimead bike as they both lunged across the line. It was officially declared a dead-heat finish.

Hislop was two points ahead of Whitham going to Knockhill and that was how it remained when they both left the Scottish circuit after sharing a win and a second place each. Hislop took the first encounter after it was Whitham's turn to miss a gear going into the Hairpin. Hizzy won the race by seven hundredths of a second despite admitting later he'd opted for a too soft Michelin front in the 'heat-wave' conditions.

Hizzy initially led the second race but a blowing exhaust took the edge off his motor to give Whitham the advantage – though the Moto Cinelli rider claimed whatever the problem with Hizzy's bike was, it did not appear to slow it much.

WHITHAM UNDERGOES CHEMO

Whitham had been complaining of tiredness and weight loss for some time and, after his vain attempt at racing a ROC in the British Grand Prix (he felt exhausted after a crash during Saturday practice), he underwent tests for anaemia and calcium deficiency. After several treatments to cure the ailments he was finally diagnosed with Hodgkin's disease and underwent chemotherapy treatment at Huddersfield Royal Infirmary. He underwent six sessions of this at three-week intervals.

Whitham was determined not to give in, and he even attempted to ride at Cadwell Park in the penultimate round but simply lacked the strength and stamina to race his Ducati.

With Whitham sidelined Hislop won all four of the remaining races in the series, two at Cadwell Park and the final two at Brands Hatch to clinch the first British Superbike title of his career, to share a place in his trophy cabinet alongside the British 250cc title he had taken in 1990.

Although Ducati machines dominated the season with Llewellyn moving into second place in the points thanks to third and second place finishes at Cadwell, there was a bright spot on the horizon for the Japanese fours. Terry Rymer was drafted into the Castrol Honda team at Cadwell after Ian Simpson had been ruled out after breaking his leg at Knockhill. Rymer scored two fourth places in his Cadwell debut but showed the potential of the RC45 when he finished second in both the races at Brands Hatch.

LLEWELLYN WINS TV SERIES

In the Shell Advance series it was the same Ducati domination. Whitham, Hislop and Llewellyn finished 1–2–3 in both races at the opening Brands Hatch round in May on the 2.6-mile GP circuit.

Whitham was again in control in the first race of the second round at Oulton in June, beating Llewellyn and Hislop, but Hizzy bounced back to win the second leg when Whitham crashed at the Avenue right in front of Rutter. The race was red-flagged and the result declared after Hislop's team-mate Stringer had crashed heavily at Island Bend.

Going into the final round it meant Hislop was on 49 points from Whitham on 45 and Llewellyn on 44 so it was all to play for. But by 23 September at Donington it was a very different story.

With Whitham undergoing his treatment for cancer and Hislop ruled out with a trapped nerve in his neck, the final meeting of the series was steam-rollered by the factory WSB Castrol Hondas. Aaron Slight won both races from Simon Crafar.

Chris Walker finished third in the first race riding Hislop's Ducati and Rutter completed the podium in the second race but Llewellyn's fifth and fourth places assured him of the title by nine points from the absent Hislop. It was a strange twist to the end of the season.

BELOW Hard-riding Shaun Muir had some spectacular races on the Colchester Motorcycles Kawasaki

The 1995 Supercup produced a thrilling Superbike encounter between Steve Hislop and James Whitham until the latter was struck down with cancer. Hislop was leading the finely-balanced scrap at the time and went on to pick up a long overdue Superbike title, his first British crown since the 250cc Supercup in 1990.

Even after winning the 250cc British title in 1990 Steve Hislop still had to fight hard to shake off his 'Isle of Man TT rider' status. He always felt no one took his short circuit ability seriously. However, his 1995 Supercup Superbike title finally laid that old chestnut to rest. His brilliantly consistent form on the well-turned-out Devimead Ducati suited his old 250cc high corner speed riding style to perfection and he made the most of it.

This year had become the 'Hislop and Whitham Ducati show.' Their incredible battles – emphasising such vastly different riding styles – will be remembered for many years. So close was the battle that they even dead-heated at Snetterton and were separated by a single point going into the penultimate round at Cadwell Park.

Sadly, Whitham by then had been diagnosed as suffering cancer and had to sit out Cadwell, even though he bravely practised. He qualified seventh but decided not to race, feeling he might not have the strength to run the distance.

So Hislop was effectively 'handed' the title. To achieve it, though, he had to work his guts out! He finally clinched it in style with doubles at both Cadwell and Brands. But the edge of victory was blunted by the bad news surrounding the Whitham camp.

"On the Monday after Brands Rob (McElnea – Whitham's Moto Cinelli team boss) rang to tell me Whit had cancer. I was gutted. Obviously I felt bad for Whit. But suddenly I had no one to race either. Winning the championship meant nothing to me. All I could think about – as far as my racing was concerned – was the next World Superbike race at Assen. I had to look forward to a new challenge.

"It's nice to have finally won the title. I've had four lean years since the 250 crown. In '91 Honda pulled me out of the Euro 250 and Endurance when I had a chance to win both titles (Honda wanted him to support Alan Carter in a bid to win the British 250 title).

"In '92 I did a bit of everything and then in '93 I had the 'bitza' RVF which was really an old RC30 engine in an RVF chassis. Tony Scott did some good work on the motor and I got some good results on that and even last year with the RC45 –

BELOW Hizzy finally shook off his 'TT star' tag by proving he was equally awesome on short circuits, given the right motorcycle

which was a bit of a nightmare – eventually came good. Tony again did the engine and I came close to pole at the end of the year.

"After last year though, I was really worried. I thought my career was over. Then the Devimead chance came up. The team was built from nothing. The bikes were late arriving so the planned testing went out of the window. We actually ran the Corsa in mid-week prior to the Spring Cup at Mallory. Then at Donington in the first Supercup I qualified well but lacked confidence on the new bike in the wet.

"But after that it became the 'Whit and Hizzy' show. I got lots of seconds but the Misano World Superbike and Shell rounds gave me the feel for the bike and I started to get some pole positions. Then I was able to run with Jamie but the only time I won was when he crashed or broke down.

"But as the season went on, I got more confidence and Martin (Bennett, Hizzy's crew chief) got the motors working well and the turning point came at Snetterton. I had a crap first race, finishing fourth after choosing the wrong compound tyre, but everything else went well in the second one and I caught Jamie. I nailed him into the Esses, held it through Corams then missed a bloody gear at the chicane and Jamie just got up with me on the line for a dead heat. But that was it psychologically. I knew I could run with him and beat him!"

At Knockhill Hislop was fast all weekend, winning the first race but Whitham passed him on the last lap of the second race. One of Hislop's exhaust springs popped off causing the motor to lose its edge but he was not giving that as a reason for finishing second.

Then came the bombshell of Whitham's illness. "I'm sure there will be knockers who will point and say, 'Hizzy only won the title because Whit wasn't there,' but the people who really matter will know I was leading the championship at the time. I think when people look back on the series in years to come, yeah they will remember Whit getting cancer but hopefully they'll also say, 'yeah, but do you remember those great races with Hizzy and Whit?' The championship title is a bit hollow though and it's sad Whit wasn't around for the final couple of races."

Even so Hislop got a rude awakening when Whitham turned up at Cadwell and pulled on his leathers – just days after his second bout of chemotherapy. "No one expected him and when I saw him I thought, 'oh no!' It was a brave decision to try it but he didn't have the strength to race."

With Whitham grudgingly accepting the inevitable, and sitting Cadwell out, Hislop's title was assured.

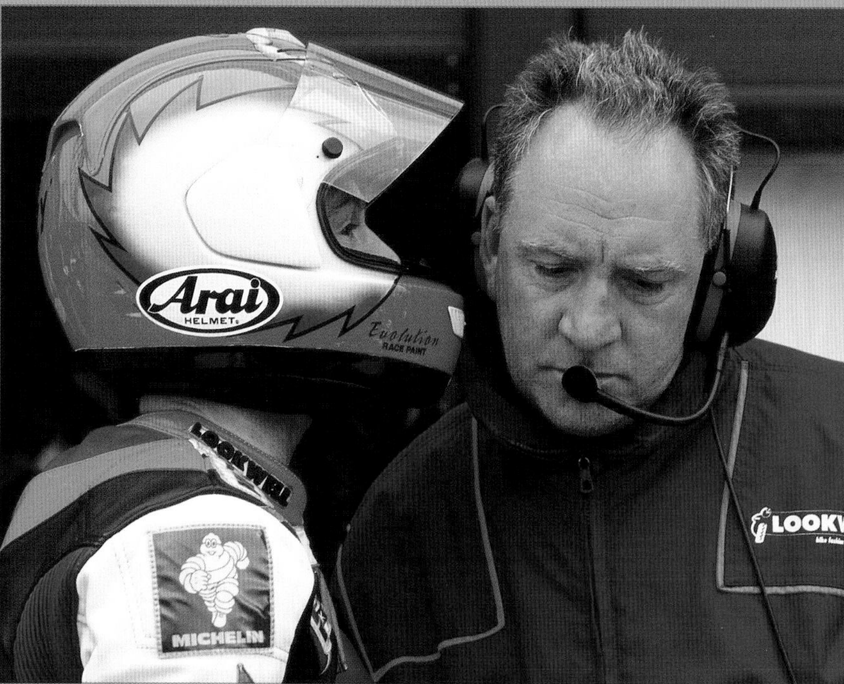

ABOVE Hislop confers with Devimead Ducati team manager Steve Horton

So now Hislop has the crown, what is the next step? The Devimead shop and race team has already been advertised for sale. Hislop's future again hangs in the balance.

"I've enjoyed being competitive and I feel I've got maybe four or five good years left in me. I've proved I can ride with the world-class superbike guys and I really want one good full season of World Championship competition with a good team before I call it a day.

"I'm not sure this team will continue. We've been let down before by several of our sponsors and I'm still owed wages. I think we've started with nothing to become one of the most professional teams in the paddock but where do we go from here? We need a major sponsor to keep the team intact.

"I'd love to continue riding a Ducati but you need factory kit parts to compete in World Superbike. The budget would need to be a big one. I've already been offered a big-money deal to stay in the UK but I really want one year in World Championship racing."

Now that Hislop finally has the machinery to match his ability – and has proven his case as one of the leading short circuit superbike exponents in the country – it is ironic that team manager Steve Horton may not get a chance to take Hislop and the rest of the Devimead team forward into an assault on the World Superbike Championship.

**This interview by Gary Pinchin first appeared in the November 1995 issue of* RPM *magazine, published by Village Publishing Ltd.*

1996

Mackenzie's first title

Although the Motorcycle Circuit Racing Control Board (MCRCB) had assumed control of the British Championship from the Auto Cycle Union (ACU) the previous year it was not until October 24, 1995 that MCRCB Chairman Robert Fearnall revealed the fine details of a radical shake-up of the entire British motorcycle racing.

The reason it took so long was that the MCRCB had taken up the reigns very late in 1994 by which time the ACU had already taken most of the major decisions concerning the championship for 1995.

So to the public watching the racing in '95 it was business as usual. The MCRCB tidied up the calendar, gave some focus to the TV coverage with the Shell International series but there was no major new sponsorship deals apart from the Triumph Speed Triple one-make support series.

Instead Fearnall and his team took a long hard look at how the championship could be improved, comparing it with the then buoyant British Touring Series which at that time warranted top level support from the major manufacturers, had the vital BBC TV package – and enjoyed massive support from the fans.

Announcing the changes to British motorcycle sport in *RPM*, Fearnall said: "We knew '95 would be difficult for the MCRCB because people could look back on the season and say, 'well, nothing's changed.' But we knew we had to tear it all apart and start again within six months so we could present our plan ready for the 1996 season – and beyond that. The ACU structure didn't allow any sort of long-term plan because of the way it (the organisation) was constituted."

N. MacKenzie
Cadbury's

PREVIOUS PAGE Ten years after he won the British 250 title Mackenzie was back in the UK, and his GP pedigree was obvious

ABOVE Niall Mackenzie and James Whitham. It was this close all year between the Cadbury's Boost Yamaha team-mates

INSET No matter how hard they raced, the friendship between Mackenzie and Whitham was never tested

CRUCIAL TV DEAL

Fearnall's long-term plan hinged on a comprehensive TV deal. For the Easter Supercup race in '95 the MCRCB paid £20,000 to BHP (Barrie Hinchliffe Productions) to prepare a pilot programme. BHP already produced an excellent British Touring Cars highlights show for BBC.

Fearnall presented the footage to David Gordon, the Editor of BBC *Grandstand*, and after several months of negotiation an agreement was struck for the BBC to cover the ten-round series with a similar highlights programme to the Touring Cars.

Each British Superbike round would get a 25-minute show during peak viewing times on the Saturday or Sunday *Grandstand* the following week of the event and, instead of straight race footage, the aim would be to include short, sharp interviews with the racers to help build the profile of the series by making the riders become household characters the TV viewers could readily identify with.

BHP would also cover the Thunderbike (similar to 600cc supersport bikes) and Superteens (a class to foster young new riders) support races, which would be included in a different package for Eurosport, the satellite TV channel.

The TV deal was so crucial that when planning the championship schedule the MCRCB left a big hole in the middle of the season from mid-June to mid-August to avoid clashing with the bigger, more popular events like European football, the Olympics, Open Golf, Wimbledon etc.

The fear was that even with this TV deal, BSB at the time was not strong enough to sustain such high-profile coverage. Fearnall, however, had faith that announcing the terrestrial TV coverage package before the winter would boost interest in the series, bringing new teams and new riders.

He told *RPM*: "The TV deal was the biggest vehicle motorcycling ever had to launch itself. Before their TV deal TOCA (British Touring Cars) only had 12 cars on the grid but eventually encouraged nine different manufacturers and 30 cars. Their highlight programme was a good vehicle to promote Touring Cars, which saw attendances jump from 5,000 to 25,000 following TV coverage. We're hoping it will be a positive method of bringing more spectators to the superbike series.

"The product for British Superbike has given the teams, owners, sponsors, manufacturers an opportunity to develop a very good British Superbike Championship and we will build new names, new characters, new stars. The grids will come and produce a competitive field. It's no problem."

With the new package Fearnall also focused attention on superbikes. For too long there had been too many different championship classes so there was never any real focus. It was a typical ACU trait – promoting the sport of motorcycling rather than trying to promote a business. By the 1990s motorcycle racing at the top level had become just that, a business, and the ACU, typically, had not moved with the times.

BSB meetings would still include 250cc, 125cc, Thunderbikes and Superteens but it was clear to everyone that these were support races while the main focus would always be the superbikes – the sole British Championship.

With a much tighter race weekend package there were casualties. Sidecar racing was kicked out. The Triumph series was moved to support a new Formula One Cup series, which had a second division-style superbike class headlining it. Supermonos – single-cylinder machines which at one stage qualified for a British title tag – were dissolved into a class with twins and triples, also at the F1 Cup rounds. The changes didn't win friends among competitors or fans of the more traditional classes, but the sport at the top level needed to move forward.

Fearnall said: "We don't run championships for the sake of it – as in the past (with the ACU). If anyone comes with a proposal and says 'try this,' we'll look at it and take it from there."

NEW ORGANISATION

It was not only the racing itself that was in for a shake-up. The MCRCB also wanted to introduce key officials into the major organisational roles and set up a new marshal's association called Racesafe. The whole idea was to ensure consistency throughout the championship. Previously there would have been different staff at each circuit.

They also standardised the pass system, paddock parking and pit allocation and planned new hospitality areas where teams could entertain sponsors and their guests. It was the level of organisation that was only previously seen at Grand Prix or World Superbike events but with some of the top UK teams annual budgets already nearing £1million it was perfect timing to take the sport to another level.

The MCRCB plans were totally embraced by the motorcycle industry. Jeff Turner, head of Yamaha's marketing at the time, responded to the news of Fearnall's plans by telling *RPM* readers: "I don't think the implications of just how important this is going to be for the bike industry are fully realised. Television will bring big crowds and we'll see bike racing surpass Touring Cars for appeal, simply because our product is better."

Simon Belton at Kawasaki UK added: "Fan-bloody-tastic. We had already decided Kawasaki should be involved in UK racing again and had already started making plans. I was a bit cynical when I heard about the proposals because there are often so many good ideas never realised but all credit to Robert Fearnall. It is wonderful news."

Neil Tuxworth, then team manager of Castrol Honda's WSB team, said: "The new TOCA-style package is the best thing ever offered in British racing."

And Colin Seeley, the chairman of FORRM, the riders group, said: "It's a fantastic opportunity for everyone in the sport. Long-term it will be good for racing and everyone will benefit. I think the industry must respond in a positive way and the manufacturers must support it. If it's handled the right way then the whole game will be raised to levels we've never previously seen in bike racing."

FIM SUPERBIKE REGS

The other big change for 1996 was a switch to the FIM superbike regulations. Previously the British series had adopted the more liberal FIM TT Formula One rules, mainly to facilitate a way to allow the highly popular Norton Rotary to run alongside superbikes.

After Honda had dispensed with his services at the end of 1995, Colin Seeley even lobbied the MCRCB for dispensation to run the all-conquering 1993 Spondon-framed Nortons again but was told, in no uncertain manner, that the only bikes eligible for BSB were those running to FIM superbike rules.

Seeley eventually struck a deal with oil company Duckhams – one of his long-term backers – to field a two-man Ducati team with Jim Moodie and Ian Simpson with a pair of second-hand bikes (one ex-Iain Duffus 916 and one ex-Llewellyn) plus a brand new bike on Michelin rubber.

Ducati again dominated the line-up – at least on paper. Ducati importers Moto Cinelli lined-up a two-man team with backing from Old Spice – but opted to use updated versions of the factory 916s that James Whitham raced the previous year until he was struck down by illness.

Moto Cinelli's Promotion Manager Eric MacFarlane, a former Yamaha factory rider by coincidence, signed Terry Rymer (who had finished the 1995 season on Castrol Hondas) and Chris Walker. By the time the season kicked off the £150,000 team would be managed by Robin Mortimer, brother of former GP privateer Chas who would later manage the team.

ABOVE Rutter raced his 1995 916 chassis – but with a 1996 uprated motor

ABOVE Whitham leads Rymer and Hislop at Oulton

Rymer had also signed for SERT, the Le Mans, France based Suzuki Endurance Racing Team but luckily only one race clashed, the Le Mans 24 Hours which meant Rymer would be dashing back for the Easter Monday Thruxton race and start from the back of the grid.

Michael Rutter continued with his McCulloch 916 (1996 engine in the '95 chassis), Dean Ashton was on the Baxi Ducati again, and Peter Graves reverted to the Italian bikes after a terrible year on Yamahas.

David Jefferies was intending to fund his own show with a Doug Holtom-prepared 916 after spending all winter driving haulage trucks around Europe for the Manton Group, a name well known as road racing sponsors. Then he secured a last-minute ride on the Medd Honda RC45.

After two dismal years with the RC45 the UK Honda importers did not even bother to run their own team. Winter rumours had suggested that after their disappointing 1995 season they would bounce back with the ex-factory Aaron Slight and Simon Crafar WSB bikes for Michael Rutter and Terry Rymer but nothing transpired.

Full factory bikes almost certainly would have been a more competitive option than the kitted RC45s previously seen in BSB.

Honda blamed a lack of sponsorship but Steve Hislop had slated the bike for its poor handling when it first appeared in 1994 and former British Champion Ian Simpson and Phil Borley had a torrid '95 with the beast. Simpson eventually was ruled out by injury so the feeling was that Honda wanted to steer clear of British racing until the factory team had turned the bike into a consistent winner.

Bob MacMillan, Honda UK's Motorcycle Division General Manager at the time, said: "It was a difficult decision but without a sponsor it would have been impossible to compete at the highest level."

The ex-team bikes instead were run by V&M for Mike Edwards while Paul Brown was signed to ride a Medd-backed RC45 for a second season but was replaced by David Jefferies just before the opening round when Brown quit to race a 600.

Although Suzuki launched a WSB team to promote the all new GSX-R750R signing Brit John Reynolds and Aussie Kirk McCarthy, the UK importers saw fit not to become directly involved in the British series. However a pair of the new GSX-Rs made the starting grid thanks to Crescent, a small, but enterprising Suzuki dealership in Bournemouth One of the GSX-R750s was for the shop owner's son Paul Denning (who was driving the entire project with an abundance of vigorous, youthful enthusiasm) and the other for Ian Cobby, a mate of Denning's and a top level club racer cum road tester for *Superbike* magazine.

Kawasaki did not have an official team in the series either but they were represented by the high-profile Nemesis team, owned by Mike Porteous and managed by Steve Horton. The ZX-7RRs sported Red Bull backing and were to be ridden by Steve Hislop and Matt Llewellyn – both superbike title winners from the previous season.

Ray Stringer set up his own Kawasaki privateer effort with backing from Keith Newnham's Sabre Airways and Shaun Muir was again on the Colchester Motorcycles Kawasaki.

BOOST FOR YAMAHA

It was Yamaha who created the biggest news when their new two-man team was announced in a lavish reception at the Hippodrome in Leicester Square, London in January. Backed by Cadbury's Boost (a new chocolate bar which the company was promoting heavily), and managed by Rob McElnea (returning to the Yamaha fold after running the Moto Cinelli team the previous year), Yamaha secured factory Yamaha YZF750s for Niall Mackenzie and James Whitham.

Whitham appeared at the team launch, still very gaunt and totally bald as a result of the chemotherapy treatment he'd undergone to rid himself of the cancer he went down with mid-way through the 1995 season.

Now diagnosed to be free from the illness, he was ready to resume his racing career. He said: "I rode one of the factory YZFs in 1993 and know what it's capable of. I can't wait to get back on a bike after what's happened in the past six months."

For 35-year-old Mackenzie it was a return to domestic racing from Grand Prix some ten years after he had won the British 250cc title. For him, the previous year's World 250 title campaign with Aprilia had been something of a disaster and he was delighted to be back racing in Britain.

LEFT Robert Fearnall. The man to thank for ensuring a prosperous future for the British Superbike Championship

He told *RPM*: "It's an exciting deal. I ended last season with zero motivation but this is the chance of a fully competitive bike. That's all I've ever wanted."

Mackenzie started the season with a win in the first race at Donington on 31 May in front of 12,500 fans. Rymer – back racing in the UK full-time for the first season since 1990 – had qualified pole but suffered a blocked fuel valve early in the first race but the Ducati rider reversed the odds in the second race, comprehensively beating Mackenzie by almost 13 seconds.

Simpson finished a consistent third in both races on the Duckhams Ducati with three more Italian-built V-twins behind him in each race to round out the top six.

The big surprise of the meeting was Steve Hislop claiming second place in the first race on the new Nemesis Kawasaki. His joy was short-lived though when the ZX-7R expired in a cloud of oil smoke when it blew up on the way to the Melbourne Loop early in race two. He was battling with Mackenzie and Rymer's team-mate Chris Walker at the time. Walker later crashed at Craner.

Mackenzie left Donington with a 13-point lead over Simpson but Boost Yamaha team-mate Whitham did not even score a point after breaking a gear lever in race one and crashing out of race two.

It was this failure to score that would ultimately lose him the title.

BELOW Paul Denning brought Suzuki into BSB with a two-man team run out of his Bournemouth-based dealership

RYMER FROM THE BACK

Rymer was a sensational first race winner at Thruxton. Unable to do qualifying due to a clash with his World Endurance commitments with the French SERT team (where he finished seventh), Rymer flew back to the UK to start the Bank Holiday Monday race from the back of the grid.

In front of 12,000 fans Rymer blasted through the pack to take the lead from Mackenzie with three laps to go at the chicane. The race was decided in the same place on the final lap when Rymer held onto the lead as Mackenzie tried to out-brake him, ran wide to allow his own team-mate Whitham to scuttle inside for second place.

Mackenzie won race two but might have been pushed harder had Rymer's Ducati cam belt not broken. Whitham and privateer Ray Stringer rounded out the podium as Mackenzie established a 34-point lead in the *Motor Cycle News* supported series with closest rival Simpson only able to score fifth and seventh place finishes.

James Whitham's emotional first race win at third-round Oulton was his first victory since winning his battle against cancer.

He told *MCN*: "This win has put everything behind me. My life is back to normal now. I had ten years of racing and winning before I became ill and now everything is back just like it should be. The nightmare is over."

Whitham finished ahead of team-mate Mackenzie and Ducati privateer Michael Rutter.

Rymer was sidelined with an oil leak in race one but used a brand new 1996 Corsa to win race two, even

OTHER HIGHLIGHTS OF '96

- Michael Doohan (500), Max Biaggi (250) and Haruchika Aoki (125) are crowned World Champions
- Valentino Rossi wins his first 125 GP race at Brno, fending off experienced Jorge Martinez
- Troy Corser takes the WSB title on a Power Horse-backed Ducati from Honda's Aaron Slight and official Ducati factory rider John Kocinski. Carl Fogarty finishes fourth overall
- Brian Morrison is crowned World Endurance Champion even though he and his Kawasaki team-mates fail to finish the final Bol d'Or round. The Scot does not even get a chance to ride in the race after the bike's axle breaks in the first hour
- Other British Champions include: Dave Heal (Thunderbike), Steve Sawford (250), Robin Appleyard (125)

though testing had been insufficient to establish a good race set-up.

Whitham beat Mackenzie to second place and moved into second spot in the points, 37 points behind his Yamaha team-mate.

A week later Whitham piled on the pressure with a winning double at Snetterton. He broke his own three-year-old lap record in the first race after opting for a soft-compound rear tyre. It went off with four laps to run but by then Whitham was so far ahead of his rivals that he was still able to cruise to a 5.7s victory over Old Spice Ducati rider Chris Walker. Mackenzie was third.

Whitham won race two but this time it was Mackenzie who broke the record. He had to switch to his spare bike when his number one machine hit carburettor problems on the grid. Mackenzie battled through to second place with Rutter completing the podium.

Rymer was fourth in both races after suffering front-end handling problems and indicated, not for the first time in the season, that the team's priority should be some meaningful testing.

Whitham moved to within five points of series leader Mackenzie after another brilliant double at Brands Hatch on the short Indy circuit.

Whitham clinched the first race by three hundredths of a second from Rymer after getting the drag to the line from Clearways on the final lap but beat the Ducati rider by a slightly more convincing 1.6s in race two.

Rymer blamed his 955cc for not having the top-end speed and power to run with the YZF750 and said he would push his team to have 995cc engines.

Mackenzie was third in both races after making his usual dramatic charges through the pack following two appalling starts.

TEAMS IN TURMOIL

Steve Hislop's season continued to be fraught with problems, even though former manager Steve Horton had been sacked and replaced by new boss Colin Wright for Brands Hatch. Hislop collided with a backmarker in race one when he was third and a pit-line fire meant he did not start race two. Team-mate Matt Llewellyn was fifth in race one.

The Old Spice Ducatis were also in turmoil. Chris Walker quit the team to race for the Elf team in 500cc Grand Prix and team owner Robin Mortimer threatened to take legal action.

Rymer was absent from the Knockhill round, instead travelling to Brno, to race the Lucky Strike Suzuki in the Czech Republic 500cc Grand Prix. He had earlier been called up to deputise for the absent Scott Russell at the Mugello GP on May 26 and then raced in Germany and England when Daryl Beattie was sidelined by injury.

Mortimer accepted his leave of absence, since Rymer had asked permission beforehand and also asked if he could continue riding for the team in the final rounds.

Scott Smart and Matt Llewellyn rode the Old Spice bikes in Scotland.

ABOVE Fifth and third places at Brands underlined privateer Andy Ward's talent in the wet

ABOVE Start at Cadwell with (left to right) Hislop, Mackenzie, Whitham and Rymer blasting off the front row. Moodie is off row two with the Suzuki

They were not the only changes for the Knockhill race. Hizzy had quit the Nemesis team, as had new manager Colin Wright. Then the team, in big financial difficulties, folded which is why Llewellyn took the Old Spice ride.

Hizzy was also sorted for Knockhill thanks to Reve Racing boss Ben Atkins who dusted down his old 1995 John Reynolds ZXR750s and had them re-liveried in Red Bull colours.

Hislop repaid him, enjoying his best weekend of the season with a pair of third places first time out on the bike, but he could not close in on the Cadbury's Boost Yamahas of double winner Mackenzie and Whitham.

Scott Smart was seventh and fifth on his superbike debut aboard the Old Spice Ducati. Mackenzie's double gave him a 15-point championship lead with four rounds to go, but within a week, that had been dramatically slashed to just five.

At Cadwell Park on Bank Holiday Monday, Whitham beat Mackenzie in the first race after damp conditions at the start turned tyre choice into a lottery.

Then the result was declared at seven laps after being thrown into chaos after three red flags due to crashes and bad weather. Whitham's intermediate front/slick rear combination worked best in the early stages compared to his team-mate's front and rear slicks but Mackenzie closed to within a quarter of a second at the line as the track dried out.

Whitham won the second race by over ten seconds from his team-mate. Rymer's return to the Old Spice Ducati team turned into a disaster with brake problems putting him out of the first race. He was fourth behind Rutter in race two.

Another double for Whitham at Mallory gave him a nine-point championship lead over Mackenzie. It was the first time all year Whitham had held the upper hand.

Hislop managed to split the Cadbury's Boost Yamahas in the first race but had to be content with third behind Mackenzie in race two.

David Jefferies scored a good fourth on the Medd Honda in race one. Jim Moodie was sixth and fifth in his first race on the G-Shock Suzuki GSX-R750. Having quit the Duckhams Ducati team earlier he was subbing for Ian Cobby who had broken his leg at Cadwell Park.

The week after Mallory Whitham broke his scaphoid when he crashed in torrential rain during the Bol d'Or but that did not stop him racing at Brands Hatch a week later.

Rymer won both races held in damp conditions, on the Indy Circuit, to strengthen his bid for third place in the championship. He edged 24 points clear of Rutter who finished third in race one but then was sidelined as his McCulloch Ducati broke a cam-belt in race two when he was set to finish second.

The star performance of the day came from little-known privateer Andy Ward with fifth and third places on his Fowlers-backed Ducati 955 to establish himself as a top wet-weather rider.

WHITHAM'S BITTER BLOW

The battle for the championship intensified as Mackenzie finished second and fourth, while Whitham was fourth and fifth, leaving them level at the top of the table on 349 points each with just one more double race round to go at Donington Park.

Mackenzie enjoyed the all important psychological break. He won the first race while Whitham could only finish third behind Sean Emmett who was back from Grand Prix action and having an end-of-season run on a John Hackett-prepared Ducati 995.

Early race leader Whitham opted for a different spec rear tyre to his team-mate and it simply did not last the distance so well.

Whitham was inch-perfect in race two but Mackenzie shadowed him all the way to secure second place – and the title, by four points.

The delighted Scot told *MCN* readers: "I silenced critics who said it was all over for Niall Mackenzie. I returned to race in Britain and to prove I am fast. When you are in GPs you become a forgotten man and no one thinks you are fast. But I did it my way. People will criticise me for not winning many races but I am the champion."

For Whitham, losing at the final hurdle was a bitter blow, especially in such an emotional season after fighting his way back to fitness from his illness. He said: "Niall's never looked like crashing and the Yamahas have been reliable all season. Between us we've had one breakdown, when my gear lever broke at the first round. If that hadn't happened, I would be champion. But after coming back from last year with the cancer and everything, it ain't so bad."

BOOST YAMAHA TECH

The bikes that Niall Mackenzie and James Whitham raced during 1996 were the former Italian Belgarda Yamaha YZF750 factory bikes ridden by Massimo Meregalli in the 1995 World Superbike season.

The bikes – worth £60,000 apiece – were not full factory bikes but did have A-kit parts from Japan and the motors were built by Bepe Russo, regarded as one of the top engine tuners in WSB at the time.

The team maintained a link with Belgarda (the Italian Yamaha importer) all year with engines freshened up by Russo.

The tried and tested YZFs allowed the Cadbury's Boost Yamaha riders to come out of the gate running while their rivals spent time in early races sorting brand new bikes.

Not only were the YZFs fast and nimble, they were also very reliable with the consistent Mackenzie scoring in every one of the 20 championship races. He also took five race wins – while Whitham scored ten.

The five-valve-per-cylinder, liquid-cooled engine developed 150bhp at 13,300rpm, compared to the SP road bike's 112bhp at 12,000rpm but it also had a good spread of power with 63.9ft lb of torque at 10,400rpm.

Camshafts, valves, pistons, crankcases, gearbox internals, clutch and sump were all factory parts, while the heads were flowed by Russo. Keihin 41mm flatslides replaced the stock 39mm carbs. Slovenian company Skorpion (which later became Akrapovic) supplied the titanium four-into-one race exhaust.

The standard YZF750SP frame was braced only at the top of the suspension cross member but the chassis had a lot of adjustability. The swing-arm pivot point was adjustable and the triple clamps were adjustable for offset between 24 and 30mm.

The standard 43mm Kayaba forks were ditched in favour of race-spec Ohlins 46mm units which were fully adjustable for compression, preload and rebound damping.

Four-pot Brembo calipers replaced the road-going six pot calipers and discs were fully-floating 320mm stainless steel rotors.

The standard road shock, with adjustments for compression and rebound was replaced with an Ohlins race shock with the same options plus ride height adjustment.

The swing-arm came out of Yamaha's A-kit catalogue and was stronger than stock as well as being fabricated by hand to tighter tolerances for racing.

Wheels were lightweight Marchesini's with the 6" wide rear and 3.5" front shod with Dunlop slicks.

BELOW The original Cadbury's Boost Yamaha team. Left to right: Barry Stanley, Adrian Marsh, Niall Mackenzie, Rob McElnea, James Whitham, 'Stuey' Smith and Mel Allen. Their YZF750s came from the Yamaha Belgarda WSB factory team

agv
ON THE EDGE
Cadbury
BOOST
BOOST
MCN
1
MOTOR CYCLE NEWS
Cadbury
BOOST

1997

Another Cadbury's Boost Yamaha success

After the successful changes implemented the previous year, including the top class coverage on BBC Television's flagship sport's programme *Grandstand*, the 1996 season was always going to be a hard act to follow – especially as the reigning BSB Champion Niall Mackenzie looked in such a strong position going into the new season with the Cadbury's Boost Yamaha team.

The introduction of a string of newcomers to the championship injected plenty of zest into the 1997 campaign. The meetings had been extended to three days in a bid to give riders and teams more time to set the bikes up properly and the paddock was buzzing with new hospitality areas that made BSB begin to look more like a high-profile World Championship circus than a domestic racing series.

Mackenzie's main rival from the previous season, James Whitham, had left Yamaha to join the factory Suzuki team so now the 35-year-old Scot had Chris Walker as a team-mate on the ex-works YZF750s.

Walker had controversially walked out on the Old Spice Ducati team mid-way through 1996 to take a 500cc Grand Prix ride with Elf, which had started as a 'wild-card' (promoter's option) ride for the British round of the World Championship and then turned into a full-time ride for the rest of the year.

John Reynolds was dumped by the Harris Performance-run Suzuki factory World Superbike team after a less-than-impressive season on the brand new GSX-R750, a machine that lacked any major development during the year and had a big void in the mid-range power delivery as well as a major handling problem in Reynolds' hands.

Reynolds came back to the UK with plenty to prove and linked up with his old mate, businessman Ben Atkins in the big-buck Reve Red Bull team riding a Ducati 996 Corsa.

In an outfit reputed to have a budget of around £1 million – the highest ever for a BSB team – Steve Hislop joined Reynolds to form one of the strongest teams in the series.

PREVIOUS PAGE The only thing different about 1997 was Mackenzie's new team-mate Chris Walker. Yamaha continued to dominate the championship

RIGHT Michael Rutter was Honda's sole factory rider in BSB during 1997. The team was run by V&M. Rutter was third in the series

There was another impressive new Ducati team on the grid. Sean Emmett came back from riding in 500cc Grand Prix to be snapped up by Colin Seeley who was now running the Darrell Healey-owned Groundwork South East team with a pair of Ducatis fettled by renowned UK specialist John Hackett.

Kawasaki returned to the series with an official team after the disaster of the privateer Nemesis effort in '96. Team boss Colin Wright gambled on former Thunderbike World series runner-up Scot Iain MacPherson who had never previously ridden a superbike, while having Terry Rymer as his number one rider. Rymer had impressed early on in the previous year with the Old Spice Ducati before spending the back end of season riding for Lucky Strike Suzuki in the 500cc Grand Prix as a replacement for the injured Daryl Beattie.

The Crescent Suzuki team lined up with Jim Moodie and Matt Llewellyn on GSX-R750s while Honda fielded just one RC45 for Michael Rutter in a team managed by V&M.

The field was boosted by a healthy contingent chasing the new Privateer Cup class with Ray Stringer's Sabre Airways Kawasaki, Dean Ashton on a Baxi Ducati, and former British Superbike Champion and former Sidecar World Champion Darren Dixon on a Kawasaki.

MACKENZIE DOMINATES OPENER

Niall Mackenzie was hell-bent on destroying the depth of talent from the very start. He went unbeaten at Donington Park in the April opener, and powered into a comfortable 17-point lead in the series. In the first race Reynolds and Hislop completed the rostrum. In race two Walker improved from fourth in race one to finish second, making it a Cadbury's Boost Yamaha one–two ahead of Rymer on the Kawasaki.

Mackenzie was unable to maintain that dominant form in the next round at Oulton Park where he could only finish fifth in the first race and third in race two. Team-mate Walker won the first from Reynolds and Rymer but any chance of a double for the Nottingham rider ended in the most spectacular way when he suffered a monumental highside in race two as he crested the Avenue at over 150mph. He suffered a

BELOW Sean Emmett was given his big break in BSB with Darrell Healey's GSE Ducati team, run by Colin Seeley

cracked bone and torn ligaments, injuries that ruled him out of the following week's Donington Park World Superbike meeting.

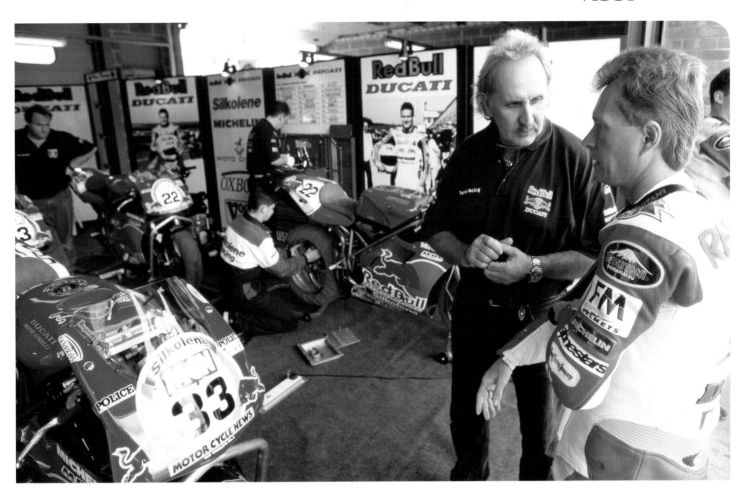

At Snetterton though Walker was back to full fitness and traded wins with Mackenzie as the Cadbury's Boost Yamaha team snapped back into top form. After looking so good at Oulton Park Reynolds had a disappointing time at the Norfolk circuit with an eighth place in race one following a clash with Rymer. Bike problems ruled him out of race two which contrived to drop him 49 points adrift of series leader Mackenzie.

Michael Rutter used the speed of the RC45 to claim third in race one but the Suzukis of Llewellyn and Moodie took third and fourth in race two. Rymer failed to finish either race and the only joy for Kawasaki was provided by World Endurance Champion Brian Morrison. The Scot scored sixth in both races. He was deputising for MacPherson who was sidelined by an injury sustained playing five-a-side football earlier in the week!

At the rain-lashed fourth round at the Brands Hatch Indy circuit Sean Emmett suffered a rear tyre puncture on his warm-up lap leaving his GSE Ducati team no choice but to replace the intermediate with a slick – even though the conditions were far from perfect. Even that could not stop him winning his first race of the year and he immediately claimed it was down to having been given 'the tyre from god.'

Walker was second from Rymer, Rutter and the now fit MacPherson. Mackenzie, struggling in the wet conditions, was only eighth and could only finish fourth in race two

ABOVE Roger Marshall (black shirt and talking to Reynolds) managed Ben Atkins' Red Bull Ducati team

LEFT Nicknamed both 'Spud' and the 'Old Trout' by race commentators, Mackenzie enjoys clinching title number two

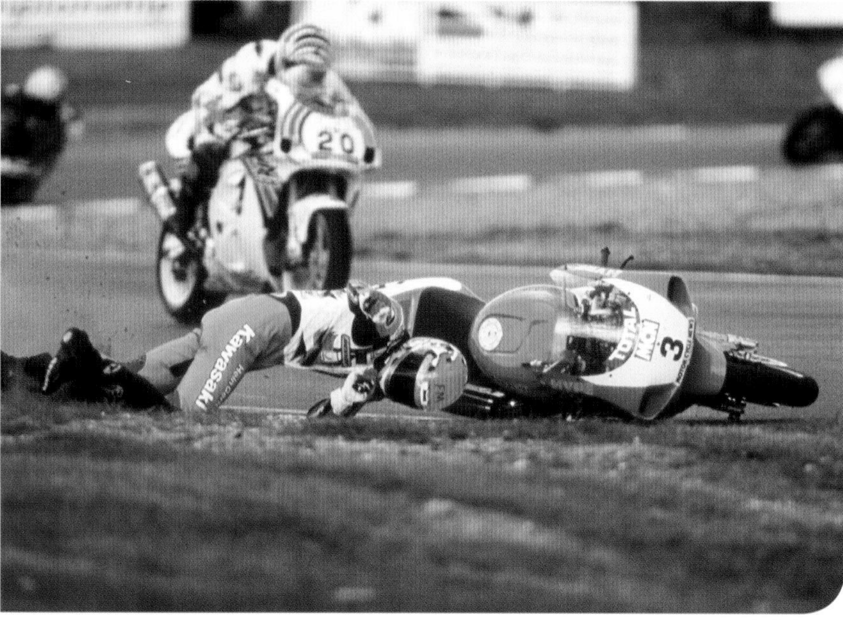

behind Reynolds, Rutter and MacPherson – his first-ever superbike podium finish. Walker was fifth but had closed the points gap from 19 to nine.

The high speed, bumpy Thruxton circuit proved to be a pivotal point in the championship – in more ways than one. Mackenzie stamped his authority on the championship winning both races. Rymer was second in both while Walker, in race one, and then Reynolds in the second completed the podium.

With Walker fifth behind MacPherson in race two, Mackenzie suddenly had a 32-point lead in the standings over his team-mate.

Thruxton was also a turning point for Steve Hislop. Struggling with the harsh power delivery of the Ducati all year, he could only finish 12th and 18th and team manager Roger Marshall was given the unenviable task by owner Ben Atkins to sack him.

Mackenzie, though, was in a different frame of mind, compared to earlier in the season, for the second Oulton Park round of the year. He won both races with Reynolds and Walker second and third respectively in each outing.

Mackenzie was charging clear in his effort to retain the crown. He was now 50 points clear of Walker and a whopping 78 ahead of third-placed Reynolds.

Team Kawasaki had a torrid time at the Cheshire circuit with both Rymer and MacPherson excluded from the first race results after a rival team protested the legality of their bikes. With the ZX-7RRs running dangerously hot, the team had removed the front mudguards to get some air into the radiators. Rymer crashed out of third place in race two when he was running third.

Rymer was not at Mallory Park for the next round. Instead Kawasaki chiefs drafted him in to ride one of their four factory bikes in the prestigious Suzuka Eight Hour Race (partnering Italian Piergiorgio Bontempi). Steve Hislop, currently out of work, was drafted in by team-boss Colin Wright to ride the spare Kawasaki ZX-7RR at the short, demanding Leicestershire circuit.

SENSATIONAL HIZZY

Typically, Hislop was sensational. Finishing third in race one and second in race two. MacPherson, on the other Kawasaki, rose to the challenge too, scoring a career best second in the first race.

Mackenzie remained imperious. No-one could match him as he scored yet another double to make it six wins in a row and edge even further ahead in the title stakes. He was now 74 points clear from Walker with Reynolds sidelined with a dislocated shoulder after crashing in the high-speed Gerrards right-hander during practice.

Mackenzie's hopes might have taken a massive knock at his home track, Knockhill when he was skittled out in a first turn crash in race one. Moodie and Emmett were also involved in the crash, but Mackenzie bounced back with his foot heavily strapped up to win the second race.

It was a great day for the Scottish fans who had already enjoyed seeing Kawasaki's Iain MacPherson score his first-ever British Superbike win in race one, ahead of Hislop who was now riding a Sabre Airways Kawasaki. Hislop was then fourth in the second race of the day, finishing behind Walker and MacPherson. The best Ducati finisher was Ian Simpson substituting for the injured Reynolds. He grabbed sixth and eighth places.

Mackenzie's championship hopes took another dive at Cadwell Park. After struggling home eighth in the first race he crashed in the woodland section during the second race and broke his wrist.

Simpson won the first race from Rutter, Rymer, MacPherson and Walker. Rutter won the wet second race to chalk up the first victory of the year for the V&M Honda RC45. With Walker finishing second, Mackenzie's points lead was down to 44, and he was considered to be a doubtful starter for the penultimate round at Brands Hatch.

Rutter's win elevated him to third in the championship but with only two rounds and four races left the title was a straight shoot-out between the Cadbury's Boost Yamaha duo.

Three weeks on and with his wrist heavily strapped, Mackenzie came out fighting to take both wins on the Kent Grand Prix circuit to wrap up the title. Reynolds was also back and finished second in race one from Emmett. Emmett was runner-up in the second race from Walker and Reynolds.

Mackenzie won the first race in the final Donington Park round but a clash with Hislop in race two meant he did not finish the season with a double success.

Instead Walker won the race from Emmett and Rymer.

Mackenzie finished the series 57 points clear of team-mate Walker while Rutter was third just 19 points ahead of Reynolds.

OPPOSITE Terry Rymer had some big crashes in 1997, including this one at Brands Hatch

LEFT AND BELOW Steve Hislop never got to grips with the fierce power delivery of the '97 Ducati (below)...
....so he subbed for Suzuka Eight Hour-bound Rymer at Mallory...
...and ended the year on privateer Sabre Airways' Kawasaki (left)

OTHER HIGHLIGHTS OF '97

- Mick Doohan wins his fourth consecutive 500cc Grand Prix title and Max Biaggi becomes the first-ever four-time 250cc World Champion while Valentino Rossi prevents a Honda steamroller, taking the World 125cc title on his Aprilia
- American John Kocinski gives Honda the WSB title after a season-long scrap with Ducati's Carl Fogarty
- Other British Champions include: Paul Brown (Supersport), Scott Smart (250cc),Darren Barton (125cc)
- In his debut season of national racing, teenage sensation James Toseland finishes third in Supersport and wins the one-make Honda CB500 series
- Fourteen-year-old Leon Haslam dominates the Gilera Scooter Championship (12 wins in 16 starts) and wins in his only round of the Honda CB500 Newcomers Cup

MOTOR
Cadbury

1998

New season, new pressures

Niall Mackenzie's two-year dominance of the *Motor Cycle News* backed British Superbike Championship was put under serious pressure when an even stronger field than ever before was confirmed for the 1998 campaign.

A lot of that pressure came from within his own camp when team boss Rob McElnea signed Steve Hislop to replace Chris Walker.

While Mackenzie was probably the highest paid rider in the series, Hislop was definitely the lowest since he put pen to paper for absolutely no salary at all.

After being sacked halfway through 1997, McElnea offered Hizzy the 'chance to put yourself in the shop window.' Hizzy was more than willing to take up the offer, relying on product support and prize money to eke out a living.

Walker switched to Kawasaki to replace Rymer while MacPherson was retained on the ZX-7R.

Suzuki, with backing from household electronics firm Sony to promote their new Mini Disc, signed Rymer and James Haydon. The latter was returning to BSB after the most dismal time in World Superbike with GiaCoMoto Ducati. His season was littered with 'dnfs' and crashes, often caused by blown oil seals or parts falling off the bike. After the tenth round at Albacete Haydon walked away from the team – while he still could.

Honda expanded its V&M-managed team to two riders with former BSB Champion Ian Simpson joining Michael Rutter on the RC45.

The GSE Ducati team also flexed its muscles – bringing little-known Troy Bayliss to the series.

The 28-year-old Aussie had finished runner-up in Australian Superbike in 1997 riding a GSX-R750 but more impressively had finished fifth in both WSB races on the same bike at Phillip Island and, in a one-off ride on a works RGV250 that most people dismissed as being totally uncompetitive, finished sixth in the Australian 250cc Grand Prix.

Jamie Robinson had a disastrous season on the RGV250 but was also signed by GSE despite having no previous experience on a superbike.

Ben Atkins' Reve Red Bull Ducati team retained John Reynolds and signed Sean Emmett.

The dozen 'factory' riders were joined by a handful of privateers including Dave Heal on a V-twin Honda VTR1000 Firestorm, Phil Giles, Brett Sampson and Max Vincent on Kawasakis and Peter Graves on a Ducati.

The limited entry was not helped by the fact that there was a new Powerbike class. This was basically for race-kitted and mildly-tuned 1,000cc production bikes running on slicks.

This class was championed by Sanyo Honda supersport team boss Russell Savory and former international racer Mick Grant (who worked with Savory) and was sort of a half-way house between the production championship and superbikes. Gordon Ritchie, writing in *Motocourse* that year summed up the series as something that: "looked suspiciously like a sop to the almighty Honda in their 50th anniversary year. The only way to make the Fireblade competitive against the new Yamaha R1s and Ducati SPSs was to tune it as if there were no tomorrow, so almost anything was allowed inside the engines. Not one of the MCRCB's better ideas."

YAMAHA'S BRANDS BOOST

The first BSB round drew just 13 entries and led to suggestions that the bikes from the Powerbike class should be incorporated into BSB to boost the ailing superbike grid count. That would have led to all sorts of complications lining up 1,000cc fours alongside existing 750cc four-cylinder superbikes.

Ironically for a class so derided at the time Powerbike actually proved the harbinger of new superbike regulations that would govern the class worldwide just after the turn of the decade. As a look into the future maybe the MCRCB plus Savory and Grant had it spot on.

Chris Walker just beat Emmett across the line in the first race of the year at Brands Hatch with Haydon making a tremendous start to his return to the British scene in third. The Cadbury's Boost Yamaha boys trailed in sixth and seventh in the first race but normal service was resumed in race two with a one–two finish. Mackenzie beat Hislop. Walker finished third to take the series lead with 41 points to the 35 of Mackenzie.

Rutter won in the wet on the RC45 in the first Oulton Park race from Suzuki's Rymer, Walker and Mackenzie but in the dry second race the rivalry in the Cadbury's Boost Yamaha camp became evident as Hislop took the race win with what Mackenzie viewed as a very forceful outbraking manoeuvre going into Lodge, the final turn. Walker was third to remain the series leader by five points from Mackenzie. Hislop was seven points adrift of his team-mate in the standings in third overall.

Emmett, had suffered a double fracture of his left arm during the Donington Park World Superbike meeting, was ruled out, so his place was taken by Matt Llewellyn who finished eighth in race one. Red Bull's other rider John Reynolds was also struggling with an ankle injury sustained at a non-championship Mallory race earlier in the month.

At Thruxton Mackenzie assumed control of the series, winning both races. Rymer took second on the Suzuki from Hislop in race one but Hizzy made it a Boost 1–2 in the second outing. MacPherson completed the podium.

Hislop won the first race at Snetterton from Mackenzie but a moment of madness from the champion in the final Russell's chicane took both Yamaha riders wide in a desperate bid to stay on board their bikes.

Hislop was already committed to the corner when Mackenzie arrived backing the YXF750 in on the limit. Hislop, according to *Motocourse*, said: "a purple exocet missile suddenly arrived at my elbow."

That move gifted the win to Rymer – the first win for the Crescent GSX-R750.

Walker finished second, Hislop third ahead of Mackenzie. Even so the defending champion still had the points lead, 151–138 over his team-mate, with Walker third on 120 points.

Hislop won the first race on the two mile Donington Park National circuit but it was a traumatic last corner after he had outbraked himself going into Goddard. Haydon was following him closely but instead of being able to capitalise on the Yamaha rider's mistake, he too shot straight on. Both recovered to maintain their positions while Walker finished third ahead of Bayliss on the GSE Ducati.

Mackenzie crashed out of race one at over 100mph exiting the Old Hairpin but bounced back to claim the second race – destroying any hopes Hislop might have had even after smashing the lap record no less than three times. Haydon was third.

BAYLISS'S FIRST WIN

For the first time Hislop had the championship lead, by seven points (183–176) after his Donington Park heroics and the team-mates were fast becoming arch-rivals as the action switched to Oulton Park for the sixth round.

Ian Simpson missed these races, and those at Knockhill after breaking his arm in a dirt bike crash. Jamie Robinson was another absentee. Having failed to make the grade aboard the GSE Ducati he was replaced by Matt Llewellyn, the Leicester rider who had become known as the Ducati super-sub in the BSB paddock. He had ridden the Red Bull bike while Emmett was recuperating from his arm injuries.

Ironically Ducati teams GSE and Red Bull shared a win apiece at Oulton Park with Troy Bayliss claiming his first British Championship victory in the wet first race from the Yamahas of Mackenzie and Hislop

In race two it was Emmett's turn. Still far from fully fit he put the rain to his advantage riding a smooth race to become the seventh rider during the twelve races held so far to chalk up a win. Mackenzie and Hislop were again second and third which meant the defending champion was back ahead of Hislop, although by only a single point.

If Emmett's performance was not the epitome of a hardman, Chris Walker went one better. He broke his

PAGES 50–51 BSB commentator Fred Clarke with the man he dubbed 'Spuds' Mackenzie on the grid

OPPOSITE Hislop was committed to the corner but Mackenzie was not about to back off going into Russell's chicane – with this resulting dual excursion onto the dirt. The move handed the race win to Michael Rutter

BELOW Terry Rymer put the new Sony-backed Suzuki into the thick of the action

ABOVE There was a dramatic shift mid-season in the Honda camp from Michelin to Dunlop as the logo on the front mudguard reveals

kneecap in no less than eight places in a first race crash but somehow found the determination to get back on the bike for race two and still finish seventh!

The podium after the first race at Knockhill was one for the walking wounded with Walker second to Mackenzie and Reynolds, still far from fit, in third.

Hislop crashed out after colliding with Emmett at the chicane but finished second in race two behind Mackenzie who left Scotland with a healthy 31-point lead over Hizzy.

Matt Llewellyn became the eighth rider during the season to win a race when he took the opening crash-strewn encounter at Mallory on the GSE Ducati.

Reynolds and Rutter – now on Dunlops after Honda's shock switch from Michelins – completed the podium but Walker looked the likely race winner until a spectacular highside exiting the Bus Stop chicane. Mackenzie was the unwitting victim of a Bayliss crash at the Hairpin but remounted to finish seventh. Hislop was only sixth.

Walker set a new lap record in race two to beat Mackenzie with Rutter again third. With Hislop back in seventh Mackenzie now enjoyed a 39-point advantage.

HIZZY HURT

The intense battle for the championship came to a sudden end at Cadwell Park when Hislop highsided at Barn Corner during Friday practice. He dislocated several bones in his right hand and damaged tendons in his left ankle but was back from hospital in time to watch the racing.

OTHER HIGHLIGHTS OF '98

- Doohan claims his fifth title after a fight with Biaggi while another Italian Loris Capirossi punts Japanese Tetsuya Harada off the track in the final race to win the 250 crown
- Carl Fogarty wins his third WSB title after a dramatic final round at Sugo – even though he had written himself off mid-way through the tough season
- Other British Champions include: John Crawford (Supersport), Woolsey Coulter (250), Chris Palmer (125)
- Steve Plater wins the undersubscribed British Powerbike series on a Sayno Honda FireBlade and Gus Scott is the runaway success story of the National Sports Production series riding a Yamaha R1
- Christian Lavielle and former WSB champion Doug Polen win the World Endurance title, but Brits Terry Rymer and Brian Morrisson (plus Aussie Peter Goddard) win the final Bol d'Or round at Paul Ricard

Mackenzie did not escape unscathed either. Walker crashed coming out of Barn in the first race and Mackenzie collected the spinning bike and also went down. He suffered a gashed foot but after dashing off to the medical centre to be stitched up, passed himself fit enough to race and took fifth place in the restart which was won by Walker.

The amazing thing was that MacKenzie's spare bike was from the 1996 season and was never used except in absolute emergency since the old-spec engine had all it's peaky horsepower delivery up at the top end making it very difficult to ride – especially after the much smoother delivery of the later-spec engines.

Walker also won the second race from Rutter and Bayliss. Mackenzie, not quite on the adrenaline high of the first race restart, was back in seventh.

It meant that with three rounds left Mackenzie had a 49-point lead in the title chase over Walker with the out-of-action Hislop back in third place.

SILVERSTONE RETURNS

Silverstone returned to the calendar for the first time in 11 years, hosting the tenth round of the *MCN* British Championship and it was James Haydon's turn for a slice of glory. He had missed the previous round after dislocating his shoulder falling down the stairs at home. Recovered from that, he took his first win of the season on the Crescent Suzuki.

Mackenzie and Rutter completed the top three while Walker and Bayliss both crashed but restarted, Walker finishing 14th with his bike stuck in fifth gear and Bayliss ninth.

Haydon crashed in race two, re-injuring the shoulder he had dislocated in his tumble at home. Bayliss took his second win of the year when he beat Walker by over a second in race two with Rutter third again.

Mackenzie finished sixth but was now looking favourite to retain his title.

Hislop bounced back in the penultimate round at Brands by winning the first race. Reynolds took his first win of the year to become the tenth different race winner of the season but fourth and third places shadowing Walker home in both outings gave Mackenzie the title.

In the final Donington Park round Walker won the first race from Rutter and MacPherson but the second race degenerated into a farce when it was declared a wet race. Even with rain clouds threatening everyone started on slicks but sure enough the rain fell and with no red flag forthcoming (once the race start is declared wet it is up to the competitors to run the tyres they think suitable to complete full race distance) it was a case of slithering around trying to stay on two wheels. Mackenzie, along with others pulled in leaving Rutter to take the win from Llewellyn and Rymer – a disappointing way to end a wild season of intense Mackenzie/Hislop rivalry, not to mention a long list of injuries, sackings, controversy and outright excitement.

The Privateer Cup, went to Phil Giles on a Kawasaki after his closest rival Max Vincent crashed out in practice for the final round on his Ray Stringer built ZX-R7.

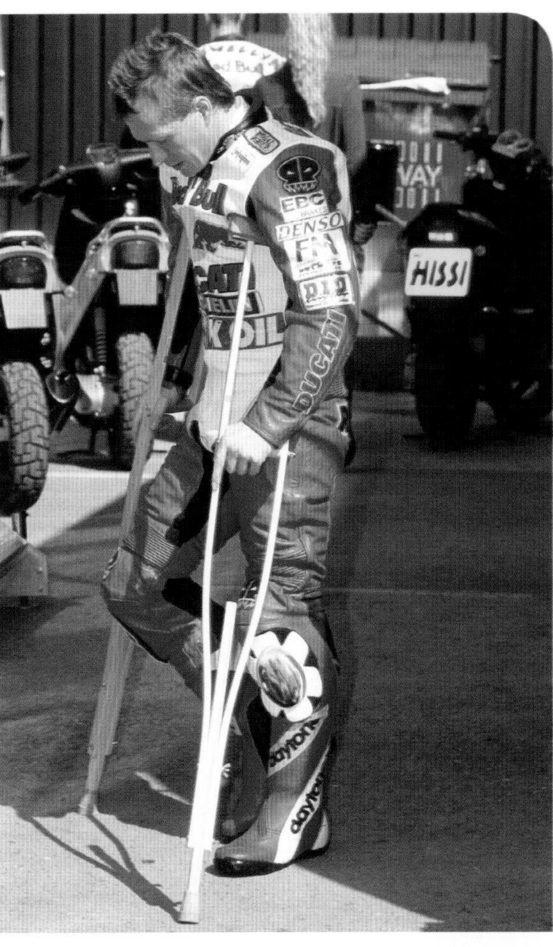

LEFT John Reynolds battled on through the year despite sustaining an ankle injury in a non-championship Mallory Park race crash

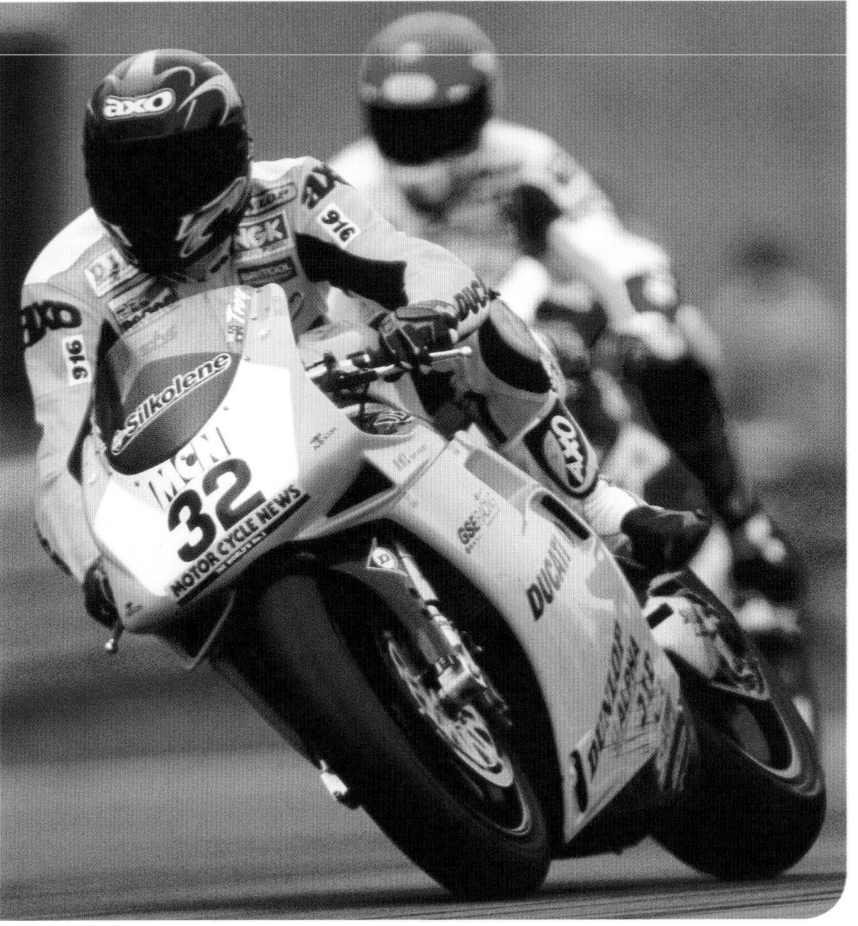

BELOW Aussie Troy Bayliss was the emerging talent from the 1998 season on the GSE Racing Ducati

RIGHT AND FAR RIGHT
Niall Mackenzie – three-times BSB Champion. Mackenzie's toughest title-winning year came in 1998 when Steve Hislop was his team-mate. That really spurred Mackenzie on!

Niall Mackenzie came back to Britain after the most disappointing Grand Prix season of his career, riding an Aprilia in the 250cc class for the 1995 season.

Racing on the big, fast and relatively safe World Championship Grand Prix circuits was one thing, but banging fairings with the hard-nosed BSB regulars on some of the narrow, tree-lined British tracks was very different.

Mackenzie took that into account when he made his decision to return.

He said: "It never really worried me about the tracks because in the back of my mind I wasn't going to push and risk hurting myself. But I have to admit there were times when I did go beyond my limits."

The YZF750s were ex-factory from the Italian Belgarda team, but being a year old, they were no longer at the cutting edge of superbike development. At least that was how Mackenzie saw it.

"While most weekends we had no real speed advantage over our rivals, we had incredible reliability. Rob's (Rob McElnea – a long-term mate from their times in GPs and now his BSB Yamaha team boss) team was so well organised and it was a real team effort.

"I think what happened was Rob went to Italy and cleared out their workshops. We had the same chassis each year. In 1997 we had updated factory engines – but only one new unit for each rider. In 1998 the bikes stayed the same all year long. We went faster each year because we got new suspension and better tyres.

"The great thing for me was that the team stayed the same – we kept our staff and that gave us a real advantage."

Mackenzie's 1996 team-mate was James Whitham who had been a BSB title contender the previous year until he was laid low by cancer.

The pair of them hit it off and have remained firm friends since.

Mackenzie said: "The time with Whitham was a lot of fun. We worked as a team, sharing information, but on track we battled it out.

"He won twice as many races as me but he missed out scoring in the first round and he knew that was a disaster straight away. For me the championship was won in the first round. I always had that cushion.

"I knew from that moment that he'd struggle to win the championship if I remained a consistent finisher. But to his credit, he fought back. At Donington we were equal on points. I won the first race and he was third. I just had to follow him home in the final race."

Whitham was plagued by a tyre problem in the first race, which effectively handed Mackenzie the title.

"Whit blamed Rob for the bad tyre choice. Rob blamed him. I chose my own tyres. I led most of the second race but he passed me and in the last few laps I was riding around thinking, 'if I pass him now and f**k it up I'll never forgive myself.' I liked him too much anyway and I actually wanted him to win the race as consolation for losing the title. Actually, I desperately wanted to win the last race!"

Whitham left the British scene, so Yamaha signed up-and-coming Chris Walker – on the say-so of Mackenzie.

"I got to know him in 1996 when he kind of befriended me, and I was keen to have him in the team. He made me laugh all season long but I had never realised how competitive he was.

"I wanted to win as many races as possible in '97 but he won races and I didn't like that. The nice thing was that it was all clean between us."

The defining point in the season was after Mackenzie crashed at Cadwell Park and broke his wrist. Two weeks later he raced at Brands Hatch.

"I'd been to Brian Simpson, the famed bone welder. He fixed it for me and I went to Brands aiming to salvage points but I got pole and two wins. Amazing considering I'd gone there just hoping I could ride!"

Yamaha signed Steve Hislop for the 1998 season, which did not sit well with Mackenzie.

"I never really disliked him," said Mackenzie. "How could I, he never had a bad bone in his body? But I never figured him out.

"I had a lot of respect for him but I liked to get on with my team-mates."

Mackenzie found it hard to cope with Hislop's infamous mood swings. "Steve was cocky when he beat me," he recalled. "What I hated most was the way he got to me. He'd be chat, chat, chat all day long when he was up and say nothing when he was down. That really upset me."

What really spurred Mackenzie was a Hizzy photo shoot for *MCN* after Donington Park.

He said: "I'd crashed out and Hizzy won the race. *MCN* ran a picture of Hizzy masking one of the digits on his number 11 plate, suggesting he had the title in the bag. I cut that out and stuck it up on the wall in my gym. That image gave me all the motivation I needed to beat him."

It was nothing new for Mackenzie to be battling with his team-mates. The new element was the amount of angst between the two.

Mackenzie recalled: "At Oulton in the second meeting of the year he beat me in race two on the last lap. I was fuming and spat the dummy claiming he'd roughed me up. It was a nothing incident really that I'd made out to be a big fairing–banging incident.

"But it was Snetterton that really scared me. He never lifted off and we both ran off the track. At the Bombhole I wanted to run into him but that would have taken us both out. Thank God I didn't do it.

"What won me the title was being totally motivated. But my motivation came from outside (supplied by Hislop) rather than from within. In my entire career I never felt like I wanted to beat someone so much. But once I'd finished racing all those feelings disappeared."

Now 37 years old many expected Mackenzie – with three BSB titles in the bag – to quit racing, even though he was still at the top of his game. He was lured into another season by the thoughts of riding the all-new Yamaha R7.

"Maybe I should have then quit at the end of 1998 but what swung it was the R7. It was the most gorgeous bike I'd seen and I wanted to race one. I turned down Suzuki and Kawasaki to ride the Yamaha but in November Cadbury's pulled out. By then any other offers I had were gone.

"All winter Rob and I kept knocking on doors to make it happen. We went to the R7 launch in Spain and took a bike. Rob made contact with Virgin and ten days before the first race we had a decision from them to go racing."

DUCA
Troy#32
RKL PRO PAINT
GSERACING
DUCATI CORSE
INTERNET
NETWORK
AUTOCOM
MCN
32
MOTOR CYCLE NEWS
THE WORLD'S No.1

1999

The arrival of GSE Racing

After three years of dominating the British scene with their ex-factory YZF750s hand-me-downs from Belgarda Yamaha Rob McElnea's team went into the 1999 season with an entirely new look.

Gone were what had become the familiar Cadbury's Boost colours. The confectionery giant having decided only in the previous December that they would not continue for a fourth year. That left Rob 'Mac' and Yamaha a major last-minute panic to secure the necessary backing for another top-line season.

McElnea told *Motorcycle Racer* magazine: "Obviously Yamaha had been making enquiries (with prospective backers in case Cadbury's quit racing) but had come up with nothing. So either we stayed at home or went racing – somehow.

"My last resort was to ring our product sponsors to see if each of them could come up with a bit more budget. My very last call was to Tom Beman of Autocom and while he couldn't help, he suggested I should ring Virgin (Autocom supplied their communications kit to Virgin for the 'limo bikes' they ran at the time).

"I got a call from Richard Branson's man who got back to us in 24 hours to say they were interested and it went from there. Virgin only had the money for a one-man team and while we could have topped it up to run two with cash from other backers, Virgin didn't want other sponsors on the bike."

It was the lifeline that the team needed, and meant that their champion Niall Mackenzie would now be racing the all-new, fuel-injected R7. Initially it was thought they would continue to get full factory bikes but the reality was that they only had access to the same customer kit parts that anyone else could buy. This meant the team would have to develop in-house since there were no full works bikes, as such, anywhere in the world.

Two bikes came from Japan, race kitted but these were no better than the bikes with engines prepared by the team's freelance engineer Stewart Johnstone of NorthMoor Engineering.

PREVIOUS PAGE Troy Bayliss smoothed the rough edges off his riding style and won the 1999 BSB title riding the INS-backed GSE Racing Ducati

ABOVE Walker leads Emmett, Reynolds and the rest of the field from the start at Mallory Park

RIGHT Walker looks straight down the lens of James Wright's camera

The 'revvy' new engine also meant Mackenzie would have to adopt a different riding style. McElnea said: "The old YZF had no mid-corner grip so Niall used to sit the bike up early and spin the rear tyre out of corners. The new bike has a 35mm longer swing-arm but the short motor (thanks to it's stacked gearbox) allows Yamaha to retain the good geometry of the old YFZ. The actual chassis feel is not that different but Niall is able to use a much higher corner speed with the R7 so he's having to ride it using a different style. It's more like a high corner speed 250 style than he's been used to in some time."

GSE'S NEW LOOK

It was not only the Yamaha team that underwent change. GSE Racing had a whole new look also. Their big problem in 1998 was that they had no clear figure-head leading the team. Team owner Darrell Healey had his business to run. John Hackett had engines to build and his own business to develop. PR man Sean Sutton was busy chasing sponsors.

For the new season Healey hired Colin Wright to manage the team. He was respected as one of the most astute managers in the business, as well as being one of the most outspoken!

Wright, in turn, hired one of his former Kawasaki engineers, Stewart Johnstone as crew chief, leaving Hackett to concentrate on building engines of the latest factory spec Ducati 998s.

The bikes sported the orange livery of British-based INS (Internet Network Services), one of the many integrated communications providers that sprang up on the back of the rapidly expanding worldwide web. The INS cash, worth an estimated £250,000 was considered the biggest non-motorcycle related sponsorship deal to hit the British Championship.

The team retained Bayliss, regarded as one of the most promising international superbike prospects but also pulled a master-stroke, signing Neil Hodgson. The 25-year-old was coming back to domestic action after six years of World Championship competition. This included three seasons of largely unfulfilled promise in World Superbike racing aboard factory Ducatis (1996/97) and Kawasakis (1998). The step back to racing in Britain by Hodgson was a determined bid to rebuild his career.

Ben Atkins' Red Bull Ducati team, managed by Roger Marshall, also had the latest-spec Ducatis for John Reynolds and Sean Emmett and opted to remain with Michelin (GSE were on Dunlops), even though the French tyres had not been so competitive during the previous year.

KAWASAKI FACTORY BIKES

With Wright going to GSE, Kawasaki hired former 500cc Grand Prix privateer Simon Buckmaster as their team manager. He had been Suzuki's World Superbike team co-ordinator but with the Hertfordshire-based Harris team no longer running the GSX-R750 programme – the Belgian-based Alstare outfit had been given that role – Buckmaster brought in several of their old crew to look after the green bikes.

Chris Walker remained with the team with Steve Hislop as his new team-mate. But that was not how it was originally meant to be. Warwick Nowland was originally brought into the team, a very early signing by Wright prior to the Motorcycle Show held at the National Exhibition Centre in November of 1998. The Australian rider was ditched without even having the chance to run a single lap on a ZX-7RR.

Kawasaki claimed 24-year-old Nowland's departure was brought about by his failure to secure a UK work permit. Buckmaster said in *MCR*: "It's not Warwick's fault but with pre-season testing imminent we had to make a painful decision to let him go."

Walker added: "Obviously there's been a lot of changes since Colin (Wright) left the team and Warwick was one of the people most affected by them. I don't know exactly what happened but I do know it's a shame because he never got a go on the bike. Now we'll never know how fast he could have been."

For Hislop, signing up to ride for Kawasaki was a lifeline. He had raced a Kawasaki in 1996 but that team experienced financial problems mid-season and the Scot only kept racing thanks to Ben Atkins providing a Kawasaki with Red Bull backing.

For 1997 Hislop had signed for Atkins to race for the Red Bull Ducati team but was sacked mid-season. Kawasaki snapped him up to ride for them at Mallory Park to replace their absent rider Terry Rymer, who was on World Endurance racing duty. He then finished the season on Ray Stringer's Sabre Airways Kawasaki.

BELOW Another James Haydon visit to the 'kittie litter'

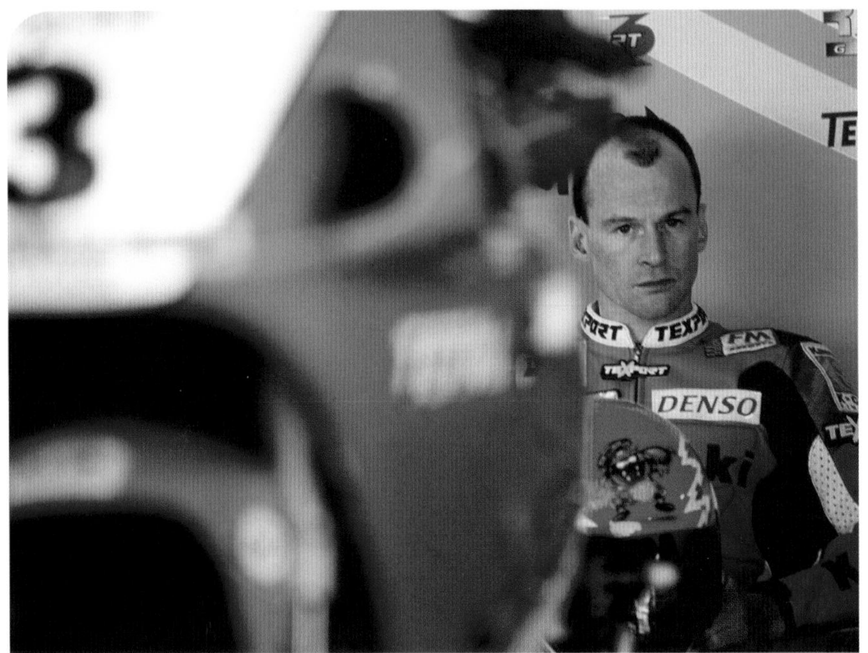

ABOVE Steve Hislop had every right to look concerned with the Kawasaki. He was never comfortable with the bike's handling and was eventually fired

In 1998 with no other offers, he grabbed a no money deal with Cadbury's Boost Yamaha and was fighting for the championship until he was injured at Cadwell Park. Without money to run two riders McElnea had no option but to release Hislop for the 1999 season.

Hizzy told *MCR*: "I'm over the moon. I was beginning to think that I might end up with nothing for this year. Yamaha might have come up with a 600 but things were desperate. I've raced the Kawasaki before and loved the power delivery. It suited me so well – just like the YZF."

Kawasaki UK secured a unique deal on equipment. They had two ex-Akira Yanagawa 1998 World Superbike full factory bikes and two factory-kitted machines – with the riders given one of each.

SUZUKI GIVEN THE WORKS TOO

For the first time since embarking on their foray into the British Championship in 1996, the Bournemouth-based Crescent Suzuki no longer had to rely on developing road bikes for racing. They secured full-on factory bikes, albeit ex-WSB 1998 machinery but also aimed to develop their own fuel-injection system using Pectel software.

In the close season Terry Rymer left the team, preferring to concentrate on World Endurance racing in 1999, and to fill the gap team boss Paul Denning brought in a virtual unknown, Marty Craggill, to race alongside James Haydon. The Australian however arrived with a strong pedigree having won the Superbike crown back home where he was a former sparring partner of Bayliss.

There were no works Hondas (or any top privateers) in 1999 but Ray Stringer assembled one of the best privateer teams seen in the championship after securing backing from finance company First National to run the promising Max Vincent and Aussie hard man Paul Young on a pair of R7 Yamahas. Other privateer hopefuls included Dave Heal on Aden Murcott's ex-Stringer Kawasaki and another Kawasaki rider, Phil Giles, the previous season's Privateer Cup Champion.

OPPOSING STYLES

There could not have been two more differing approaches to winning races than those seen in the first round at Brands Hatch. Neil Hodgson was keen to prove the doubters wrong, and provided a classy display of cool and calculating riding to claim the first race while James Haydon used his typically aggressive full throttle, wild sliding style to win the second.

Haydon almost crashed out of the first race when he tried to steal a couple of places from Walker and Reynolds by going inside them into Surtees. He had to run onto the grass to save going down but that dropped him to fourth.

Walker finished second with Reynolds third but Haydon bounced back to win the second race under a lot of pressure from Walker. Hodgson, enjoying his return to the British scene completed the podium to leave Brands with a single point advantage over Walker.

Haydon's new Suzuki team-mate Marty Craggill did not have such a good weekend. He crashed in qualifying and had a footpeg spear his thigh

muscle. Although he managed to finish 12th in the first race, the injury would haunt him for much of the season.

The biggest shock of the first round was the disappointing performance of the Yamaha R7 in Mackenzie's hands. It lacked power and proved unreliable even compared to the privateer First National R7 of Paul Young.

Haydon took the championship lead in front of a record-breaking 20,000 crowd at Easter Bank Holiday Monday Thruxton after finishing second to Troy Bayliss in a five-bike scrap for the lead in race one and then won the second after another five-rider battle. Bayliss looked set to make it a double but out-braked himself into the notorious chicane which let both Haydon and Walker through.

Haydon led the points on 81 to Walker's 76 with Bayliss starting to look like a major threat in third on 63 and Hodgson back to fourth with 52.

A Bayliss double at Oulton Park followed by another win at Snetterton plus a second place behind Reynolds in the first race set the Aussie up with a 24-point championship lead after four rounds.

Walker's title hopes went off track a little, especially at Snetterton where his Kawasaki (along with all the other fours) was something like 5mph down on the Italian V-twins through the speedtrap.

BAYLISS'S POINTS LEAD SLASHED

After a three-week break the championship took a dramatic turn at Donington with Bayliss crashing out of race one in a mêlée triggered by Hislop, which also took out Reynolds. Bayliss could only finish sixth in the second race and saw his points lead slashed to one!

Walker was beaten by Haydon in a first race thriller but looked set to clear off into the distance in race two until tyre problems forced him to back off. He finished fourth.

The race was won by Reynolds after pulling off a sweet pass on Haydon at Goddard on the final lap. The standings could hardly have been closer: Bayliss 168, Walker 167, Haydon 163!

BELOW John Reynolds finished third in the series on the Red Bull Ducati

Silverstone was the end of the line for Hislop and Kawasaki. He had struggled all year to come to terms with the ZX-7RR. The problem was that having one factory bike and one kitted bike per rider meant it was impossible to do any back to back testing. After Oulton Park the team gave him both factory bikes and Walker took the kit bikes, which he preferred. Hizzy initially looked more comfortable with this arrangement, grabbing two fifths at Snetterton but the much stiffer works bike still did not help him become the front-runner everyone felt he should be and his best effort at Silverstone was a distant eighth.

Then Kawasaki UK organised an evening test session at Donington Park, when he was preparing to set-off for one of his World Endurance commitments at Spa. He refused to do the test because he didn't feel there would be enough time to learn anything meaningful and, after setting pole at Spa, heard that his job in BSB was over.

The championship saw Bayliss back to his best at Silverstone, nailing another double in a day dominated by Ducatis. Reynolds and Hodgson completed the podium in race one but Walker finished second in race two, determined to put one over on Reynolds who had taken him out at the Hairpin in the first race.

Haydon had an off-day crashing out of the first race in a spectacular highside going into a corner then falling foul of tyre problems in race two. That meant Hodgson was now third in the points standings but the series was coming down to a straight fight between two riders, Bayliss and Walker, with the Aussie having the edge 218 to 187. Both, however, were to falter in the next two rounds.

RED BULL TEAM FIND FORM

Oulton Park was not too bad for Bayliss – sixth and second but Knockhill was a total disaster with a clutch problem hampering him to an eighth in race one, followed by no points in race two when he was caught up in a Haydon crash.

Walker scored well – a second and three thirds – but even four podiums meant he fell prey to the flying Reynolds.

In fact both Red Bull Ducati riders hit top form. Reynolds won the first Oulton Park race from Emmett but dropped back to third in race two behind his team-mate and Bayliss. At Silverstone they continued their assault with Emmett winning one race and Reynolds the other.

That meant Bayliss still held the points lead with 256 – 17 up on Reynolds with Walker a further six adrift. Knockhill was also Mackenzie's first podium of the year with a second place in race two on the R7.

Haydon won the first race at Mallory Park from Emmett, Walker and Bayliss but Reynolds was back in front in race two from Bayliss and Walker.

At Cadwell Park Hislop was drafted back into the action, riding a second Virgin Yamaha for three good reasons: to help speed development, to give Mackenzie added incentive and hopefully to give the sponsors (and

BELOW Lots of worried faces in the Virgin Yamaha garage – and with good reason. After enjoying un-rivalled success with ex-factory YZFs, the new R7 took ages to sort

ABOVE Bayliss in the rain at Donington

fans) something to get excited about in what was a frankly disappointing year with the new bike.

Hislop wasted no time settling back into the groove setting the pace on both Friday and Saturday as well as finishing fifth and fourth in the races to complete an inspired return to racing.

At the front line of the battle though Walker took his first win of the year in front of the huge 30,000 crowd – by far the biggest turnout of the year – while Bayliss, fourth in the first encounter, took the second race from the Kawasaki rider to establish an 18-point lead in the series.

Walker kept the pressure up, winning the first race at Brands Hatch but Bayliss finished second after Hodgson had slowed to allow his team-mate through, a move which did not go down too well with the fans.

Walker's challenge faltered in the second race though when he was forced to retire with a clutch problem.

Reynolds and Emmett netted a one–two for the Red Bull team but GSE's Bayliss took third ahead of Hodgson again to retain a healthy 23-point lead going into the final round.

Bayliss clinched the title in the first race with a safe sixth place, even though Walker won it. Hodgson, with no longer any team orders to worry about led a GSE Racing one–two across the line in the second race to sneak into fourth place overall in the points ahead of Haydon who had a disappointing final three rounds in the championship. Bayliss had finished his business in the series and was on the move for the following year.

OTHER HIGHLIGHTS OF '99

- Alex Criville wins the 500cc Grand Prix title but Repsol Honda team-mate Mick Doohan's career ends with a crash at Jerez
- Aprilia's Valentino Rossi and Emilio Alzamora (Honda) claim the 250cc and 125cc World titles respectively
- Carl Fogarty takes his record-breaking fourth World Superbike title
- Iain MacPherson is runner up to Frenchman Stephane Chambon in World Supersport
- Other British Champions include: John Crawford (Supersport), John McGuinness (250cc) and Darren Barton (125cc)
- The Superbike privateer championship is won by Aussie Paul Young
- Brit Terry Rymer (and Frenchman Jehan D'Orgeix) win the World Endurance title riding for Kawasaki

4
MOTORBIKESAU.com

2000

BSB rivals get tough in 2000

Winning the title set Bayliss up for graduation into the World Championship as a factory rider with Ducati Corse. GSE Racing boss Wright, looking for a big name replacment, signed up Niall Mackenzie to ride alongside Hodgson and they had similar 168bhp Ducati 996s to those that factory riders Carl Fogarty and Bayliss were running in the World series.

The Red Bull Ducati team switched from Michelin to Dunlop and signed James Haydon to partner Reynolds.

Chris Walker switched to Crescent Suzuki to ride their National Tyres Clarion-backed GSX-R750. The team opted not to run the latest 2000-spec engines and at 'only 163bhp' their 1999 power unit was marginally down on the Ducatis but Walker and new signing John Crawford could make the most of the bikes' nimble handling thanks to the latest Showa suspension and Brembo brakes.

Walker said the bike did not have as much grunt as the Kawasaki he rode the previous year but was a much better balanced machine than the ZX-7RR he had ridden in 1999.

With no Mackenzie, Virgin Yamaha's line-up on a pair of R7s consisted of Hislop and Paul Brown who was an old Yamaha sparring partner of McElnea's from the Loctite Yamaha days when Brown raced a TZ250.

The other top R7-based outfit was Ray Stringer's Level 3 Yamaha team. He signed 25-year-old Michael Rutter who was returning to British racing after a fruitless year in the 500cc Grand Prix on a Millar Honda V-twin. Rutter had many positives from that sortie into the World Championship and he maintains to this day the experience taught him so much about racecraft and bike set-up, even if the machine he had been riding was hopelessly outclassed. Even though he was on a privateer bike this time around, Rutter was still considered a force, having finished sixth overall in the 1998 championship on a Honda RC45. His team-mate was 30-year-old Aussie Paul Young.

PREVIOUS PAGE Neil Hodgson came back to Britain to rebuild his career and with the backing of the GSE racing team that's exactly what he achieved

OPPOSITE The second race at Oulton Park was always going to end in tears. Walker (left) and Hodgson had already banged fairings at Lakeside and the Hairpin when they tried to outbrake each other into Lodge on the final lap

There were three so-called 'factory' Hondas in action. The reality was the bikes were little more than customer-kitted privateer VTR1000 SP-1 V-twins run by top class teams. Paul Bird's Vimto-backed team signed 19-year-old James Toseland and the more experienced Sean Emmett while Harris Performance fielded 22-year-old Shane Byrne. None of the three riders was even able to exploit their natural talent on a bike that never lived up to the hype. Put simply, it handled well but was massively down on power to its rivals by as much as 15bhp! Both Toseland (broken leg mid-season) and Byrne (spinal injuries and lacerated liver at Thruxton) would suffer serious injuries during the year.

Kawasaki's ageing ZX-7RR was given massive 50mm upside-down WP forks for 2000 and radial-mounted huge AP six-pot brakes. The team made a great start to the campaign with Steve Plater leading Aussie team-mate Peter Goddard (who did a development year on the Aprilia RSV1000 in the 1999 WSB season) to a one–two finish in the non-championship Mallory Park 'Race of the Year' but that was about as good as it got all year.

RED BULL WIN BOTH BRANDS RACES

As the season's action began for real, with the opening round of the British Championship at Brands Hatch the Red Bull Ducati team could not have asked for a better start. Reynolds won the first race, Haydon the second. Any celebrations were muted, however, as their Ducati 748-mounted Supersport team-mate Ian Simpson suffered a badly broken leg in an horrific crash at Clearways.

In the first superbike race Kawasaki's Goddard crashed on the sighting lap when his engine cut out going into Graham Hill Bend but he started the race on his spare bike. Walker had the holeshot start only for the race to be red-flagged due to a crash. He led again in the restart from pole man Hislop but Reynolds closed them down and took the lead from Walker at Druids. Walker and Hislop completed the rostrum.

In the second race Reynolds almost crashed out after clipping the grass at Clearways and then again at Druids after a near highside – but somehow he bounced back into the saddle. Haydon – fifth in race one – took the race honours. Hislop was second and Neil Hodgson was upbeat after finishing third (he was fourth in race one) on the INS Ducati. Mackenzie had struggled on his debut, finishing sixth in the first race and crashing out of the second. The disappointment for the triple champion would continue most of the year.

WALKER'S SUZUKI BLOWS UP

Chris Walker's Suzuki suffered a spectacular engine failure in the first race at Donington Park. Either a valve broke or a valve seat failed but either way his race ended in a plume of smoke at the Foggy Esses.

The race was won by Reynolds but Walker bounced back to win the second race from championship-leader Reynolds. Hodgson was again on the podium with second and third places in the respective races and now sat second in the points. Reynolds led on 83, Hodgson was second with 65 and Walker third on 56.

BELOW A youthful James Toseland made the superbike ranks in 2000 with the Vimto Honda

After finishing sixth in race one at Donington Park Emmett declared the SP-1 to be lacking in power, not just against the Ducatis but also against the fours. "It's really stable on the brakes and turns well," he told *MCN*. "The slipper clutch means you can brake hard without worrying about the back end jumping around but it's just down on power."

Haydon won the first race at the bumpy, super-fast Thruxton circuit from Walker and Hodgson while Reynolds finished fourth. The race had been run in two parts after being red-flagged for a Shane Byrne and John Crawford crash at the chicane. Byrne suffered two fractured vertebrae and mis-alignment of his spinal column, plus a lacerated liver. He later described that as the most painful injury of his career and also one that he thought might kill him!

The second race was red-flagged on lap two with Crawford again at the centre of the action. This time his GSX-R750 engine had blown up and dumped oil on the circuit.

The race was restarted but came to a halt after 13 of the scheduled 20 laps due to rain and Hodgson was credited with the win from Hislop and Reynolds. Haydon was fourth and Walker fifth, a result that dropped him to fourth in the points.

RIVALS TOLD TO CALM DOWN

After Thruxton the riders were told to calm things down. Reynolds had complained about Hodgson's alleged forceful passing at Brands Hatch. Hislop tangled with Walker at the Club chicane which prompted Virgin boss McElnea to claim Walker "was riding like a motocrosser!" Hislop was non-plussed: "They can have a meeting and talk about it but you might as well talk to a wall. If a rider wants to ride hard he will."

Maybe everyone had forgotten the warning because three weeks later at the Donington Park World Superbike round Hodsgon beat Walker in a sensational second race which saw the pair of them smashing into each other, both riders taking unbelievable risks to stay in front of the other. The championship's own hardman Noriyuki Haga was involved in the scrap but even he backed off when he saw the lengths the Brits were prepared to go to.

Pierfrancesco Chili actually looked the likely winner until he crashed his Suzuki and that left the way open for the Brits to score a popular one–two.

Hodgson, the race winner, joked: "I had a great race with Chris. It's good to see he's not changed at all – he's just as dangerous as ever. He's the only man on earth who makes Haga look like a safety conscious rider!"

Any smiles seen on the podium at the Donington circuit soon disappeared in the next British round at Oulton Park.

Hodgson won the first race from Walker but tempers flared after the pair of them clashed in the closing stages of the second race.

On the last lap they banged fairings at Lakeside and the Hairpin. Then, as they tried to outbrake each other at Lodge, they collided again, both running off the track. Hodgson stayed on board to cross the line fourth.

ABOVE John Reynolds somehow managed to save this near highside at Brands

RIGHT James Haydon celebrates after his Thruxton success

Walker finished 13th and his Suzuki team protested. The Ducati rider was handed a 36-second penalty, dropping him to 14th place.

Hodgson's team boss Colin Wright lodged an appeal against the penalty that effectively robbed his rider of a 12-point difference between fourth and 14th plus the one point Walker would have lost being demoted one further place to 14th.

Wright said: "We genuinely feel a miscarriage of justice has taken place and if it goes against us and Neil loses the championship by less than 12 points, in our eyes we will have been robbed."

The on-track clashes showed that Hodgson had ditched his old Mr Nice Guy persona and he refused to back down when confronted about his riding. He told *MCN*: "Chris accused me of turning in too early but I didn't. I was still on the straight and moving across to defend the inside line. We both went for the same piece of Tarmac. It was a racing incident. I don't ride dirty so I don't see why I should change my riding."

Walker, always concious of public opinion, tried to avoid further confrontation and said: "We're both right at the top of our game. We both want to be winning races and be the top man in Britain. Neil's a great guy and I'm sure he feels the same. Racing's racing."

The appeal still had not been heard when the fifth round of the series took place at Snetterton and Hodgson was again subjected to judicial procedures. This time, he fell foul of the authorities for giving his team-mate Niall Mackenzie a lift back to the pits after his Ducati had broken down in morning warm-up. He was fined £1,000 for that indiscretion.

Hodgson was also given a six-month suspended race ban but this was lifted after Wright protested.

The matter clearly wasn't going to worry Hodgson who claimed the first BSB pole of his career. However, he had to give best to Walker in the restarted first race when he missed a gear out of the final corner.

Reynolds won the second race after making it through the backmarkers better than Hodgson. Walker was third and the championship battle had closed up. Reynolds led on 194 points, with Hodgson on 173 and Walker 151.

HODGSON GIVEN HIS POINTS BACK

On the Wednesday before the Silverstone round the GSE Ducati team won their appeal against the penalities imposed after the infamous clash between their rider, Hodgson, and Walker at Oulton Park. Not that that calmed the action down one little bit on the race track.

Hodgson beat Walker in race one but the pair were again subjected to a controversial incident in the second race when Hodgson crashed out at Abbey. The pair of them clashed at the apex.

Hodgson claimed in *MCN*: "I was the fastest rider all weekend and was clearly knocked off."

Walker reponded: "It was all over so quickly I don't know what happened. Neil was coming past me and we collided. I was just concentrating on staying on for some points. To get the win was fantastic. It's hard trying to look happy in second place."

Walker won race two from Haydon and Hislop – but fifth-placed Reynolds still led the series with 221 points from Hodgson 209 and Walker 195.

At Oulton Park, for the second time in the season, Hodgson was on pole for the third round in a row but he stalled on the line and was sent to the back of the grid. Something similar had happened to Haydon at Silverstone two weeks earlier and after the chaos it caused, championship officials instigated a new rule saying if it happened to anyone else they would have to start from the back of the grid.

When the lights turned green Hodgson rode like a man possessed, going from last to first in just eight laps! Haydon won a two-man scrap for second with Hislop. Walker was fourth from Reynolds and Mackenzie.

Walker beat Hodgson in the second race by two tenths of a second but with Reynolds only third, Hodgson claimed the championship lead for the first time all year with 254 points, six clear of Reynolds and 21 ahead of Walker.

With the lull in domestic action, Hodgson set up his future in the World series with first and second places in the European round of that championship at Brands Hatch. Hislop, Haga and Colin Edwards all crashed out at Paddock in the first race and Hislop suffered a broken neck. Unbelievably the injury was not diagnosed until the week before the Mallory Park BSB round in September and that meant he would miss the rest of the season. Incredibly, Hislop had tried to ride in front

BELOW The under-powered SP1 was not a user-friendly motorcycle – as Sean Emmett found to his cost at Oulton Park

ABOVE Chris Walker's BSB title hopes disappear in a cloud of smoke at Donington

ABOVE RIGHT Walker, in tears, trudges past masses of well-wishers on his way back to the pits

of his local fans at Knockhill but withdrew after a couple of painful laps in practice. Doctors later said that one false move could have paralysed him!

Walker won both races at the Scottish venue to close Hodgson's championship lead to a single point.

Walker was over 20 seconds clear in race one from the Level 3 Yamaha duo of Rutter and Young who were having their best race of the season. Hodgson had to be content with sixth place but was second in race two. Haydon completed the race two podium.

Amid continuing rumours that Hodgson was going to ride in the World Championship in 2001, the two pace-makers on the domestic front shared the spoils in the ninth round at Cadwell Park before Walker turned the tables at Mallory Park. He finished second to Hodgson in the first race but won the second from Reynolds, with Hodgson having to be content with third. It was an amazing performance by Walker who was riding with several broken bones in his right foot and a broken left hand after crashing in mid-week testing. Adding to his discomfort, he was also diagnosed as suffering from food-poisoning at the meeting. His heroic performance gave him the championship lead by a point from Hodgson as they headed to Brands Hatch for the penultimate round of the series.

The championship rivals had mixed fortunes on the Indy circuit. Walker crashed out of the wet first race while Hodgson finished sixth. The race was won by acknowledged 'rain-master' Michael Rutter from Haydon, Reynolds and Anthony Gobert – the Aussie who had been brought in to replace the injured Hislop on the Virgin Yamaha.

Gobert looked a potential race two winner until he crashed on oil and the race was won by Walker from Rutter and Reynolds. Hodgson crashed at Graham Hill Bend and that gave Walker a 21-point lead in the series and now the Nottingham rider only had to score two third places at his local Donington Park to be assured of the title.

WALKER'S HOPES GO UP IN SMOKE

Hodgson – armed with Troy Bayliss's factory Ducati 996 for the finale – clawed nine of those points back by winning the first Donington Park race while Walker was content to finish third behind Reynolds. It meant that the local rider to the Leicestershire circuit was still 12 points clear going into the second race, but no one could have predicted the outcome.

Walker was running a comfortable fourth, just enough to seal the title, when his bike began making ominous noises with six of the 22 laps remaining. The rattles quickly turned to a billowing plume of smoke. With little more than two laps – or seven miles of racing – remaining, Walker pulled over at Redgate and parked up. His championship hopes had literally gone up in smoke. It was the second time during the season his GSX-R750 had died in a cloud of oil fumes at this circuit.

Distraught after coming so close to clinching the title, Walker trudged back to the pits in tears and said: "It's hard to take comfort from securing second place in the championship as we were so close, but I'll bounce back. I can't think about the future at the moment. I need to get over this first."

Hodgson finished second to Haydon in the race but it was enough to give him the title by eight points (422–414).

He said: "I knew I needed a lot of luck to win the title and that's what I got. I really feel for Chris. He's ridden so well all year."

Reynolds confirmed his third place in the championship with second and third places at Donington. Hodgson's team-mate Niall Mackenzie announced his retirement after finishing fourth in the second race.

The 39-year-old Scot said: "It's the right decision. I've got friends from Grand Prix who have been forced to retire through injury. I don't think Carl Fogarty saw his career ending that way (through injury). This is my 20th season of racing. I know I can be as fast as anyone but I'm not prepared to make those silly moves any more. The longer you race, the more chance there is it will happen to you. Joey Dunlop's death didn't influence my decision but it does make you realise what can happen."

Going into 2001 the British scene would have a very different look with Hodgson moving on, into the World Championship together with the GSE Racing équipe on HM Plant-backed Ducatis, Walker off to Grand Prix riding a Shell Honda NSR500 and no Mackenzie, well not as a regular anyway!

OTHER HIGHLIGHTS OF '00

- Kenny Roberts wins the 500cc Grand Prix title riding a Suzuki RGV500
- The 250cc World title is decided in the final inches of the last race at Phillip Island in Olivier Jacque's favour. He beats his Yamaha team-mate Shinya Nakano across the line by 14 thousandths of a second! Italian Roberto Locatelli wins the 125cc title
- Carl Fogarty suffers what turns out to be a career-ending crash in the first WSB round in Australia. Colin Edwards wins the title for Castrol Honda
- Other British Champions include: Jim Moodie (Supersport), Callum Ramsey (250cc), Kenny Tibble (125cc), David Jefferies (Superstock)

BELOW Steve Hislop looked to be turning around Virgin Yamaha's fortunes with the R7 until his WSB crash at Brands which left him with a broken neck

ABOVE Bayliss did the business on the track but behind closed doors he had a few intense discussions with his team boss

Colin Wright enjoys an enviable reputation as one of the most efficient road racing team managers in the business. He is noted for his straight talking, no-nonsense, almost confrontational style of management but it obviously works. He has led Kawasaki UK and GSE Racing to British Superbike titles and enjoyed success in the World series running GSE as a satellite team to the official Ducati Corse factory squad.

In 1997 he helped Kawasaki become a major player in the championship again but then, against all the odds, the long-time Kawasaki man switched to manage Darrell Healey's GSE Racing team for the 1999 season and has been there ever since. Under his leadership, the team has taken the British title three times, first with Troy Bayliss in 1999 and then Neil Hodgson in 2000. On the back of those successes, the team graduated to become a major player for three seasons in the World Championship, operating as a privately-run Ducati satellite équipe . The team took a year out in 2004 but bounced back in style to win the 2005 BSB title with Gregorio Lavilla.

SMOOTHING OUT BAYLISS

"Troy took no time at all to gel with the team. The thing that always impressed me was that he'd do laps in his mind sat on the bike before going out for each session. He'd come into the pits, sit on the bike and shut his eyes, then he'd do a full lap sat there, making all the gear changes, braking etc.

"Troy was an excitable and eager personality and couldn't wait to get out on the bike. Because of that excitement he wanted to be the fastest as soon as he got out of the garage. And he'd get frustrated if he wasn't.

"He was probably the least technically minded of the three riders we had in those two seasons and that led to his frustrations.

"We went to Knockhill with Troy leading the championship by 46 points but the team had four DNFs that day which was unheard of for us. Mallory he got a fourth and a second and went to Cadwell with only 18 points in hand and rode like an amateur.

"Whether it was the title race getting to him or what I don't know but he was missing apexes, running onto the grass. So I collared him and said, 'back off mate, you need to calm down and think about what you're doing out there.' And he just flew at me saying: 'Get this f**king bike sorted and I'll ride it.' To which I replied: 'No one can sort that bike out the way you're riding the f**king thing.'

"It was a totally confrontational situation and all it did was to antagonise Troy more. I've had confrontations with every bloke that's ridden for me but I've also had a good relationship with all of them. I don't believe you can have that sort of relationship without the confrontation. It's actually healthy to be able to do that, providing you're big enough to accept your faults and do something about correcting them.

"Troy and I both realised after that confrontation that we both needed to treat each other in a different way. I realised confrontation didn't work with him, where it had with other riders.

"Troy and I both sat down after Cadwell to work out how we could make things better. He partly accepted he was riding like a dick. I accepted that antagonising him wasn't going to motivate him to ride any better. That was the only time we had a cross-word – and he went on to win the title."

RESURRECTING HODGSON'S CAREER

"Neil Hodgson had reached a point in his life where he realised it was time to either resurrect his career or get out of the sport. We spent three days together at my house, getting to know each other. I wanted to understand what made him tick. We came away with a much better understanding of each other.

"In 2000 when he was battling with Walker he didn't cope at all well with the pressure initially. At Knockhill Walker kicked his arse in damp conditions. Neil had always claimed he was good in the wet but that clearly wasn't the case at that time.

"The thing that annoyed us was the way he sulked so badly. He refused to go to the podium and instead went back to his motorhome, got changed and went home. He didn't say goodbye, nothing.

"We got packed up and then set off and I rang him. I pointed out that not only had Chris beaten him on the track, he'd got the better of him psychologically. I told him if he maintained that attitude, then he would lose the title.

"The positive was that Neil listened and agreed 100% that his anger and aggression were affecting his performance. After our 'chat' he channelled his anger in my direction. We always had massive rows but the good thing was neither of us took it personally.

"By the end of the 2000 season Neil was the BSB Champion. I felt sorry for Chris (Walker) – for about ten seconds. There were about ten of us on the pit wall. We spotted a puff of smoke when Chris downshifted a gear too many. Inside I was elated but there were half a dozen cameras on us so we had to contain our glee!

"I'm proud not only that we won the title, but what we did for Neil obviously helped him develop as a rider because he later became a World Superbike Champion.

THE ONE THAT GOT AWAY

"Bearing in mind Troy was gone, Niall Mackenzie was on our shortlist with John Reynolds and Chris Walker for 2000. I'd offered Walker £100,000 but Denning countered that with a bigger offer and Chris went where the biggest money was.

"We could have gone for a younger rider but that would have been a risk. And signing Niall, a former BSB Champion, was big news for the team. Half way through the year though we realised it wasn't such a wise choice.

"Mid-season we had a meeting and I told him I thought he should retire. It was a hard thing for me to say but we were trying to think of a way out of the situation (without the adverse publicity of sacking such a popular figure). It wasn't working for Niall and it wasn't working for us. He wasn't getting results and he'd had a lot of crashes so I certainly wasn't going to sit there and avoid the issue.

"I asked Niall if there was anything we could do to help him and he said he needed more time on the bike. But he didn't want to retire so we decided we'd stick it out until the end of the season. This all happened before Knockhill and, to be fair, he qualified pole there and was running second or third until he crashed.

"Niall was shocked I'd even consider suggesting he should quit. But the truth is that if we'd had another rider lined up to replace him, we'd not have come out of the meeting until he had agreed to quit racing!"

BELOW Colin Wright (left) with right-hand man Stewart Johnstone in the GSE Racing pit

agv
OGK
DENSO
Hislop
MDS
MOTOREX
monstermob

2001

The JR and Hizzy show

Anything after the captivating and often crazy scrap for the 2000 title between Neil Hodgson and Chris Walker was going to be a hard act to follow, particularly since the champion Hodgson had moved with the GSE Racing team to the World Championship and Walker had gone to Grand Prix on a Honda NSR500.

Added to that, a much thinner grid than in recent times did not help. Not only had two major protagonists moved on, Suzuki had slimmed to fielding only a single rider and there was still no major Honda team in the series. However, Jos Foulston, the Championship director did not see a problem and in a preview to the series he told *MCN*: "I believe the teams that are signed up for this year mean the series is even stronger than last year."

He tipped Reynolds and Haydon to battle for the title – and, along with the fans, relished a scrap between the two very different personalities that obviously did not gell well together in the Red Bull team the previous year.

Foulston also pointed that Emmett was back with Red Bull, that Plater was the best of BSB newcomers on a Kawasaki and Steve Hislop would go well on a Ducati. At least he got that right.

Pre-season favourites had to be Ben Atkins Red Bull Ducati team with brand new 996 Corsa customer bikes for John Reynolds and Sean Emmett – especially after JR set the pace in a pre-season test at Albacete.

Reynolds' 2000 team-mate James Haydon had signed for the Virgin Mobile Yamaha, and along with their other new signing Jamie Robinson, they respresented the youngest 'factory-backed' BSB team ever at 26 and 25 years of age respectively.

McElnea's team took their truck to Italy to bring back a pile of ex-Belgarda factory parts used by Vittoriano Guareschi in the 2000 WSB season, including power-enhancing stuff like special pistons, fuel injection and throttle bodies.

The man McElnea could not find a place for in 2001 was Steve Hislop. After finally being given the all clear in late December from doctors that the neck injury he

PREVIOUS PAGE AND ABOVE Steve Hislop (MonsterMob Ducati) and John Reynolds went at it like this almost all season. And this is just the start of the season at Donington Park!

suffered at the Brands World Championship round the previous year had finally recovered, Hizzy agreed a deal with Paul Bird to race in his new-look MonsterMob Ducati team – the title sponsor specialising in mobile phone ring tones and logos.

HIZZY'S EX-HODGSON DUCATIS

Bird originally planned to buy a pair of the ex-Red Bull bikes but instead secured the ex-Neil Hodgson GSE Racing Ducati 996s from the previous season.

Hizzy told *MCN*: "I'm happy to find out I've a good bike, a good team and a great shot at winning the title. When Yamaha told me there was no chance of staying with them I was worried I'd be left without a decent ride."

Hizzy's bike had the latest factory 42mm Ohlins and radial mount Brembos – identical to the kit used on the works Ducati Corse WSB bikes. Hizzy also opted to run a 16.5" front wheel instead of the 17" version after testing them back-to-back at Albacete.

Hizzy added: "Once we made the change I felt right at home on the bike. It falls into turns much better and you can feel the contact patch when the bike is on its side (fully leant over)."

Enzo DiClementi's Dienza team took delivery of the other two ex-GSE Racing bikes (those run by Niall Mackenzie) and signed 1997 British Supersport Champion Paul Brown for his first full season on a V-twin superbike. His only previous experience on a twin came at the Bol d'Or on a Honda Firestorm.

Kawasaki signed Michael Rutter alongside Steve Plater and kicked off the season in style with a resounding 1–2 in the non-championship Mallory Race of the Year. The ZX-7RRs were fitted with the same 50mm WP forks that Gregorio Lavilla was running on the factory bike in WSB and they also had the latest AP Lockheed brakes complete with special twin master cylinders feeding the individual calipers.

2000 Supersport champion John Crawford was Crescent Suzuki's sole BSB rider on a Clarion-backed Suzuki GSX-R750 though the team also fielded up and coming John Crockford on Superstocker GSX-R1000, and Karl Harris on GSX-R600 in Supersport, while former triple British Superbike Champion Niall Mackenzie was signed as stand-in rider for the superbike effort.

The privateer entry was led by another emerging talent, Shane Byrne on Rick Cappella's Performance House Suzuki GSX-R750. Others helping to bolster the grid included: Hawk Kawasaki duo Mark Burr and Gordon Blackey, David Wood on Aiden Murcott's Myco Kawasaki, plus Lee Jackson, Francis Williamson and Steve Marks on Yamahas.

TEAM DISSENT THREATENS RACE

Foulston inked a four-year TV deal with BBC and introduced Superpole, the rider by rider final qualifying system run previously in WSB and designed purely for TV. He said of the 'innovation': "We want to make BSB more of a weekend of entertainment for the people who pay to come and watch racing."

Despite his continued upbeat approach to running the series, behind the scenes things were anything but upbeat, and there was a distinct possibility that the season would not even start at Donington Park thanks to dissent among the teams concerning the 2001 contract Foulston had offered to them.

The teams were concerned on three different counts:

1 That under the terms of the contract they had to provide their riders to the organisers for three promo days per year, free of charge.
2 The series promoters wanted to hold rights to videos and photos which teams might not have access to even for their own promotional purposes.
3 The teams were to have no hospitality passes provided at all. The previous year they were allocated 40 per year but now would have to pay extra.

Virgin Yamaha boss Rob McElnea said in *MCN*: "We need to sit down and sort this out. I can't sign the contract as it is."

Buckmaster commented: "We won't even be at the official launch unless there's compromise over certain issues. We're prepared to pay entry fees but want something back."

Paul Bird added: "We won't be signing the contract and I don't know anyone who will under these terms."

A week later Foulston had yielded to the team's concerns and it was business as usual. Well, not quite as usual because before the season had even started there was intense discussion regarding new technical rules for the 2001 incorporating a 1,000cc top limit for all bikes.

This was something being considered for WSB to be implemented for the 2003 season but the BSB option was quite different in bike specification. The WSB rules were to allow open engine tuning and then, to keep the fours and twins competitive, there would be air restrictors to curb the power output of the fours. The rules were not scheduled to come on line until 2003.

The BSB proposal to the manufacturers (UK importers rather than Japanese factories) incorporated a blend of supersport engine rules (ie limited tuning and more use of stock engine internals) and superbike chassis for the triples and fours. The British series wanted the new rules implemented for 2001. The only common rule between the two championships was a 162kg limit for all machines.

Doug Barnfield, the man charged with drawing up the new BSB rulebook, said: "The FIM is too slow in making decisions and their proposals appear expensive. Not only that, the Japanese manufacturers don't appear too interested in the proposals."

McElnea and Denning both expressed concern about moving too far away from the FIM rules but agreed technical changes would be inevitable to safeguard the future of the class which had become the domain of fantastically expensive factory bikes.

By the end of March, and the start of the new season, it was certain 2001 would be the last year of the existing 750cc fours/1,000 twins rules for BSB.

BELOW Hizzy tells Stuart Bland (left) and Phil Borley just exactly how it is

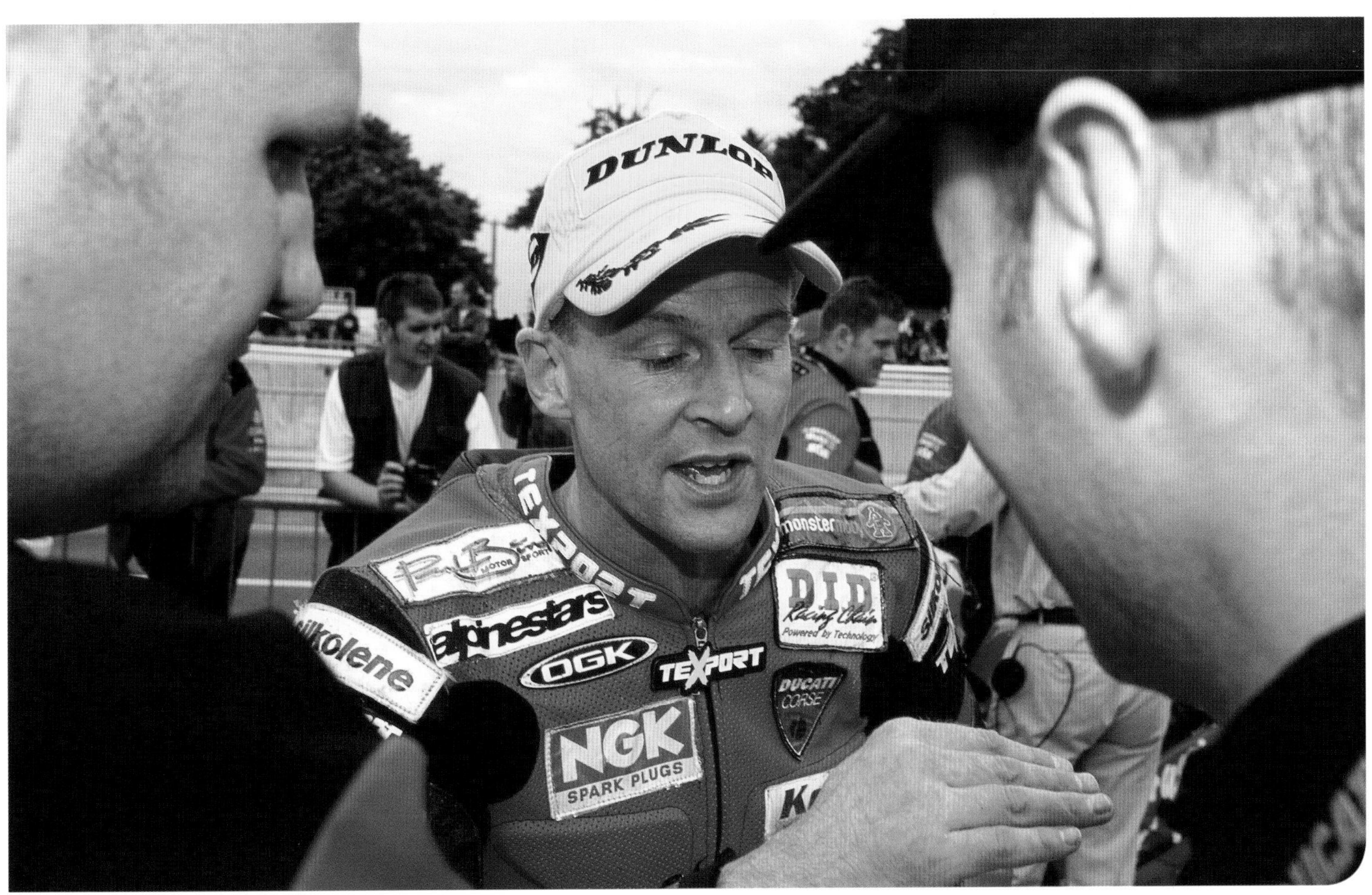

REYNOLDS AND HAYDON SCRAP KICKS OFF SERIES

Like Foulston many expected the real championship battle would be between Reynolds and Haydon and it certainly looked that way after the first round at Donington Park.

Haydon was battling with Reynolds in the first race until he slipped off at the Melbourne Loop and hurt his ankle. Race two and it was the two of them at it again, with Reynolds completing the double.

Hislop finished second in race one, third in race two but admitted he was still far from confident on the Ducati because he was still running Hodgson's setting since he had run out of time to experiment with something that suited his high corner speed style better.

John Crawford enoyed a good debut on the Crescent Suzuki with a pair of third places but JR, with his maximum, had a 17-point lead over Hislop going to the second round.

Hizzy had brand new £15,000 Ohlins 46mm factory forks with lightweight magnesium bottoms for Silverstone and was clearly much more at ease on the V-twin. Hizzy grabbed pole by more than half a second from Reynolds but the Red Bull rider still managed to beat him in the first race but Hizzy took revenge in race two to score his first victory of the year.

Crawford was third in race one but Haydon completed the podium in race two – quite a feat after a huge crash in qualifying. Already suffering from his Brands Hatch ankle knock, Haydon highsided at Luffield and somehow managed to end up under the bike as it ground along the track surface. Amazingly Haydon escaped with nothing more than torn neck muscles but the crash was so spectacular it even made *News at Ten*!

Steve Plater was not so lucky when he highsided in the first race at 140mph and sustained a broken right ankle and left wrist plus concussion. The crash looked like it might have far worse consequences.

Plater aggravated his arm injury after another crash in practice at Snetterton and was not able to start the races.

Haydon also suffered another monster crash in qualifying and the team had to contend with three blown motors but Haydon still bounced back to claim a pair of third places.

HIZZY COMES INTO THE FRAME

The front end of the field was all about Reynolds and Hislop again with the Red Bull Ducati team claiming a pair of wins, albeit by a tenth of second each time.

The new 1,000cc rules package for 2002 was also announced at Snetterton but some felt they should have gone futher than supersport engine tuning. Crescent boss Paul Denning said in *MCN*: "I'm all for the new rules but I'd also like to see quickshifters and narrower crankcase covers to cope with the extreme lean angles a superbike chassis will allow." V&M's Jack Valentine added: "I'm looking forward to the new class but want stronger clutch baskets to cope with the extra horsepower the 1,000cc fours will produce."

The championship might have quickly developed into a two-horse race between the most experienced runners in the series but that did not stop a whopping 20,500 crowd turning up for the first Oulton Park meeting of the year.

With the huge success of their V-twins in superbike worldwide Ducati were struggling to cope with the huge demand from customers and teams like Red Bull and Monstermob were forced to run engines close to the recommended mileage limits between rebuilds. Reynolds suffered three engine failures at the Cheshire circuit and Hizzy's engines were right on the mileage limit but he still took pole by almost a second from JR.

Hizzy won both races but only after the MonsterMob team had picked up a fresh engine from their workshop near Preston overnight and installed it ready for the races.

OPPOSITE Reynolds – pure class and a determined bastard who never knew the meaning of defeat

BELOW The battles continued at Oulton Park. Hizzy leads JR onto the start/finish straight

agv
Red Bull
DUCATI
CORSE
DENSO

ABOVE Rutter was drafted into the Hawk Kawasaki team while the works team sorted their finances out after the promised sponsorship money failed to arrive

ABOVE RIGHT Talented Jamie Morley was given a shot on the works Kawasaki at Oulton Park

Even then there was drama for the Scot. He had a seven-second lead in the first race but had to back off when his new motor started to overheat. Then he had to complete race two with his old high-mileage engine.

Haydon had another high speed get-off – this time a 130mph crash at Knickerbrook in race one which damaged his left hand a little more than he realised. When he arrived at the start line for the second race he pulled in the clutch only to feel a pop as his knuckle broke.

The high-point among the rest of the runners was 25-year-old Jamie Morley's promising debut on the works Kawasaki in place of the injured Plater. He was only 2.5s off pole and finished seventh in race one.

Brands Hatch provided the setting for the second successive Hizzy double (after another sensational pole position performance) to take a 13-point lead in the series over Reynolds after the Red Bull rider failed to finish race two when an engine bolt worked loose.

The meeting was marred by some horrendous crashes. Sean Emmett ran into the back of Haydon's R7 at Hawthorn and both went down at around 140mph. Emmett initially admitted it was his fault – but then blamed Haydon for closing the door on him. Crawford also came off at the same place in race two. He jumped off when he went onto the grass at 160mph! None of the riders was injured.

The real downer of the event was news of financial problems for the factory Kawasaki team and privateers Performance House, which meant the careers of Michael Rutter, Steve Plater and Shane Byrne were in jeapordy.

HIZZY OUT-SMARTS REYNOLDS

Over 24,000 fans turned out at Thruxton to enjoy two amazing eight-rider scraps at the front of the superbike races. Plater took pole but had to be content to finish second to Hislop in race one. Reynolds took the second slipstreaming stunner from Haydon and Rutter with Hislop relegated to sixth.

Round seven was back to Hizzy's favourite Oulton Park track, with a ten-point lead in his pocket and with 25,000 fans watching he took both race wins, out-smarting title challenger Reynolds.

Hizzy said in *MCN*: "It's getting silly out there. We're going to have to consult all the old videos to work out the best places to pass and plan our tactics up front. But what do you expect? You've got two guys on similar bikes trying to outsmart each other.

"If this carries on we're going to fall out big time, but it's hard to complain when we're good friends, but also professional on the track."

Reynolds agreed and said: "I suppose Steve's right, we are going to fall out if this carries on. I rode my butt off out there. In the second race I thought I had him covered but I never expected him to pass where he did."

Hizzy actually passed his rival on the inside drive to Druids where the more conventional (and much safer!) line would be around the outside at Clay Hill.

Hizzy admitted: "I never planned it. I was going for a nice wide sweep around the outside but saw a gap and went for it."

It was enough to give Hizzy a 23-point lead in the series.

As feared, Team Kawasaki's dire cash crisis caused by the non-arrival of the promised instalment of sponsorship money from Transatlantic Finance meant they had to put their season on hold.

Rutter was lucky to secure a ride on a spare Hawk Kawasaki. It suffered a misfire race one but he was able to finish a strong sixth in race two.

At least he raced. Team-mate Plater was sidelined, as was Shane Byrne. His Performance House team did not have the cash to race at Oulton Park either but they were back in action for Knockhill and Byrne would go on to win the Privateer Cup title.

Kawasaki were back too, but only with Rutter and only because one of their secondary sponsors, ceramics company Tau Ceremica stumped up enough cash for the team to see out the season with a one-rider effort.

Niall Mackenzie made a one-off appearance on the Clarion Suzuki. The popular Scot qualified second and finished an impressive fifth and fourth in the races but said afterward that his racing career was finished. He joked: "If I ever do this again, shoot me!"

Reynolds halted Hizzy's run of form by winning both races at Knockhill in front of a bumper 20,000 crowd. He also owed his Red Bull team-mate Sean Emmett who managed to demote Hislop to third in the first race. That allowed Reynolds to close within six points of the championship leader.

The Cadwell Park grid was also boosted by the return of Steve Plater who signed up to race for the Virgin Yamaha team for the remainder of the year. He scored a pair of eighth places at his home venue.

An incredible 33,500 crowd saw Hizzy back to his best, claiming pole position and two wins. Reynolds was beaten by Haydon in race one so the points gap was now back to 20 and JR said: "You can see why Steve's such a legend because to see him through the woodland section of the course is simply awesome. Nothing seems to faze him."

Reynolds clinched pole at round ten Brands Hatch – but only by 15 thousandths from Hizzy and the pair traded wins to maintain the status quo going to Mallory Park.

CALL IN THE FAITH HEALER

It was at Brands that 39-year-old Hizzy admitted to have special help in his corner, and from an unlikely source. He was consulting a faith healer called Jon Hargill, and the rider claimed he had eradicated pain in his spine, a hangover from his crash at Brands Hatch the previous year.

The pair of them met in the Isle of Man after Hargill had been treating a cancer patient.

Hizzy said: "I was sceptical at first but I'm willing to believe he has special powers. He lays his hands on my head and talks to me, reassuring me everything is going to be okay."

Even when Hargill couldn't go to meetings he would lay his hands on a piece of paper then post it to Hislop

BELOW James Haydon came so close to giving Virgin Yamaha a race victory at Mallory

who could then benefit from his 'healer's' energy field.

While most people, used to dealing with the high-tech world of motorcycle racing, dismissed such hocus-pocus, Hizzy – even according to his own MonsterMob team – seemed happier, more confident and more focused after Hargill had performed the 'laying on of the hands.'

It was Reynolds who could have done with a miracle cure at Mallory Park. He highsided at the Bus Stop chicane in qualifying and severely sprained his left ankle – so badly he initially thought it was broken.

For the first time all year, it looked like someone else apart from Reynolds or Hizzy might win a BSB race. Haydon led the first race by three seconds from the gritty Reynolds, heading for his first Virgin Yamaha R7 win, only to crash out in the 130mph Esses. He was unhurt but Rob McElnea and his team were distraught.

Hislop only finished third with tyre grip problems in race one but bounced back to take the second race with Reynolds, really struggling from his sore ankle, back in fifth.

Paul Brown scored his best result all season with second place – his first podium of the year – but all eyes were on the championship table with Hizzy now a commanding 25 points ahead of Reynolds.

Rockingham was next. The shiny new, modern facility designed to host 70,000 race fans that Foulston viewed as his jewel in the crown. He told *MCN*: "The facilities are first class. We're delighted to be taking the series there. It's a fresh challenge for riders and a fantastic spectator venue."

OTHER HIGHLIGHTS OF '01

- Valentino Rossi clinches his first Grand Prix 500cc title after an epic three-way Italian battle with Max Biaggi and Loris Capirossi as the title is decided in Australia with the closest-ever race finish in the series
- Daijiro Katoh (Honda) and Manuel Poggialia (Gilera) win the 250cc and 125cc titles
- Former BSB Champion Troy Bayliss claims the WSB title but another former BSB Champion Neil Hodgson is proclaimed Britain's new hero after finishing fifth in the series on a GSE Racing Ducati
- Karl Harris wins his first British Supersport title, 15-year-old Leon Camier claims the 125cc series and Adrian Coates is the British 250cc Champion

BELOW 2000 British Supersport Champion John Crawford on the ex-factory Clarion Suzuki GSX-R750

He might have seen it that way but the circuit was far from popular with the majority of riders or teams. They had no complaints about the fantastic pit facilities, or the nice flat paddock area. Nor could anyone argue that the spectactor facilities were not top notch with plenty of immaculate toilets, a nice clean restaurant and good parking. The actual viewing area however was confined to the front straight, opposite the pits. Where the bike action really mattered was the infield and no spectators could get there.

From a rider's perspective there was the wall. The retaining wall on the outside of the first corner and the last corner. Rockingham was built primarily for American-style oval racing and the plan was to host a lucrative round of the US-based Indy Car championship and that required not just a strong concrete retaining wall but also a tall safety fence to prevent the 200+mph cars from the tipping into the crowd.

The road circuit for bikes and national car racing was built as an after-thought but the design incorporated the entire front straight of the oval course plus the first and last corners. At each end of the straight makeshift chicanes were marked out, using plastic kerbing and the concrete walls were lined with plastic safety bales, designed to prevent riders or bikes hitting the solid concrete.

Perhaps if there had not been any major dramas Rockingham would have been accepted as a welcome addition to the championship but there was a major incident and it could not have had a bigger impact on the series.

John Crawford's first race crash brought out the safety car with Reynolds leading from Hislop. When the course went green Hislop set up to pass the Red Bull Ducati on the exit of the chicane but Reynolds missed a gear and the MonsterMob Ducati piled into the back of Reynolds' and crashed heavily (see separate panel).

With Hislop on his way to hospital, Reynolds finished third and second to retake the lead in the championship by 11 points and with Hizzy out for the rest of the season, the championship was virtually decided.

Sean Emmett took the first race – his first victory all year – and the first time a rider other than JR or Hizzy had won a race! Rutter claimed second place ahead of Reynolds but went one better in race two, scoring his and Kawasaki's first win of a troubled season. Reynolds was second with Emmett, riding shotgun, in third place.

Speaking to *MCN* readers from his hospital bed on the Monday after the crash, Hislop said: "John rode well and pushed me real hard all year. My injury doesn't take anything away from his achievement. I want to see him go out and win both races at Donington for me."

Reynolds did exactly that but had to work for his second race victory after a thrilling scrap with Haydon, Rutter, Crawford and Plater resulted in him taking the flag by 0.16s from Haydon.

It was a great way to end the season even though Hislop's unfortunate accident at Rockingham had robbed the fans of what could have been a real nail-biting climax to a season dominated by the two oldest players in the championship.

ABOVE Steve Plater had some good rides on the Virgin Yamaha

ABOVE LEFT Reynolds celebrates his title in the now time-honoured fashion with a Number One tee-shirt

It might have cost £50million to build Britain's first brand new, purpose-built race circuit in decades but Rockingham Motor Speedway lurched from crisis to crisis even before the fateful British Superbike round in September.

The ambitious project was to host American-style oval track racing around a 1.5-mile course with a concrete retaining wall around the entire perimeter.

Within the oval there was a road course with eight different permutations with BSB running on a 1.74-mile layout that incorporated the front straight of the oval with chicanes at each end leading riders from, and back onto, the straight.

Midlands-based businessman Peter Davies came up with the idea of building the facility on a redundant 300-acre steelworks site on the outskirts of Corby and building work started in 1999.

Guy Hands, a top man at Japanese investment bankers Nomura, invested a further £34million of his own cash into the project and by January of 2001, Davies had been ousted and replaced with David Grace, a former Managing Director of the Scottish and Newcastle pub chain. He was a massive motorsports fan and a former British Hillclimb Champion.

The inaugural Indy Car meeting just eight days before the 2001 BSB round was fraught with problems as two practice sessions were cancelled due to moisture seeping back up through the track surface – even though there was no rainfall! The race was eventually run but cut from 500 miles to 340.

Even during pre-event testing top BSB riders voiced concerns over the safety issues of how the road course joined the banked oval, and the fact that there was no gravel trap, just a concrete retaining wall. If that was not enough none of the riders had anything positive to say about the tight infield road section.

John Reynolds commented: "Where we ride up on to the banking and come down onto the infield is dodgy. If you lose control at the front of the machine at the end of the banked section and fall, then you go straight into the wall that lines the track. It needs changing before we race there or somebody could be really hurt."

The initial test was on a 2.05-mile course and the first bike meeting was meant to be an MRO race but that had to be cancelled when the ACU refused to issue a permit on safety grounds.

The track was then reconfigured over a 1.74-mile layout with some £38,000 spent on the modifications and safety barriers but when practice started for the first BSB round concerns were still being voiced by riders and teams about its suitability as a bike racing circuit.

BSB staff worked flat out with the circuit owners trying to make the course as safe as possible. They worked with riders to design the make-shift chicane at each end of the straight and even insisted on parallel lines being painted along the entire straight – one white one and one yellow to mark the edge of the course and keep riders away from the wall. Anyone running over the yellow was subject to a penalty. Even so, there was only so much the BSB staff could do.

Friday practice passed without major incident but Saturday was hit by rain,which caused the track to flood and the morning sessions were wiped out. Superpole was cancelled in the afternoon, replaced by regular qualifying.

Hislop's crash came in the first BSB race. Reynolds and the MonsterMob Ducati rider were battling for the lead when John Crawford crashed and while his bike was removed from the circuit, the safety car was in play.

As it pulled off and the race went green, the field accelerated down the front straight and started to peel off into Turn One, a fast chicane with a fifth gear exit.

As both riders accelerated through the left to right flick where the bikes would be going from third to fourth at around 120mph, Reynolds suddenly slowed, almost as if he missed a gear, and Hislop, right behind him, had nowhere to go and clipped Reynolds' rear tyre.

Reynolds was sent into a high-speed wobble by the force of Hislop's collision but managed to hold onto his bike, but Hizzy was flicked off the right-hand side of the bike. As he fell, his right foot folded under his leg and then the rest of his body slammed down onto the track surface, shoulder first.

He and his bike sped across the track in a shower of sparks and disintegrating bodywork. The bike clouted the large, plastic Recticel safety barrier, lifting it up and Hizzy followed it in, disappearing under the huge plastic bale.

His injuries included a shattered right ankle, broken right tibia, broken right collarbone and concussion. His season was over, along with his title chances.

A circuit spokesman claimed: "We are as saddened as anybody about the crash and have begun an investigation into the accident. But in our opinion Rockingham is the safest track in Europe.

"When Hislop and his bike hit the specially-designed barrier it did its job and limited further injury."

Hislop always maintained his leg injuries were caused when he hit the wall foot first but having seen video evidence it was apparent the ankle injury was sustained as he fell from the bike, as was his broken collarbone.

Having said that, he appeared to come to rest against a concrete wall. That was something that should not have happened. He was racing at a brand new, purpose-built circuit, which should have incorporated every conceivable safety feature. The problem really lay with the fact that the circuit was built primarily for racing cars, and bikes were simply an afterthought.

In the fall-out following the crash, *MCN* branded Rockingham as having "the scariest corner in Britain" – and rightly so.

Hislop himself had misgivings about the course from the beginning. He said in *MCN*: "I said all along that corner was dangerous and I was right."

Rival Yamaha rider James Haydon added: "I had expressed some concerns about the place, which unfortunately proved to be well-founded. It's a shame because the facilities were fantastic."

Opinion between the Red Bull riders John Reynolds and Sean Emmett was divided – Reynolds did not like it, Emmett loved it, while their team manager Nigel Bosworth said: "I felt we were skating on thin ice throughout the weekend. It seemed most of the paddock didn't want to be there so that must have suggested something."

Virgin Yamaha boss Rob McElnea added: "I went to Rockingham with an open mind but came away thinking too many compromises had been made. I wasn't happy seeing my riders put in a situation where they were unhappy about being there. I don't think that we can go back there until the whole place has been reviewed."

Rockingham remained on the BSB schedule for two more years.

OPPOSITE Rockingham had great facilities but the racetrack left a lot to be desired – especially the concrete wall on the outside of the oval

BELOW Starting from the pit lane was another unusual aspect of the new circuit

MCN
FM
Rutter
OGK
Silkolene
MCN
2
FUCHS
DUNLOP
kes

2002

Hizzy's command performance

By the end of 2001, the World Superbike Championship was in a sorry state and the BSB promoters, as well as most people involved in the racing industry, considered WSB's long-term ill-fortune could have a devastating effect on the British series.

There had been a lot of discussion about the future of the class at world level because it was patently obvious the 1,000cc V-twins had a distinct advantage over the 750cc fours.

Many feared for the future of the series, especially with the stagnant Grand Prix series now revitalised by the buzz surrounding the new 990cc four-stroke formula that would commence in 2002.

While the world's major manufacturers geared up to build exciting new MotoGP bikes, in WSB both the ZX-7RR Kawasaki and GSX-R750 Suzuki were hopelessly uncompetitive and the only Yamahas in the field were privateer R7s.

Benelli's 900cc Tornado Tre triple was not in the same league as some privateer fours and the new Foggy Petronas FP1 had not even passed homologation in time for the series.

The field was predictably dominated by V-twins, mainly Ducatis plus a pair of factory VTR1000 SP2 Hondas for Colin Edwards and Tadayuki Okada. Even Troy Corser on the works Aprilia's RSV1000 60-degree V-twin failed to live up to his season-opening Valencia double victory.

There were plenty of ideas of how to level the playing field once more: allow the fours an interim increase of 100cc displacement, penalise the twins with more weight, reduce the weight limit of the fours, fit the twins with air restrictors. The Flammini brothers, however, who ran the series for the Octagon Group, did not appear to have any clear direction to take the series out of the doldrums and to rejuvenate what had been the most fiercely competitive racing class in the world.

In BSB it was a very different story. Unbeknown to the general public, series boss Jos Foulston and Stuart

PREVIOUS PAGE It was another year of Ducati: Hislop leads Rutter and Emmett – all of them on the Italian V-twins

ABOVE British Champion John Reynolds faced a tough year of development with the new Rizla Suzuki GSX-R1000

Higgs (BSB clerk of the course and Foulston's right hand man and, most would agree, the driving force behind the series) had spent the second half of 2001 discussing the future of the British Championship with all of the manufacturers, sponsors and team bosses and came up with a plan to run outside of the rigid FIM rule book by allowing the latest breed of 1,000cc four-cylinder bikes into the 2002 series – something that had been mooted for WSB in 2003.

However it did not stop there. They decided on a total revamp of the entire BSB series. Not only were there new superbike rules, they ditched the 250 class completely (so those with two-stroke twins' only salvation was the amateur-status MRO series) and reduced the 125cc, supersport and superstock classes to national status. The idea was to build the prestige of the superbike class.

BMP was not just worried about Ducati dominating BSB. They knew the bulk of the BSB teams were teetering on the brink of financial ruin with the exorbitant costs of running pure-bred FIM-spec superbikes. And they were also only too well aware that the vast gulf between the so-called 'factory-backed' teams and the privateers was robbing the championship of its spectacle. They gambled that robbing the British tag from the support classes would encourage some of the better-backed supersport teams to switch to the main class.

Foulston told *MCN Sport* magazine: "The changes implemented meant I wasn't the most popular person in the paddock but it was either get on and do it or watch the series die. We had to cut costs to make the feature class more attractive to some of the top teams from the support classes."

The aims were to reduce costs and increase entries by limiting engine tuning of the 1,000cc fours to supersports spec while allowing them to run superbike-spec chassis. BMP felt this should allow the big bikes to compete alongside the existing superbike 1,000cc V-twins and 750cc fours even though they were allowed more freedom of engine tuning under the existing FIM regulations.

The pistons, conrods and crankshafts of the new 1,000cc fours had to remain stock with not even any lightening or polishing permitted. Things that could be modified or changed included: increased duration of the cams (but stock lift), higher compression, gas-flowed but otherwise standard cylinder-heads, different fuel injection software, different gearbox ratios – and slipper clutches. The package of engine-related changes, plus a specially designed racing exhaust system, was thought to give the 1,000cc fours a potential 185bhp, about 20bhp more than the old 750s and some five bhp more than the best Ducatis.

The 1,000cc fours were also allowed superbike-style chassis, which meant while frames including the swing-arm pivot point had to be stock, they could be braced. Stock suspension, brakes and wheels could be replaced with aftermarket parts. Weight limit for the new bikes was 162kg while the twins limit was increased by 2kg from 2001 to 164kg and the 750 fours were allowed to run at 159kg (three kilos lighter than the FIM rules).

The whole idea was that even though there was no FIM homologation guideline to follow, the BSB 1,000cc four-cylinder rules drawn up by series technical director Doug Barnfield would be easy to police.

Crescent Suzuki, Virgin Yamaha and MotoPower Honda were the top names among a host of teams embracing the new rules. No sooner had Foulston announced the new rules the previous July, Suzuki started development work on their 2002 Rizla-backed bike for British Champion John Reynolds and Karl Harris, the 2001 British Supersport Champion on a GSX-R600.

Yamaha could have continued with factory-backed R7s but instead made a late call to develop their own R1 for Steve Plater and surprise signing Simon Crafar even though the 32-year-old Kiwi had not raced in 18 months.

The R1 fold was boosted by a satellite team run by Colin Appleyard who signed former 250 rider Darren Barton (27) and 22-year-old Scouser Paul Jones.

Although the UK Honda importers continued to give BSB a miss, privateer team MotoPower decided to convert a pair of 1,000cc four-cylinder FireBlades into new rules BSB bikes for the promising Gary Mason and experienced Matt Llewellyn. Of the top teams only Hawk Racing continued with an FIM-spec ZX-7RR superbike – but only because Kawasaki had no suitable 1,000cc road bike to use. They signed 31-year-old Aussie Glen Richards from the Sanyo Superstock/ Supersport team and 21-year-old Mark Burr.

SUZUKI'S EARLY START

The Rizla Suzuki was first seen on track at the Brands Hatch Suzuki GSX-R festival at Brands in August 2001 but was basically a mildly-tuned 170bhp GSX-R100 engine in a GSX-R750 superbike chassis with Showa suspension. The 2002 GSX-R1000 racer had Ohlins 43mm WSB upside down forks and AP monobloc radial-mount calipers. Rear shock was also WSB-spec Ohlins.

Cast magnesium wheels were swapped for forged magnesium Oz wheels, which were fractionally lighter but also stiffer.

The team tested pre-Christmas at Almeria and again at Albacete in March and the motor was developing closer to 180bhp thanks to new cams, revised compression ratio, new injector bellmouths and a new airbox. A Motec engine management system replaced the stock system and gave a much wider range of adjustment of the fuel and ignition curves than the stock system. But even then British Champion John Reynolds suggested in *MCN* that new bike was not ready to go head-to-head with the well-sorted Ducatis.

Rizla were not the only Suzuki team embracing the new rules. Scottish businessman Alistair Flanagan's ETI team signed John Crawford from Rizla Suzuki to race a V&M-prepared GSX-R1000 while a new team backed by a recruitment company called Grafters fielded 33-year-old Aussie Paul Young and 35-year-old Neil Faulkner. Young had won the British Superstock title the previous year riding a

BELOW Richards highsided at the bottom of the Cadwell Park's Mountain but escaped injury thanks to landing on the very top of the crest

GSX-R1000 while Faulkner had club racing experience having raced a Yamaha R1 in the MRO Powerbike series the previous year.

YAMAHA LATE BATTLE

Virgin Yamaha took delivery of their bikes just two months before the start of the year and basically had to go it alone with development since no one in the world was working to BSB-type 'superstock' rules.

Engine development was carried out by Kev Stephenson. He raised compression from 11.5:1 to 13:1 and fitted stainless one-piece valves made by REC. The team received some race kit cams from Japan but Stephenson also developed his own and increased the power up to 167bhp @ 12,200rpm – 37bhp more than stock – and 20bhp more than the old R7 race bike. Torque was 82ft/lb from 9,000 to 10,000rpm – comparable with a 998 Ducati. Kit gearbox parts were used and a slipper clutch was fitted. An R1 race kit engine management system was retained and R1 racing project leader Jiro Ozaki, made several trips to the UK bringing new ECUs with revised ignition and fuelling maps.

One of the biggest improvements in performance came from fitting the 2002 Akrapovic exhaust, which gave a six to seven bhp gain.

The chassis was modified by Harris Performance. The stock frame was braced at the swing-arm pivot point and by adding a crossbrace to the rear ride height mount. They also fitted yokes with adjustable inserts to allow the steering axis to move forward 7mm (from 23mm out to 30mm) and tip the steering head angle from 23–25 degrees.

Harris made a smaller diameter swing-arm spindle to fit eccentric adjusters into the existing swing-arm pivot hole (which was not permitted to be modified under the rules). That allowed them to drop the swing-arm pivot point by 25mm and allow the suspension to move through it's full stroke in a bid to improve traction.

PRIVATEER HONDAS

Some felt that MotoPower were on a hiding to nothing with the CBR900RR FireBlade. The 954cc engine was almost 50cc down on its rivals and team boss Russell Savory had no financial or technical help from Honda.

However Savory's connections with Honda Europe and long-term friendship with FireBlade project leader Tadao Baba, meant he did enjoy some limited technical support.

The bikes continued to sport Sanyo livery, who backed the team in its supersport heyday, but the reality was that the team was now part-owned by rock star Mark Knopfler of Dire Straits fame and it was him who was bank-rolling the effort.

A massive bike fan, Knopfler went to several BSB races when his schedule permitted but kept a very low profile, preferring to enjoy his hobby rather than bask in his fame.

The Blade started the year with high compression and a rev-limit of 13,800rpm to get the grunt out

BELOW Hislop winds his Ducati through a ridiculous Rockingham kerbing. Very few riders or teams had very positive things to say about the new venue – apart from the state-of-the-art pit facilities

of corners but the team found it responded better to lower compression. By reducing it from 13:1 to 12.2:1 it knocked off some of the grunt but gave the engine more rpm – a 14,400rpm limit – and better top end.

Savory added: "We saw between 165–175bhp at 14,400rpm on the dyno and I'd say our bike produced about the same horsepower as the R1 but not quite the grunt."

The blueprinted engine featured gas-flowed cylinder head, special one-piece stainless steel valves and springs. Savory tested 14 different pairs of cams (with more duration but stock lift as per the rules), spending at least two to three hours per camshaft on the dyno to find which worked best.

The crankshaft assembly was balanced (with stock rods and pistons) which entailed buying boxes of standard pistons and finding four with identical weights, since lightening of internals was prohibited.

In a bid to find extra grunt, Savory made his own high velocity airbox fed by carbon air ducting. He also developed his own programmable electronic engine management system, including a datalogger.

Although the team had HRC race-kit slipper clutches, close-ratio kit gearbox ratios never arrived so for the first half of the year the riders had to put up with the widely-spaced stock ratios. By mid-term, Savory replaced them with close-ratio gears he commissioned from transmission specialists, Quaife.

While the majority of the BSB grid ran Ohlins suspension, MotoPower had WP backing and used their Dutch-made inverted 50mm forks and rear shock. They used Oz mag wheels and tiny 210mm twin double disc Beringer brakes.

Savory never considered bracing the standard Blade frame or the swing-arm but fitted Italian-made Robbi triple clamps with adjustable offsets.

KAWASAKI – TIGHT BUDGET

With no suitable 1,000cc Kawasaki in the range, Hawk were stuck with the ageing ZX-7RR. They also operated on one of the tightest budgets of the top teams in BSB but did a fantastic job in keeping Kawasaki competitive in the series.

Their limited finances meant some of the major engine components like the crankshafts, crankcases, cylinder heads were up to four years old, even if the major internals like Pankl conrods, kit pistons, valves springs, guides and kit close-ratio gearbox and Suter dry clutches were brand new. The best engine builder John Trigger managed to squeeze from the old 750cc motor was 153bhp on the dyno but where the Kawasaki really lacked was grunt off the tighter corners.

The one big plus in Richards' favour was the ZX-7RR chassis, which allowed the Aussie to make up some serious ground on his rivals into and through each corner.

Incredibly, the team used frames from as far back as 1997, although team boss Stuart Hicken did admit that he had bought two new ones prior to the start of the year.

The frames were identical to those anyone could order from a Kawasaki dealership. Hawk dipped them

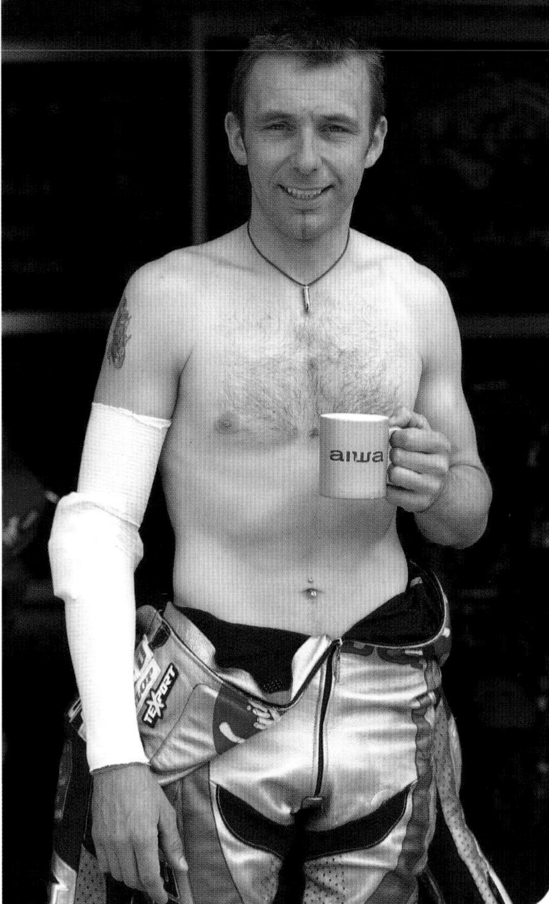

ABOVE Plater lies prone after a race one Rockingham crash coming out of the final turn...

LEFT ...but ten minutes later is enjoying a cuppa before the next scrap

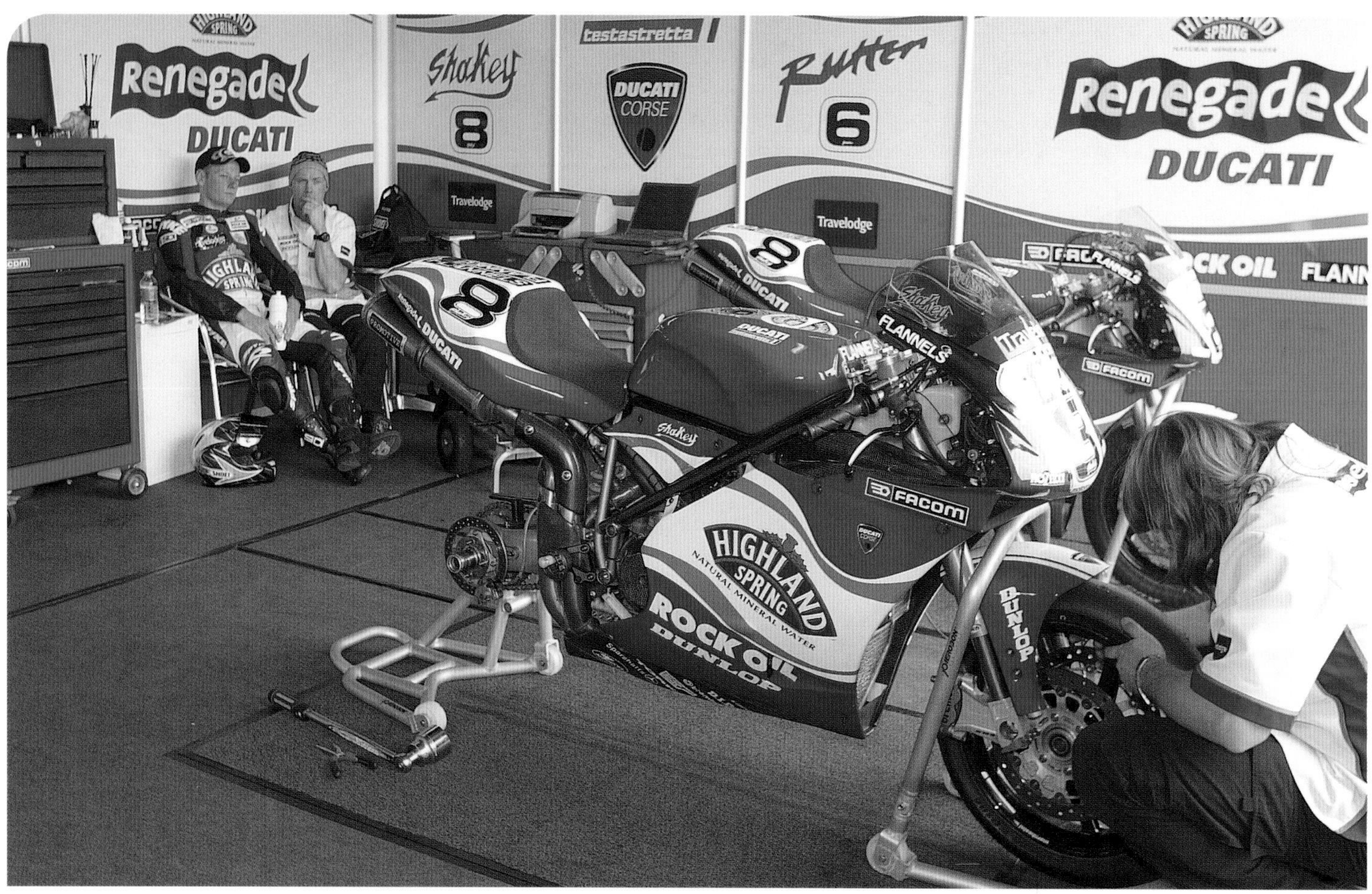

ABOVE For a new team Renegade Ducati were a force to be reckoned with from the start

to remove the paint, drilled out the rivnuts (threaded inserts in the frame which components are bolted into) and replaced them with weld-in threaded bosses. They did not even add bracing.

The swing-arms were of 1996 vintage, incorporating a fabricated shock mount rather than those with the later cast-in mounts. Hicken reckoned the early design offered more feedback. Richards had the choice of the latest-spec WSB Ohlins with radial mount Brembos or 2001 forks and conventionally-mounted brakes but had no real preference for either. Hicken – a former suspension technician – overcame any potential shock fade by asking Ohlins to develop a longer shock body to accommodate more oil.

DUCATI STRENGTHS

Generally the new rules were welcomed but the Ducati threat was still as strong as ever. MonsterMob Ducati and Mark Griffiths' new Renegade team had the very latest 998RS models with the Testastretta (narrow head) cylinder heads and these were said to be the same specification as the factory bikes Aussie Troy Bayliss took to the 2001 WSB title.

After being thwarted by injury in his title bid in 2001 Steve Hislop, now 40 years old, was back fully fit and as determined as ever to win the title on the MonsterMob Ducati.

The Testastretta was a radical departure for Ducati when it was introduced in 2001. Twenty replicas were built for distribution worldwide, of which just six came to the UK. The Testastretta produced 174bhp at 12,200rpm, some 6bhp and 200rpm more than the old 996RS.

The later engine had a 100mm bore and 63.5mm stroke compared to the previous 98mm bore and 66mm stroke – and lighter pistons were used. The included-valve angle was reduced from 40-degrees to 20, hence the 'narrow head' term, with the flatter combustion chamber shape giving a more efficient burn. The narrowed valve angle also allowed Ducati to increase the valve sizes from 38mm to 40mm for the inlet and from 30m to 33mm for the exhaust.

There were also new Weber Marelli single fuel injectors for the 60mm throttle bodies replacing the previous triple injectors.

The power delivery of the new engine was much more aggressive than the previous 996 as Hislop told *MCN*: "Last year's power delivery with the triple injector engine was so smooth but not only was this year's engine more peaky, it had the single injector which made it so harsh off the bottom end of the rev range. It took a lot of work by Mark (Richardson – the team's data man), messing with the mapping to overcome."

The Testastretta chassis featured the same geometry as the 2001 bike so Hislop and the team just had to concentrate on getting the chassis to suit the new power delivery.

Hislop ran the same suspension as his 2001 bike, even using the smaller 42mm Ohlins instead of the 46mm forks that came with the Testastretta. Renegade opted to keep theirs stock.

Hislop's bike also sported tiny 290mm rotors everywhere except Donington, Snetterton and Rockingham when he went to 320mm discs to cope with the heavy braking areas. The lighter weight of the smaller discs allowed Hislop to flick the bike from side to side much easier.

Steve Hislop's 2001 Ducati 996RS was also in the field, ridden by Dean Ellison. The ex-Hodgson 2000 title-winning bike had been bought by Danny Gallagher who had run Ellison the previous year on a D&B Honda SP1.

The other top team with the Testastrettas was Mark Griffiths' new Renegade team. Griffiths had backed Nigel Nottingham's privateer Yamaha in 2001 but this was his first venture as a full-blown team owner with backing from mineral water brand Highland Spring. He signed the experienced 30-year-old Michael Rutter from Kawasaki and the 2001 BSB Privateer Cup champion Shane Byrne (25) and retained Nottingham but in a managerial role.

Another new team was IFC, which signed Sean Emmett and Paul Brown. The team was managed by former racer and engine tuner Ray Stringer but the IFC tag came from International Flying Centres, a Lincolnshire flying school owned by Dave Copley and Alan Shepherd.

When the riders signed they had been promised the same new Testsatrettas that MonsterMob and Renegade had but because Ducati Corse never received any down-payment on the new bikes from the team they did not allocate any bikes or even engines to them.

With no possibility of new bikes IFC bought the 2001 title-winning Red Bull Ducatis 996RSs from Ben Atkins.

The backing for the team was said to be coming from an American sponsor and the team claimed it would be the biggest sponsorship deal ever seen in the series – so big that they planned to expand to a four-man team and run two 'junior' riders, Jamie Morley and Kenny Tibble. At 27 Morley was hardly a junior but was a protégé of Stringer's and came highly-rated with experience in supersport and superstock. Tibble was 21 and a former 125 British Champion.

Everything was arranged very late. The riders' deals were only finalised a month before the first race. Delivery of the bikes was only taken a week before the first race and there was only enough equipment for the two senior riders.

It meant Emmett and Brown would go into the first race with absolutely no testing, while Tibble would just have to sit in the garage and watch. Morley managed to secure a ride with Padgetts on their GSX-R1000.

Curiously the IFC bikes were painted plain white and sported just the black company logo. There was no hint of the American title backer and when quizzed about it, Copley simply said that they money was delayed and was due any time. It was an eleventh hour move to finally have the bikes at Silverstone for the opening action.

BELOW Sean Emmett leads Steve Hislop. If it had not been for IFC's financial problems Emmett could have taken the title chase to the wire

HISLOP'S FIRST BLOOD

Despite his lack of testing Emmett was on the pace from the start, qualifying second to Hislop and then winning the first race after the MonsterMob rider was held up by backmarkers.

Hislop blamed himself for not being aggressive enough in traffic and had to be content with second place. However, he was not going to make the same mistake in race two and bounced back to dominate the two-part race winning by seven seconds from Reynolds. The race had been stopped after John Crawford crashed and was briefly rendered unconscious.

Emmett was third in race two so Hislop left Silverstone with a four-point lead over the IFC rider but his team were confident about their title prospects, already talking enthusiastically about getting a new Testastretta in time for the next round at Brands Hatch.

Reynolds should have been happy with his fourth and second places but had already realised that the 185bhp that the team had now extracted from tuning the new GSX-R1000 was actually too much and while the team got the bike working over the Silverstone bumps, it did not want to turn as quickly as the Ducatis. Yamaha too had serious handling problems and while Plater's aggressive riding netted third and sixth places, team-mate Crafar struggled to come to terms with the unwieldy R1.

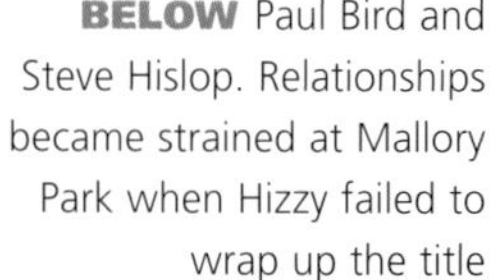

BELOW Paul Bird and Steve Hislop. Relationships became strained at Mallory Park when Hizzy failed to wrap up the title

Considering how well their Ducati rivals went in the first round, Renegade did not have a happy start to the series with Rutter and Byrne having to start from the pit lane after team boss Nigel Nottingham failed to have them out of the pit lane within the allotted time. They finished seventh and fifth respectively. Byrne crashed in race two but Rutter was fourth. Nottingham did not remain as manager for too long.

Hislop set a blistering pace in the series, winning the next two races at Brands Hatch to build a 21-point lead over nearest rival Emmett.

At Donington Park the Renegade team finally came good with Byrne and pole-sitter Rutter sharing a win apiece. Plater finished second in race one to score Virgin Yamaha's best result of the year.

The post-race Donington talk was Byrne's name being bandied around as Britain's next big hope and how his zany post-race, stand-up wheelies and burn-out celebrations were attracting an increasing fan base.

Hislop was third in the dry Donington first race, sixth in the second as the weather turned foul. Reynolds crashed heavily at Redgate in race one and was so severely concussed doctors ruled him out of the second race – even though he was keen to saddle up again.

At Oulton Hislop beat Rutter in race one but the Renegade man turned it around in the second race, although Hislop was stalking him until the race was stopped. Emmett was third both times so Hislop now enjoyed a 34-point lead in the series.

The second race was cut short at eight laps after Reynolds' Suzuki blew up spectacularly and dumped most of it's oil on the track. The slick brought down Dean Ellison, Gary Mason and Reynolds' Rizla team-mate Karl Harris who badly broke his left wrist, right scaphoid and collarbone. He also broke his nose and suffered concussion in the 100mph smash. Despite a massive clean-up job the Bank Holiday Monday meeting had to be abandoned after Clerk of the Course Stuart Higgs consulted several of the top stars who deemed the track surface unsafe.

The Oulton disaster prompted Rizla Suzuki to drop their GSX-R1000 red line from 13,200rpm to 12,700rpm in a bid to keep the engines reliable but behind the scenes team boss Paul Denning was lobbying for a change in the rules to allow the 1,000cc fours to run aftermarket con-rods for the sake of safety.

At Oulton Emmett's team continued to insist that the new Testastrettas for him and Brown would be arriving – and that their 996RS machines would be ridden at Snetterton by Morley and Tibble.

No one was surprised when they failed to arrive but Emmett's performances at Snetterton proved that he did not need a Testastretta anyway.

Emmett had complained bitterly at Oulton that his bike was no longer a match for the newer Ducatis of Hislop, Rutter and Byrne, but here he won the first race of the day convincingly from Reynolds then took race two after Reynolds crashed out.

Steve Plater put the Yamaha R1 on the third place podium spot in race one, ahead of Hislop but the order was re-shuffled for race two with Hislop second, Rutter third (after a dnf in race one) and Plater fourth.

ABOVE Hislop and Reynolds were the main protaganists for the 2001 season, but JR spent most of the year helping develop the GSX-R1000, while Hizzy became the man to beat on his Ducati

LEFT Hislop celebrates his well-earned title success on the podium at Donington Park

Hislop had been spooked by new high-profile Dunlops that had been used previously in WSB. The tyres had been brought in specially to cope with the high temperatures generated on the fast course but Hislop struggled all weekend to get his bike set up to suit them.

Hislop now led the so far Ducati-dominated championship with 189 points from Emmett's 172 while Rutter was a distant third on 130.5.

Then at Brands Hatch, Hislop struggled with a tyre problem in race one and only finished twelfth but typically bounced back to finish second in race two – beaten by Emmett who had failed to capitalise on Hislop's first race problems when his ageing Ducati blew a clutch oil seal.

Emmett won the race with a typically gutsy overtaking move at Dingle Dell on the last lap to close the points gap to 16 and then told *MCN*: "My bike is the bollocks. Even if I get a new Testastretta I'm not sure I'll want to ride it as much as I want to ride this one."

He knew he was pushing Hizzy to the limits too and added: "I could see Hizzy was struggling all weekend. You can see he's losing it. Give me a couple more meetings and I'll have broken him completely."

The battle for the title was briefly overshadowed in the first race when Reynolds chalked up the first win for the 1,000cc four-cylinder in BSB – snatching the lead from another 1,000cc four, the R1 of Steve Plater, on the last lap.

In a sensational race that saw the pair swapping places in outrageous places, Plater looked to have clinched it when he nosed ahead of the Suzuki at Dingle Dell – only for him to miss a gear at Stirling's and let Reynolds by. Reynolds said: "What a relief. We knew this year was going to be tough developing a new bike and we've had some ups and downs but we've done it at last."

Although Rutter netted two third places at Brands Hatch he never looked in contention but he certainly

BELOW Plater takes time out to say 'Hi!' He helped put the Virgin Yamaha team back in the limelight with some aggressive and determined riding on the R1

bounced back into the frame for the title with a double at Rockingham.

Emmett was third and second, Hislop was second and fourth so the IFC rider pulled another three points back, 246–233 but Rutter was looking threatening in third with 212.5 points.

Hizzy was back to his best at Knockhill, winning the first race from Emmett and Rutter but then it turned sour in race two. On the limit under braking in race two while battling with Hizzy for the lead Rutter was out of shape going into the Hairpin behind Hizzy. His Renegade Ducati hit a bump, went sideways so Rutter let off the brakes and by the time he was back on them was running into the corner far too fast with Hislop right in front of him and about to turn in.

With nowhere to run Rutter hammered the brakes as hard as he dared but still clipped the rear tyre of Hizzy's bike and sent both of them sprawling. With the help of the marshals Hizzy dragged his bike out of the gravel to finish what might have been a vital seventh while Rutter sheepishly climbed onto the tyre wall, seemingly out of harm's way, only to incur the wrath of the partisan local fans.

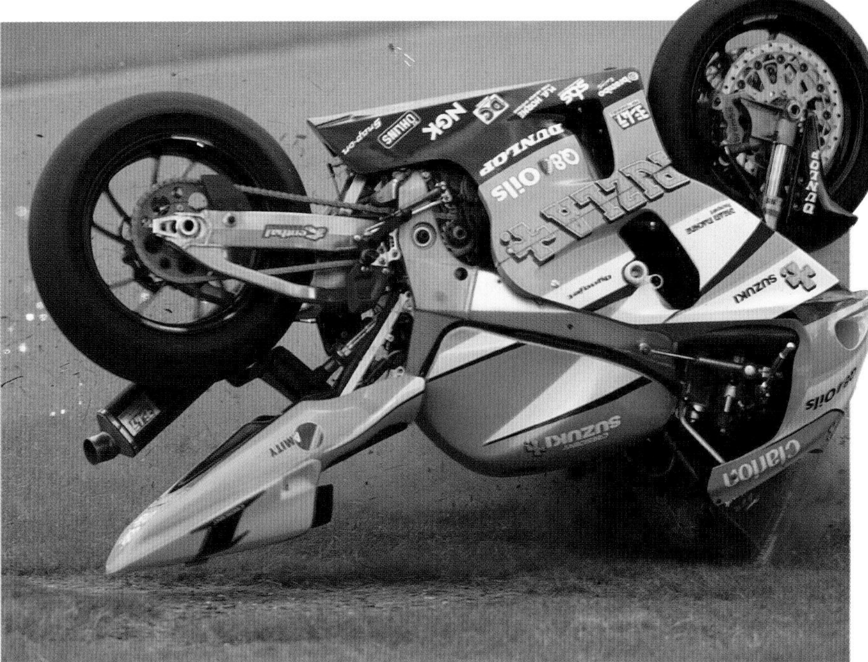

ABOVE It seemed like Reynolds's number one plate had a curse on it at times

Rutter later apologised to Hislop and told *MCN*: "No one is more sorry than me. I don't normally do things like this." Hislop revealed that Rutter actually said: "you can shoot me, hang me or even kick me in the balls. He was really sorry about it and, to be honest, it was a racing incident."

It certainly was but what few people realised was that Hislop had broken his collarbone in the crash. A week later he revealed: "I broke through the callus from the Rockingham crash the previous year but luckily the break barely separated and I heal fast anyway."

IFC RACING PULL OUT

It was not only the championship leading Hislop who was in trouble. Even though Emmett had closed the gap to 11 points after second and third places at Knockhill, he was complaining that his old bike was no longer competitive.

Emmett, however, would not be receiving the Testastretta he had been promised. His entire future was plunged into question when IFC Racing quit racing after Knockhill.

All the paddock talk suggesting the team had no money from the very start of the season had seemingly been spot-on.

Copley even told *MCN* that the IFC bikes would sport new livery for the Snetterton round – in a relaunch of the team, and then repeated time and again that the money was on its way.

The truth was that the financial stability of the IFC Ducati team had been in doubt ever since Stringer confirmed his plans to field a massive four-man team at an NEC racing car show in January.

Running four riders was always the sort of massive undertaking that even megga-bucks full-factory MotoGP teams shy away from so for a BSB team to do it was unthinkable.

The team missed pre-season testing due to non-arrival of the funds and were only able to field Emmett and Brown at Silverstone after 41-year-old businessman Dave Copley – the driving force behind the new team – put up his own property as security against the £600,000 needed to release the Red Bull Ducati team equipment from Ben Atkins' workshop.

The backing for the team was to have come from a group of private investors behind the Imperial Flight Centres venture. According to Copley, the multi-million pound project aimed to establish up to six flying centres in the UK and IFC plans to buy up and renovate disused WWII airfields.

There were two parts to the project, the first being to offer recreational pilots a complete package of a network of airfields each with full clubhouse facilities. The other aimed to develop each site into a working WWII museum with a range of relevant aircraft for static and display purposes.

Such a project including as many as six airfields would have required huge investment, believed to be in the region of £120 million, and, while Copley has never been willing to name the investor behind IFC, another key person in the team privately revealed he had been told it was from the American government, wanting to preserve its WWII heritage in the UK and said the delay in transfer of funds was caused by the US economy being in disarray following the atrocities of 9/11.

Most BSB experts felt the entire project was a 'flight of fantasy' and dubbed the team 'In Financial Crisis'.

As a means of promoting the project IFC pledged to back the Ray Stringer-managed Ducati team to the tune of £2.5 million over three years – which explained why the team even considered running four riders.

Copley owned Sandtoft Airfield in Lincolnshire and said he had been working on the IFC deal for ten years – and that it would have taken a further three years for all the flight centres to be in operation once the funds were released.

He also claimed the full funds for the aviation project were not due until the end of 2002 but he had worked hard behind the scenes to secure some of the money early to ensure the bike team could start the season.

The team had been caught between a rock and a hard place when the season was about to start on 1 April at Silverstone. No money had been paid to them.

Stringer admitted: "We were put in a difficult position at the start of the season – 'do we miss Silverstone and throw any chance of the title out of the window – or do we go, knowing, so we thought, that the money would soon arrive?' With hindsight we should not have started the season but we were told the money was on its way. We did everything in good faith."

Emmett served a writ on his old team for non-payment of wages but bounced back with Virgin Yamaha at the next round. A chance meeting in a Chertsey pub secured him the ride. Virgin team boss Rob McElnea was on his way back to his Scunthorpe base after a meeting with Yamaha and pulled into the pub for a quick leak – only to bump into Emmett who was having a quiet beer.

When McElnea heard Emmett's plight with the IFC team he offered him a ride on his Appleyard Yamaha satellite team to replace the struggling Paul Jones.

After one brief evening test at Cadwell, Emmett went to Thruxton and finished third in both races to keep his title hopes alive. With Hislop second in both races to Renegade Ducatis (Rutter in the first one, Byrne in race two) it meant Emmett only dropped eight points to his rival so left the high-speed Hampshire circuit still only 19 points adrift with four rounds left.

He told *MCN*: "If I can still win the title it will be incredible. I'm still up for it and it's still wide open."

Hizzy responded at Cadwell Park by winning both races and shattering the lap record. He had said the demanding Lincolnshire circuit would sort the men from the boys but he was head and shoulders above everyone.

The record 30,500 crowd on Bank Holiday Monday saw what he said was a new Steve Hislop. "I've been sick of the way the season's gone," he told *MCN*. "I was going forward at every round until we got to Snetterton and then it all went pear-shaped with tyre problems there and at Brands. Then I got hit off at Knockhill so I'm out to get a grip on the season. I'm Mr Angry and intend to stay that way."

Byrne beat Rutter to second in race one, Rutter reversed the odds in race two and Reynolds was the top four-cylinder rider thanks to a new 13,200rpm limit the team could run with the aftermarket Carillo billet chrome-moly con-rods that were allowed as per new rules changes Denning had championed for safety's sake and increased reliability.

Reynolds ran them for the first time in the previous round and the engine performance was now up to a reliable 187bhp – allied to the different Yoshimura cams and new fuel mapping which he had run at Rockingham where the bike had suffered another bottom end failure.

Emmett struggled at Cadwell with fifth and sixth places and was now a distant 48 points down on the series leader with three rounds left.

Hizzy piled on the pressure, claiming pole, smashing the lap record and winning the first race at Oulton Park, another of the technical circuits that he excelled on. However a potential double went begging when his bike quit in race two, the victim of a mysterious electrical problem. His first mechanical dnf in two years of racing a Ducati was caused by a cam sensor failure.

It was not only a disastrous second race for Hislop. Rutter's Ducati was slowed by a broken exhaust. He finished fifth. Renegade team-mate Byrne was sidelined by a clutch failure.

That left the 1,000cc fours in control and for the first time since the new rules were introduced there was not one Ducati on the podium.

Steve Plater (30) scored his first-ever British superbike victory, after John Reynolds mis-judged a desperate bid to pass him into Lodge on the final lap. It was also the first win for the R1 and Yamaha's first BSB victory since Niall Mackenzie won on the YZF750 at Brands Hatch at the end of the 1998 season.

OPPOSITE MotoPower Honda rider Gary Mason had this monster crash at the Thruxton Chicane

BELOW When IFC finally fell apart, Emmett switched to a Virgin Yamaha and showed his remarkable versatility – adapting quickly to the four-cylinder bike

Reynolds finished second and Simon Crafar equalled his best result of the year with third place on another of the Virgin Yamahas.

Emmett again struggled with his R1, injuring his hand in a massive highside during practice. He wound up with ninth and sixth in the races but now lagged 56 points behind in the title chase.

HIZZY FALTERS

Hizzy should have wrapped the title up at Mallory Park but was well below par with sixth and fifth places. He had a tyre problem in race one but all weekend he struggled to negotiate the hairpin on the single injector Testastretta. The engine management system controlling the fuelling just could not cope with the 4,500rpm at 30mph around the tightest turn in BSB. It meant Hislop would trickle around the corner only to face being highsided as the power came in a big rush as soon as he opened the throttle. The fours definitely had the upper hand.

Hislop was not the only one to struggle. Like the MonsterMob team, the Renegade crew spent hours re-mapping their fuelling in a bid to make the bike more comfortable to ride for Rutter and Byrne.

It paid off when Rutter scored third in race one then took the win in the second – his first victory since the Thruxton first leg.

Plater won the first race and was third in race two to maintain his good end of season form with the Yamaha.

After Mallory Park the first signs of a deterioration in the relationship between Hizzy and team boss Paul Bird began to show.

Hizzy admitted he had ridden badly at the Leicestershire circuit and Bird, instead of placating his rider, openly agreed with him. Paving the way for potential changes, Bird told *MCN* that there was no certainty Hislop would be riding for him again in 2003 – and that he was considering all the options open to him.

In the background of the poor Mallory performance and Bird's revelations Hislop went to Donington needing just 13 points to be assured of the title. He was sensational during qualifying when he lapped the track in 1:31.45 – faster than even Valentino Rossi had managed setting pole at the British Grand Prix earlier in the year with far more favourable conditions and a bike that boasted 40bhp more horsepower and 19kg less in weight.

Hizzy clinched the title with third place in race one behind Rutter and Reynolds but it was purely academic as Emmett had highsided early in the race on the exit of the Esses and badly shattered his left wrist and broken his collarbone.

Rutter also won the second race with Hislop second but the title was his to end seven years of anguish since his last BSB title. Hizzy said: "It's been a long time since I could enjoy a moment like this. It's been uphill and down dale over the years but after what happened last

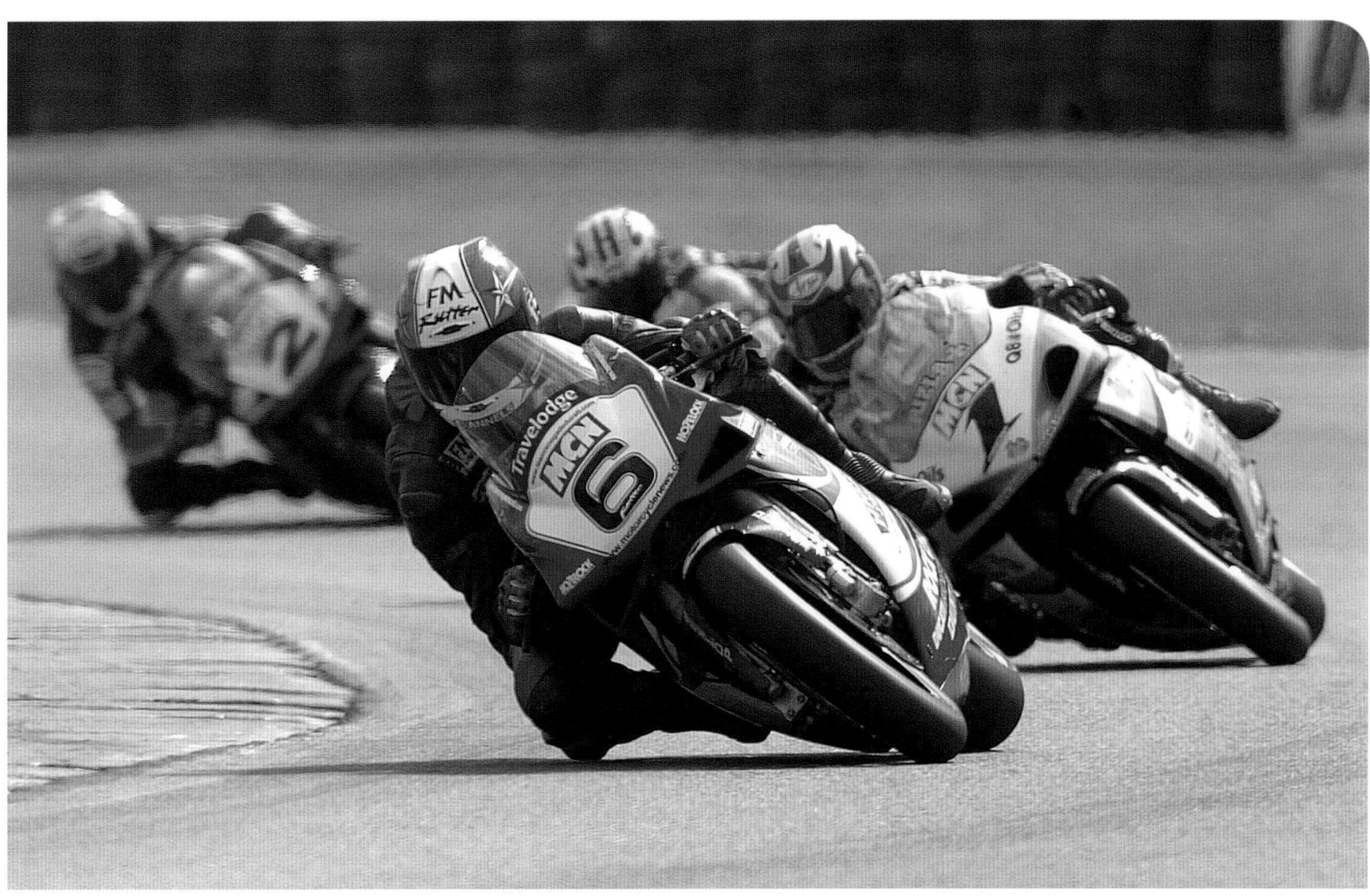

year I was determined to start the season in style. The trouble was I made it hard work for myself, with the high profile Dunlops introduced at Snetterton affecting me for a couple of rounds. But after what happened at Mallory I came to Donington like a man possessed. I wanted to win the title in style by smashing the lap record as well as winning the race but I didn't quite have the grip on Sunday that I had during practice."

Bird was choked to the point of tears after the race and Hislop said: "Birdy said that as soon as the title is wrapped up we'll talk about next year so hopefully we can get the job sorted quickly and I can look forward to defending my number-one plate."

However a week after winning the title Hislop was told by Bird that his contract would not be renewed for 2003 because the team wanted to sign a younger rider and embark on a new three-year plan move into World Superbike action.

Bird's decision incurred the wrath of the BSB race fans but Hislop did not seem too bothered once the initial shock had worn off. He told *MCN*: "If you think I've been strong the past two years then watch me in 2003. The shock decision to dump me has set me my biggest challenge ever, although I've no idea who I'll ride for. Just watch me next year – I'll be unbelievable.

"I'm looking at all the options: who has the best bikes, the best team structure and I'm talking to everyone. I just want a competitive package. Then the rest is up to me." A strange and disappointing way to end his title-winning year.

OTHER HIGHLIGHTS OF '02

- Castrol Honda's Colin Edwards wins the WSB title after an amazing nine-race unbeaten winning streak at the end of the year to beat Ducati's Troy Bayliss. Neil Hodgson finishes third overall
- Valentino Rossi wins the first MotoGP World championship riding a V5 Honda – taking his career GP win tally to 50 (11 MotoGP, 13 500cc, 14 250cc, 12 125cc)
- 21-year-old Nicky Hayden wins the AMA Superbike title riding an SP2 Honda to earn himself a MotoGP ride in 2003
- Steve Hislop's MonsterMob team-mate Stuart Easton wins the British Supersport series on a Ducati 748. Chris Martin takes the 125 title, and TT record-breaker David Jefferies is the British Superstock Champion riding a Suzuki GSX-R1000
- Chinese team Zangshen win the World Endurance title with a Suzuki GSX-R1000. Riders are Stephane Mertens, Warwick Nowland and Igor Jerman

ABOVE Michael Rutter became a regular race-win contender once the new Renegade Ducati team got into gear

OPPOSITE Shane Byrne was the revelation of the year on the Renegade Ducati

Steve Hislop was at the peak of his career in 2002.

Not only had he bounced back from some pretty serious injuries sustained in the previous year to enjoy his best season ever, wrapping up his second British Superbike title, but what really underlined his amazing talent was his breathtaking lap of Donington Park. Incredibly, at 40 years of age he lapped the 2.5-mile Grand Prix circuit faster on a Ducati V-twin superbike than Valentino Rossi had aboard his awesome HRC factory Honda RCV211, which arguably was the most potent, most exotic MotoGP bike in the world.

Hislop scorched around the undulating circuit in 1:31.45 during the first session of Saturday qualifying for the final British Superbike round. Rossi's pole time for the British Grand Prix earlier in the year was 1:31.56.

But Hizzy managed the feat on a Ducati 998 with 40 less horsepower and 19 more kilos than Rossi's RCV.

After his amazing lap Hizzy told *MCN*: "I said I wanted to come here and better my WSB Superpole time of 1:32.62 and I secretly had the ambition of getting into the 1:31s. When Troy Corser set the lap record he took a superbike around faster than a 500cc two-stroke so I wanted to lap faster than a Grand Prix four-stroke! It was just a personal thing."

Hislop was riding high and after finally winning the British title, seven years after his last major success, he should have been able to secure a fat retainer with a number-one plate attached to the front of his bike.

But that was not the case.

Hislop said: "I should have had a manager who could have sorted all my riding contracts and financial deals for me – and taken the pressure off my racing."

According to Hislop himself, Honda politics dominated his early career, and after brief spells with Yamaha and Norton, in 1993 he was lured back to Honda. Hizzy finished runner up in the British series and sixth in the Supercup, and for 1994 was given what appeared to be an exciting new RC45 – but it turned out to be a dud. As usual Hislop could not hold back in his criticism of the bike.

He said: "There was a problem with the RC45 handling. Everyone worldwide who raced them had problems. I said it publicly but Honda said I shouldn't have told anyone. I was tenth and struggling so I said 'we have a problem.' It didn't steer. I hadn't suddenly lost my ability to race!

"At the end of the RC45 year I was sacked – after all the hard work done trying to sort the bike out."

Hislop was also the scapegoat in a couple of highly-publicised mid-season sackings, notably in 1997 from the Ben Atkins Ducati team, and again in 1999. Both times Hislop was failing to get results with bikes that were difficult to ride – he liked to feel comfortable on a bike.

After he won the 1995 British Superbike title riding a Devimead Ducati, the same management team tried to put together Nemesis Kawasaki, with the support of the UK importers. Before the '96 season started, Nemesis had gone bust and it was Atkins who saved Hizzy's season.

Hislop said: "I had a fantastic relationship with Ben in '96 on the Kawasaki. He brought John (Reynolds) back from GPs. We got 995 Ducatis. 'Fantastic,' I thought, then I got thrown off during the very first test and suffered concussion.

"All season we needed to improve the suspension and soften off the power.

"JR was either scoring results or in the medical centre because he was riding beyond the limits of the bike. I wasn't going to do that. I wanted to iron out the problems. The bike was out of control so I wasn't going to stick my neck out. Ben sacked me at Thruxton."

Good end of season results on Ray Stringer's private Kawasaki prompted Rob McElnea to offer Hislop a Cadbury's Boost YZF for 1998. The deal was a place in the team but no salary. Hizzy was a title challenger until he broke his wrist at Cadwell.

"Rob said, 'the bike's here'. Put yourself back in the show window. But Rob lost Cadbury's backing in 1999 and struggled to get Virgin on board for the following year so he couldn't offer me a ride

"I got the Kawasaki ride at the last minute and a salary of £10,000 as Walker's team-mate."

A new suspension linkage Hislop asked for did not arrive until June and he was ordered to attend a one-hour evening test at Donington Park, the night before he was due to travel to Spa for a 24 hour race with Kawasaki France. He refused to go and was sacked.

He said: "One hour wasn't long enough to sort the problems we had and I really didn't need to confuse matters with the Monday night test at Donington so I said I'd rather not do it."

Hizzy then received the call from McElnea who now had enough Virgin cash to field a second bike. He broke the lap record first time out testing at Cadwell Park and earned a full-time ride for 2000.

His promising start to the year on the R7 ended with a broken neck in the first corner of the Brands Hatch WSB race where he was competing as a 'wild-card' rider.

Hizzy said McElnea was unsure that he would still have the desire to mix it after such an horrendous crash but the veteran Scot bounced back with Paul Bird's team in 2001 and looked set to win the title until he was the unwitting victim in a crash at Rockingham.

Once more Hizzy summoned the motivation to have another crack at the title and in September 2002 at Donington Park he finally pulled it off.

Even then Hislop's career looked ready to take another turbulent turn. Team boss Paul Bird was elated with the success but had already been suggesting prior to the final race that he might be looking for a younger rider in 2003.

LEFT Hizzy's favourite trick was to set the pace first thing Friday morning then watch the monitors, until it looked like his time was coming under threat

OPPOSITE Hislop through the woods at Cadwell Park. He loved the place

Hislop, 41 in January 2003, was adamant that he would defend his *MCN* British Superbike title, even though he was not sure who he would be riding for.

His passion to race burned as fiercely as ever, but there was another underlying reason for his desire to carry on racing. He had to if he wanted to secure his financial future, not just for himself, but for his two young sons Connor and Aaron.

Hislop signed to ride the Virgin Yamaha for 2003 but never gelled with the four-cylinder machine and was sacked.

He picked up a ride with ETI that was to have reunited him with his 2002 title-winning bike at Oulton Park on August 10.

Sadly, two weeks before he was due to race Hizzy died when the helicopter he was piloting crashed on the outskirts of Hawick, his hometown.

This material is taken from an interview with Steve Hislop conducted by the author for MCN *in the week following his 2002 British Superbike title success. A few days later Hislop learned that his contract with MonsterMob Ducati was not going to be renewed for 2003. Published with kind permission of* MCN.

SHARK
DUNLOP
monstermob
MOBILE FUN
Silkolene
coopers
DUNLOP

2003

Shakey's stepping stone to MotoGP

The 2003 British Superbike season had plenty to boast about with no less than six riders lining up on full factory bikes.

Honda signed Steve Plater to ride the Castrol Honda SP2 which the previous season had powered Colin Edwards to the World title. Hawk Kawasaki riders Glen Richards and new signing Scott Smart had the ex-factory ZX-7RRs from Harald Eckl's German-based Kawasaki team. 2002 British title winners MonsterMob Ducati had a pair of 998RS F02s for their new rider Shane Byrne and Renegade Racing also had two F02s for Michael Rutter and Sean Emmett.

Then there was the growing breed of 1,000cc four-cylinder bikes. Suzuki factory bosses in Japan placed their top test rider Yukio Kagayama in the Rizla Suzuki team alongside John Reynolds – a move that ensured the team received the very best technical backing and factory parts to push on development of the GSX-R1000 in its second year of superbike competition.

Virgin Yamaha scooped up British Champion Steve Hislop after he had been ditched by MonsterMob. He was seen as the ideal candidate to get the best out of the R1 – and a perfect mentor for his less experienced team-mate Gary Mason.

It certainly added a lot of kudos to the series when Honda Racing boss Neil Tuxworth revealed plans for the Louth-based team to race in the domestic series. The Japanese factory had withdrawn official support from the World Superbike Championship and rumours suggested that the team (which had previously run the highly successful WSB effort) would race in BSB for one year then return to WSB in 2004 – even though Tuxworth had publicly announced that Honda Britain's commitment to BSB would be for a minimum of three years.

The SP2 V-twin differed greatly from the Ducati way of doing things. For starters the Honda had a bore and stroke of 100mm x 63.6mm compared to the Ducati 998 F02's dimensions of 104mm and 58.5mm. The SP2

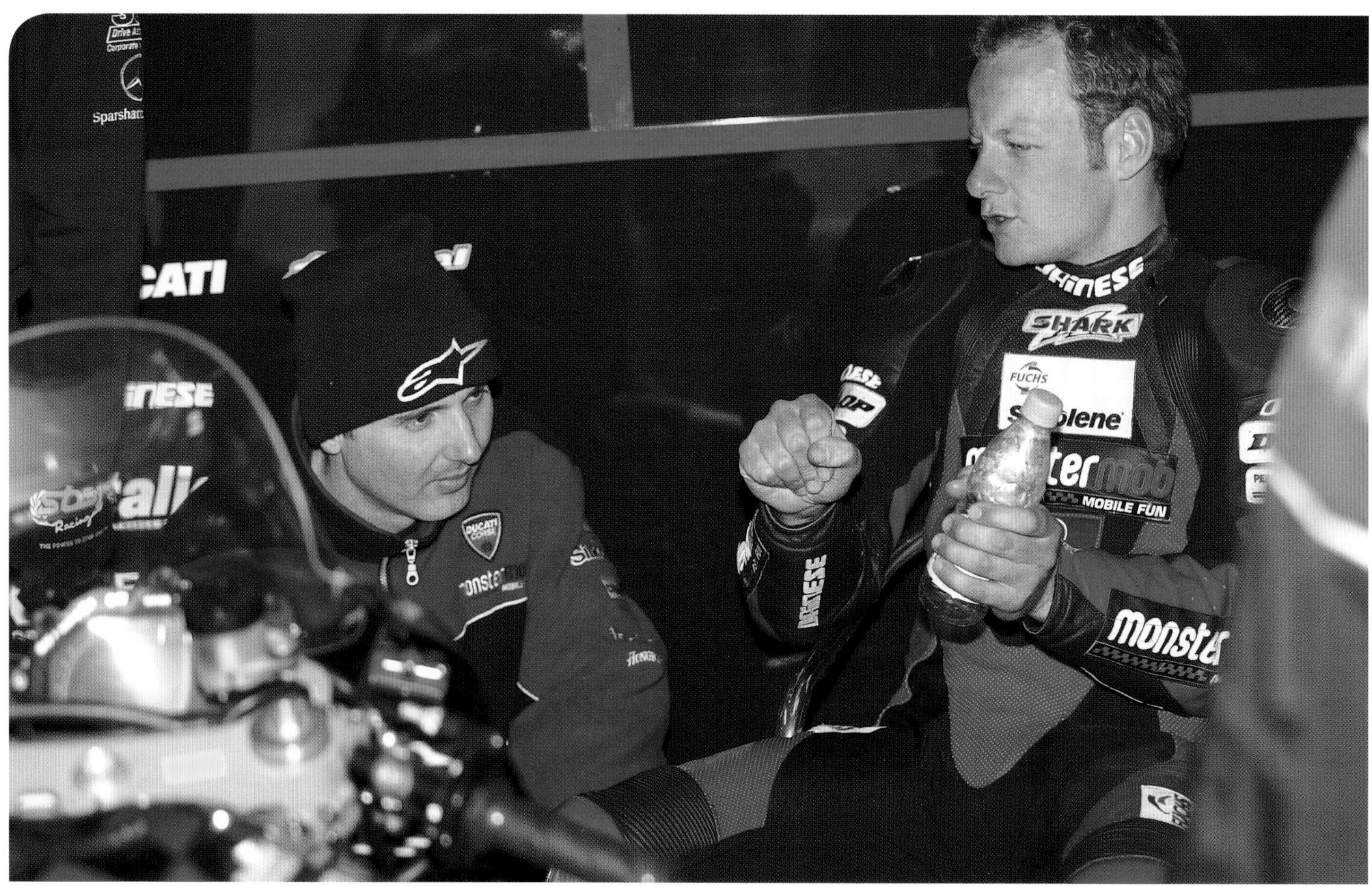

PREVIOUS PAGE Shane Byrne set such a relentless pace early in the championship, he effectively had his rivals beaten mid-way through the season

ABOVE The studious Phil Borley (left) was instrumental in Shakey's title success. Byrne relied heavily on the set-up skills of his crew chief

with conventional double overhead cam driven valve gear produced around 180bhp at 12,000rpm whereas the desmodronic Ducati boasted 188bhp at 13,100rpm.

The SP2 fuel system featured 62mm Keihin throttle bodies and a fully integrated HRC engine management system that did not require any mapping from track to track – unlike the infinitely-adjustable Magneti Marelli system on the Ducati which could be modified by means of a lap top to suit specific gears in specific corners.

While the 998 continued with the trademark Ducati trellis tubular steel frame, the SP2 had a beefy cast aluminium twin-spar frame with the engine hanging from aluminium lugs instead of cast lugs on the previous year's bike. The lugs incorporated pinch bolts so instead of fixing the engine to the frame as a stressed member, the engine was effectively suspended from the frame – the aim being to give the rider more feedback from the extra flex.

The Honda ran factory Showa forks with titanium nitride-coated stanchions to reduce stiction while the Ducati had 42mm Ohlins forks with external gas cartridges designed to prevent gas contaminating the oil and thus give more consistency over race distance.

Brakes on the SP2 were conventionally mounted six-pot Nissins gripping 320mm rotors. The Ducati had radial-mount four-pad Brembos and an option of 305mm or 320mm discs.

The rear of the SP featured a conventional twin-sided swing-arm with a Showa factory shock and two choices of linkage. The Ducati still had a single-sided swing-arm and Ohlins factory shock with just one choice of linkage. Both bikes used wheels made by Marchesini but while the Honda came with cast ones, the MonsterMob bikes used forged versions and Renegade stuck with the original five-spoke cast wheels the bike raced on in WSB.

The biggest difference between the MonsterMob 998RS F02s and those in Renegade's colours was that MonsterMob boss Paul Bird, thanks to his 2002 title success with Steve Hislop, was able to secure a deal with Ducati Corse for two brand new bikes built from spares, whereas the Renegade bikes were second-hand factory team bikes from the 2002 season. MonsterMob also seemed to have a more readily available supply of spare engines and other vital parts suggesting the team had a bigger budget and better factory contacts than the relatively new Renegade outfit.

Renegade also kept two of their 2002 customer-spec 998R Corsas. Initially team boss Mark Griffiths planned for Rutter to have both factory bikes and give the Corsas to new-boy Emmett, which made sense. At least that way each rider had two identical bikes to work with. But Griffiths changed his mind after pressure from Emmett and gave each rider an F02, thus rendering the spare Corsa useless since it was impossible to back-to-back test anything with two such different bikes.

Griffiths admitted: "I could imagine how Sean would feel, starting the season, knowing he was on an inferior bike. I couldn't let that happen."

It was a decision that Griffiths and his riders would come to rue.

There were two other competitive Ducatis in the series: the ex-Hislop 2002 title winning 998R Corsa bought by ETI team owner Alistair Flanagan for John Crawford. The other was an even older example, an ex-Hodgson 2000 996 Corsa ridden by Dean Ellison in the colours of Danny Gallagher's Team D&B.

Crawford's bike was said to put out around 176bhp and while outwardly there were no massive differences between his bike and the F02s, internally there were.

Just about every engine component in the F02 was different accounting for a difference of 12bhp over the 998 Corsa. The F02s revved higher, therefore generating more heat and had an additional cooling duct directed at the rear cylinder cam belt. On the factory bikes this was a rather tacky-looking corrugated rubber hose but MonsterMob replaced theirs with a specially-made carbon duct.

Power delivery of the F02s was said to be much more rider-friendly and their Magneti Marelli engine management system was much more sophisticated than that of the Corsas. Another area where MonsterMob held an advantage in experience over Renegade was that they employed (on a freelance basis) a specialist data technician in Mark 'Mr Bean' Richardson (a full time Jaguar Cars research technician) to fine-tune the system. The F02s also had different throttle bodies than the Corsas though the 60mm choke size was the same.

Other differences included an improved dry clutch on the F02 and 65mm exhaust header

LEFT Shakey in his 'check me out' title winning t-shirt

BELOW Rutter (No.2) chased Byrne early in the year but wilted under the pressure

pipes compared to 60mm on the Corsa. The MonsterMob bike had Blue Flame-badged cans – allegedly made by the company to drawings supplied by Ducati. Renegade used the Termignonis the bike was delivered with.

The F02's gas forks differed to the conventional 46mm Ohlins on the Corsas – as did the swing-arm, which was wider to accept wider wheels. MonsterMob used the same factory Ohlins shock that was on Hislop's 2002 bike.

HAWK'S FACTORY KIT

Facing such an arsenal of V-twin power the fours had to fight back and Hawk Kawasaki had access to factory equipment for the first time. Even so, if there was an underdog tag in BSB, Hawk's Kawasakis would have worn it. Their liquid-cooled, in-line, 73mm bore, 44.7mm stroke four-cylinder ZX-7RRs were not just the only 750cc superbikes left in the BSB paddock, they were also the only bikes left running on carburettors (old 41mm Keihin flatslides from the 2002 bike at that)!

Much was made of the fact that they inherited piles of ex-Chris Walker works Kawasaki parts from Eckl. The truth was that they had to sort through the mountain of bits to find the most suitable parts and incorporate them into the finely-balanced ZX-7RR package. Richards rode the wheels off that bike, to take seventh place in the 2002 series.

Using the factory crankshaft allowed them to experiment with external flywheel weights – a heavier flywheel supposedly gave them some of the low-down grunt the old bikes were lacking. Richards tried it, but went back to a lighter crank so he could keep the rear tyre spinning.

The team's engine technician John Trigger said: "Kawasaki may have used heavier flywheels to get more grip and improve drive but we run the older chassis so that was never an issue for us. Glen keeps the motors spinning anyway. He doesn't grunt them out of corners like maybe the Ducatis or even the Suzukis do. We don't have the low to mid-range power to do that anyway. We lightened the new crank, though, to help turn the bike (rather than reducing inertia to improve rpm pick-up)."

Although he used factory parts, Kawasaki kit pistons, Pankl rods and race kit cassette gear cam drives, Trigger also relied on Hawk's own camshafts, cam timing and combustion chamber shaped to ensure the power delivery suited the British tracks which are generally bumpier and tighter than the smooth, flowing fast WSB circuits.

Hawk initially used the 2002 factory Akrapovic exhaust but reverted to a twin-pipe system at one stage in the year in the search for more throttle response. It was not until a break in the BSB schedule at the end of May that they found time for a trip to Slovenia to develop a new 4-2-1 system with improved bottom end delivery.

No matter what they tried, however, the inherent fault of the ageing design meant the lack of grunt out of corners would hamper the Kawasaki riders all year.

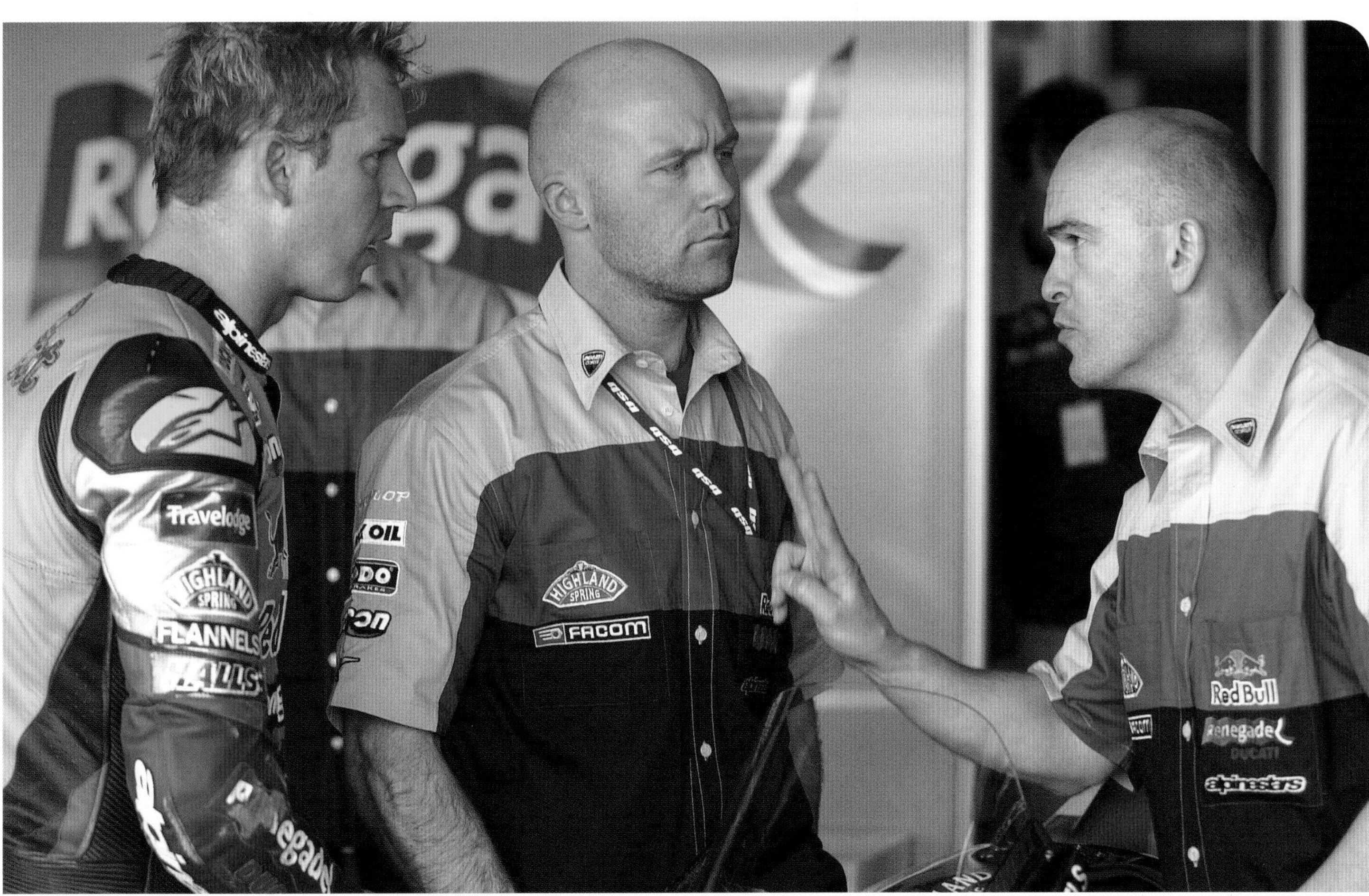

The saving grace was the impeccable handling of the bike. Ironically they ditched the super-stiff factory frames and kept the stock road-going ZX-7RR frames they used in 2003. Neither did they run gas forks the factory team had used, preferring instead to use conventional Ohlins which also came from the factory team but with the damping from Richards' 2002 bike transferred across. They did however use the stiffly-braced but lighter factory swing-arms from the works team but with team boss Stuart Hicken's special longer Ohlins shock permitting more oil to prevent overheating.

SUZUKI REFINEMENT

Kawasaki were up against it though, and not just from the Ducatis. A rule change for 2003 allowed the fast, but fragile 1,000cc fours to run aftermarket pistons and there is no doubt that it benefited the Suzukis.

In 2002 the Rizla team restricted their GSX-R to 12.3:1 compression for safety but really wanted to go to at least 13:1. Using cast Yoshimura pistons allowed them to go to 14:1 in 2003. Although they experimented with this throughout the season and ran up to 0.5:1 less compression at tighter tracks like Rockingham, to take some of the edge off the mid-range, making it easier to crack open the throttle out of tighter corners.

The pistons were also 20 grammes lighter than the standard pistons and had a thinner compression ring (0.8mm v 1.0mm). The team continued to use Carillo after switching mid-way through 2002 from stock parts when the rules changed to allow aftermarket rods – also on safety grounds.

Rizla employed Finn Erki Siukola as their full-time engine management technician. The Motec system they used was as complex as those used in MotoGP offering infinite adjustment of the ignition and fuel maps. The system was also linked with the ramp-style slipper clutch to control the massive back torque reaction of the big 1,000cc engine on the overrun going into corners – something the team would continue to develop all year.

The 2003 GSX-R1000 frame had the same cast steering head, and swing-arm pivot plate as the previous year's bike. While geometry was unchanged the frame spars were a different design, based on the MotoGP GSR-V design – each extrusion incorporated three internal reinforcing ribs, dividing each spar into three compartments for a much stiffer fame.

Throughout 2002 Reynolds struggled to control his bike late in the races once initial tyre grip had gone. Development continued all year with shock valving, ride height and an adjustable swing-arm pivot to keep the bike ridable even after tyre grip was past its best.

Reynolds' crew chief Dave Marton said: "Any chassis (set-up) changes we made were minor. Oulton was the only place we moved the swing-arm pivot point – but generally we were into really small adjustments. JR's a bit old school and tends to like to leave things if they work but I'm more for changing stuff to see if we can improve the bike even more."

OPPOSITE Team mates... but not for long. Rutter leads Emmett at Oulton Park

ABOVE Tensions flare as Sean Emmett is balled-out by team boss Mark Griffiths (right) as mechanic Chris Anderson looks on. Emmett was later given his marching orders

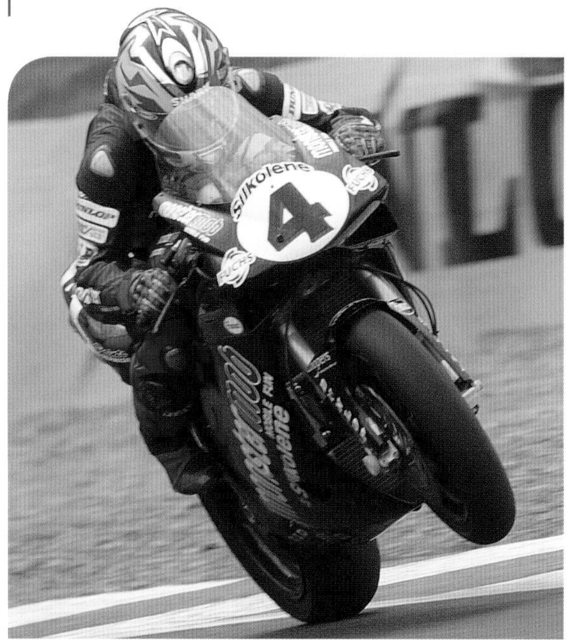

RIGHT Byrne 's aggressive style and out-going character won him a huge legion of BSB fans

YAMAHA PROMISE

Towards the end of the 2002 series Virgin Yamaha looked to be heading in the right direction with their new R1. The bikes turned tighter than the 998 Ducatis and their motors were bullet-proof. Steve Plater won races and along with Sean Emmett they made the bikes look seriously competitive.

The team's engine man Kev Stephenson did all the engine preparation in house and it seemed that all was needed was to build on lessons learned in 2002.

Compression was raised from 11.5:1 to 13:1. Pankl con-rods replaced the stock rods the team used all through 2002 even after the mid-term rule change that allowed them to use aftermarket parts.

Stephenson improved engine breathing with revised porting and valve seat designs. He also fitted REC stainless one-piece valves. New cams were developed and the package of improvements hiked power to 182bhp at 12,800rpm – 10bhp and 500rpm more than before.

Virgin ran a Yamaha kit engine management system early in the year but it was very restrictive in terms of the amount of adjustment available and relied on Jiro Izaki, the Japanese engineer overseeing the R1 race project, bringing new ECUs with revised ignition and fuelling maps from Japan to upgrade the system. Later in the year the team would switch to a Motec engine management system, allowing an infinite range of adjustments to the injection and ignition curves.

There was also a new ramp-style slipper clutch with six ramps, replacing the three-ramp Marcel Garcia (Yamaha France) design used in 2002 and new gearbox ratios offered overcame the narrow spread that hampered the team's riders at certain tracks in 2002.

The chassis was largely unchanged from the previous year with the team working closely with Harris Performance the previous season to develop a heavily-braced frame and fit the headstock with adjustable inserts in the yokes to allow the steering axis to move forward 7mm (from 23mm out to 30mm) and tip the

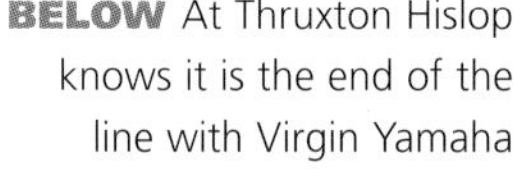

BELOW At Thruxton Hislop knows it is the end of the line with Virgin Yamaha

ABOVE Rutter, Byrne and Reynolds inches apart in a typical BSB scrap. Awesome.

steering head angle from 23–25 degrees. Because the rules said that the swing-arm pivot point in the frame could not be machined, Harris made a smaller diameter swing-arm spindle and fitted eccentric adjusters that allowed them to drop the swing-arm pivot point by 25mm.

The 2003 swing-arm was made to exactly the same dimensions as 2002 – 10mm longer than stock and one kilo lighter – but Harrris added extra webbing inside the fabrication to stiffen it further.

Mason stuck with his 2002 chassis settings but Hislop made big changes to get the bike steering quicker. Stephenson said: "Hizzy lowered the rear to speed up the steering. It always seemed that the R1 had a bit too much weight on the front."

SHAKEY START

Byrne left Silverstone leading the championship after winning the first race from Kagayama, Richards and Rutter. Then he finished a close second (0.15s) behind Rutter in race two with Richards again on the podium with the ZX-7RR.

But the field had been decimated by a series of crashes and dnfs. Reynolds was one of two Silverstone non-starters through injury (Renegade's third rider Nick Medd was the other). Reynolds broke his collarbone when he highsided at Brooklands on his flying lap in qualifying.

Sean Emmett also crashed in qualifying and again in the first race, this time in a three-bike, first-lap crash that also claimed Plater and Jon Kirkham. Emmett was ruled out of race two with an oil leak and Plater also crashed in race two but remounted to finish 10th of the 12 finishers.

The second round at Snetterton was blighted by catastrophic tyre failures in the first race. Nearly every rider was affected by the problem caused, according to the Dunlop technicians, by a dramatic change in temperature from qualifying to race day.

As a result, fast starter Byrne was robbed of a potential double win. With three laps of the race left, his tyre began to break up and as he slowed to control the bike, Rutter caught and passed him with two laps left.

Rutter had been canny enough to anticipate tyre wear problems and geared his bike to pull only 11,000rpm in sixth gear instead of 12,800rpm – which still allowed him to run a strong race-long pace.

At the request of Dunlop the second race was shortened from 25 to 20 laps, and with the temperatures dropping slightly later in the afternoon tyre problems were no longer an issue.

Rutter crashed out of the second race with what looked like a slipper clutch failure going into Sears and Byrne won by over 10secs from Emmett on the second Renegade Ducati.

Byrne now had a 27-point lead in the championship – yet he had not been regarded as the championship favourite in the run up to the start of the season. However, when he went pre-season testing it became

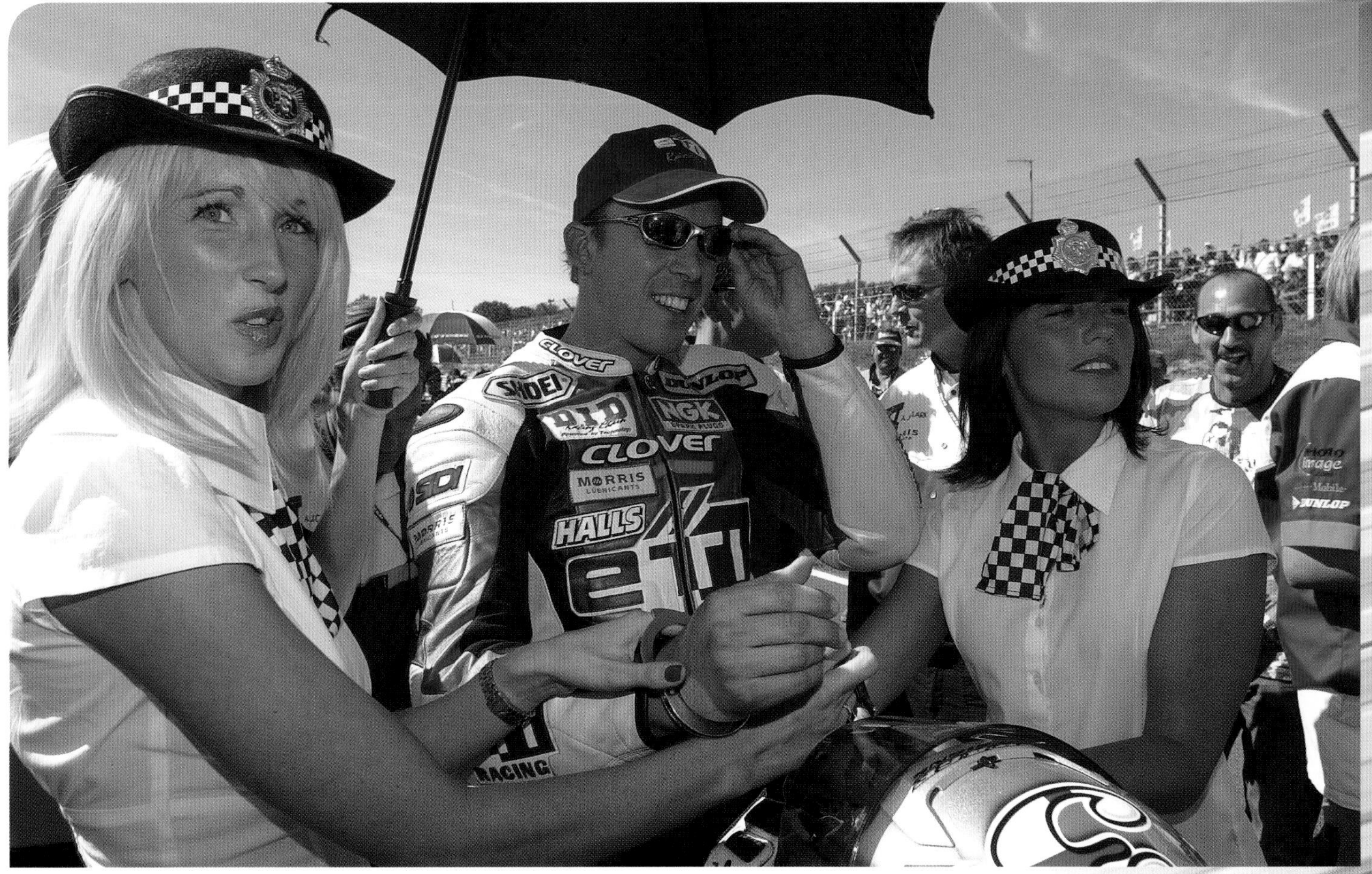

ABOVE Emmett is nabbed by 'the cops' on the ETI Ducati at Brands Hatch. It was a light-hearted taunt after he had taken a Renegade Ducati in lieu of wages he claimed the team owed him prior to his departure from their ranks

OPPOSITE Rutter speeds past a forlorn backdrop of a Rockingham stadium

clear that joining the title-winning MonsterMob team was going to suit him.

They turned up a day later than everyone else at Valencia and left a day early after the crew were satisfied they had a good base setting.

With MonsterMob, Byrne was able to rely on the tight-knit crew to give him the tools for the job all year. In Borley he had a meticulous engineer who also experienced British Superbike and Supersport successes as a rider. While Byrne did not have a great mechanical sympathy, he was more than capable enough to furnish Borley enough feedback to ensure the bike was always set up to perfection.

Stuart Bland was an excellent team coordinator and a good chassis man and Richardson was one of the most knowledgeable engine management technicians in the series.

The team also knew what it took to win championships. They had won the previous year's title with Steve Hislop – and would have won it in 2001 had Hizzy not been hurt at Rockingham.

During his time at Renegade – a team that lacked experienced technicians in 2002 – Byrne often copied team-mate Michael Rutter's settings and then had to ride around any problems he encountered. Not the ideal way to go racing.

So Byrne was not considered as a title favourite – not because he lacked pace, but because he lacked consistency and did not really have the experience to run in a one-man team. At least that was the general feeling among his rivals.

BYRNE'S WINNING STREAK

If people did not think Byrne was capable of winning the title after the first two rounds, then he certainly changed their minds in the second Snetterton race. That victory set him on an unbeaten eight-win streak that finally came to an end in late June when John Reynolds beat him into second place on the Brands Hatch GP circuit.

Byrne's first double of the year came at the Thruxton third round – he headed off Hislop by five seconds in the opener, and then Rutter by a little under three seconds next time out. There was more of the same at Oulton Park. There, he won the first race by over six seconds, swapped to his spare bike after Borley suspected a gearbox problem with the first choice machine and then won by over 10 seconds.

It was at this race Byrne explained his new-found consistency. He told *MCN* readers: "I'm thinking more about my racing a lot more now. And, I know it sounds daft, but I'm feeling a lot more relaxed. Before I just tried harder and harder and never really progressed.

"I've got the best bike and I'm with the best team. I don't have to take the risks that I used to. When you're riding an old bike like I was a couple of years ago you just have to push harder and harder to stay in touch. And sometimes you don't get away with it."

By the end of the Oulton Park weekend Rutter, the more obvious pre-season favourite, was watching his season fall apart. At the Cheshire circuit he could only finish second and third and was already admitting he

2
Red Bull
ROCK OIL
FACOM
FLANNELS
renegade
2

RIGHT Plater had to adapt to the Honda SP2 V-twin and make the bike work on Dunlops (after WSB Michelins in 2002) but finally won on the bike at Oulton Park and Cadwell Park

BELOW Richards leads Plater. The Aussie Hawk Kawasaki rider finished fourth overall in the series on the ageing ZX-7

could not run with Byrne because his bike was down on power compared to the MonsterMob F02 – even though on paper they supposedly had identical bikes.

Where Rutter, and Renegade's, effort struggled was the late arrival of their bikes. They did not get them until the day of the series media launch at Donington Park and Rutter claimed just two brief sessions of track time was not enough to set the bikes up – even though team boss Mark Griffiths dismissed the criticism.

What really hampered Rutter and his team-mate Emmett was not having two identical bikes to test. By running one F02 each, they were clocking up high mileages which meant reliability would soon come into question and the team appeared short of fresh engines.

As Shakey continued to rack up the wins in the first half of the year Renegade's challenge fell into disarray.

Rutter gambled on tyre choice in the wet first race at Knockhill but the conditions changed and he ended up finishing 20th. Then his motor blew spectacularly in race two. Speculation was rife that the equipment was too high on mileage. By now the riders had agreed between themselves that Rutter would have both F02s while Emmett would take both Corsas.

Shakey's two wins in Scotland meant he was now 104 points clear.

At Brands Hatch Byrne crashed in qualifying, hard enough to knock his spine out of line but after physiotherapy he won the first race by a tenth of a second from Reynolds but saw his winning streak come to an end when Reynolds reversed the result in race two.

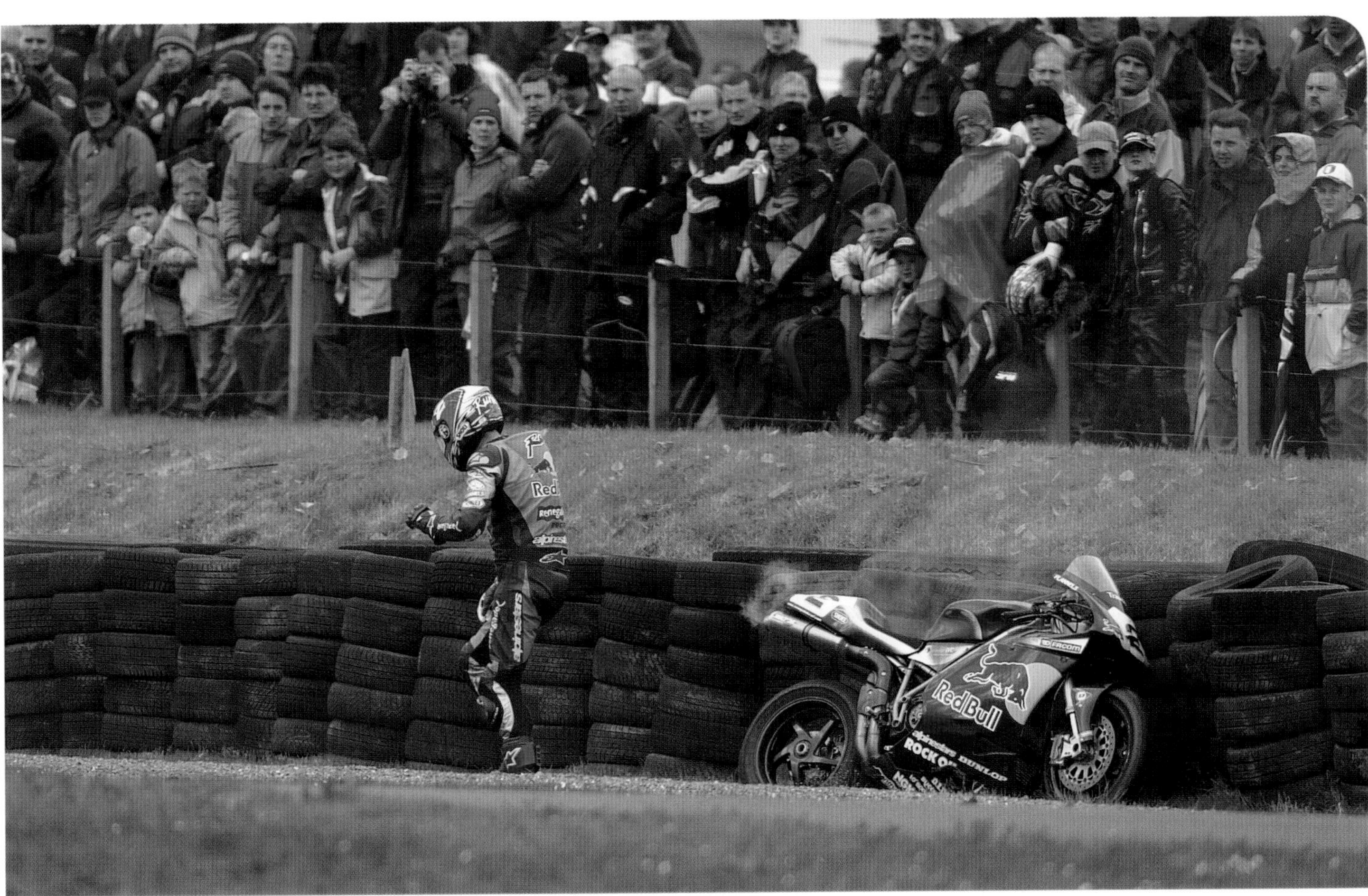

By now Byrne was 133 points clear of Rutter who suffered yet another disastrous first race when he was forced to retire with a faulty plug lead. He finished third in the second race but was over 15secs behind the two front-runners.

The Renegade team really hit rock bottom at Brands Hatch when Emmett was sacked after a disagreement with Griffiths when the rider arrived late for the pit lane walk-about. Emmett was reinstated for the afternoon's racing following the intervention of Linda Pelham from Red Bull, the team's primary backer but during the following week, Griffiths had decided his original decision should stand and promoted Leon Haslam, the team's rider in British Supersport on a 748 Ducati, to the BSB ranks.

REYNOLDS' SECOND HALF DRIVE

With Rutter no longer a serious threat the only rider left to challenge Byrne on a regular basis was Reynolds in the second half of the season. By then it was too late to mount a serious championship bid but it might have been a different story had the Suzuki rider not broken his collarbone at Silverstone.

Reynolds was back racing just two weeks later at Snetterton and ignored the agony to claim a pair of third places but a week later the high speed bumps of Thruxton were simply too much and he could only garner four points from the meeting.

Reynolds gradually recovered his strength, as second place in the second Oulton race showed. He finished third and second at Knockhill, second and first at Brands but then suffered a dip in form at Rockingham while his team-mate Yukio Kagayama stormed to a pair of wins – the Japanese rider's first BSB race victories.

The Rockingham meeting (the third annual visit to the Corby-based circuit for the BSB circus) almost did not happen at all after freshly painted lines on the track surface failed to dry out quickly enough. The lines, painted by track staff on the morning practice was due to start, were to mark the edge of the race track boundary and keep riders away from the concrete retaining wall. As soon as practice began, riders started crashing and a quick inspection revealed the paint had not dried out.

Two full days of qualifying and three races on the Sunday were lost as BSB officials battled against the odds to run the British Superbike races.

Even with a lack of circuit knowledge the extrovert Kagayama thrilled the 16,000 fans with his aggressive brand of riding to take the two wins, building on his reputation as a massive crowd-pleaser.

He said: "As soon as I saw the track I felt confident. It's much like Motegi, my favourite track in Japan."

While Kagayama starred, Steve Hislop continued to struggle to adapt his style to suit the four-cylinder R1. After 10th and 11th place finishes Virgin Yamaha team boss Rob McElnea sacked him.

Hizzy quickly fixed himself up with a ride on his old title-winning bike with ETI Ducati and was planning to make his debut at Oulton on 10 August alongside Sean Emmett who had joined the team to race at Mondello.

ABOVE Rutter's bike expires at Knockhill and with it so did his title hopes

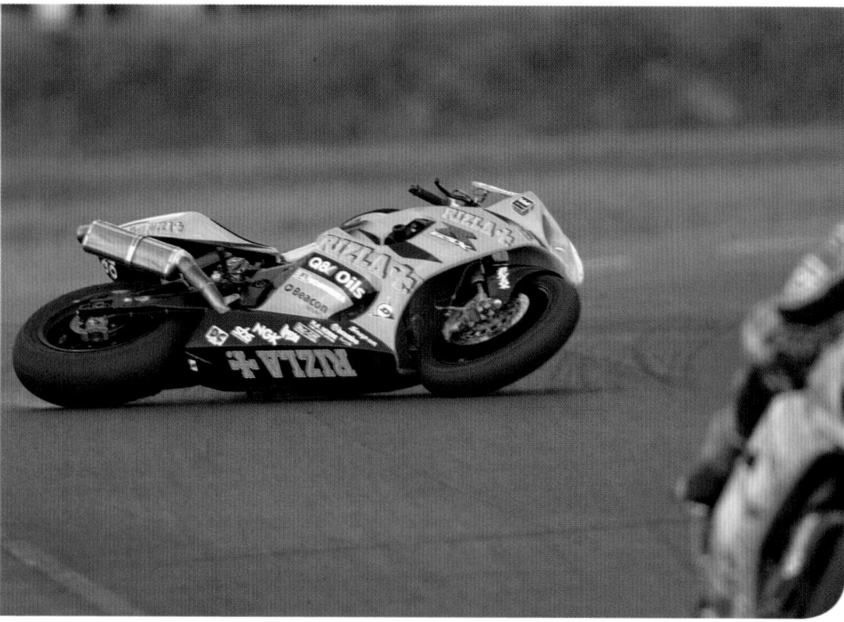

Sadly Hizzy never had a chance to make his reacquaintance with his old bike when the helicopter he was piloting crashed just minutes after take-off from his hometown of Hawick. He was killed instantly. British racing lost a real character as well as one of it's best racers.

Reynolds could only muster two fifth places at Rockingham. For the first half of the year he had suffered from a lack of strength to flick the GSX-1000 from side-to-side because he liked the pegs mounted high for good ground clearance. At Rockingham, which featured several fast changes of direction, his crew chief Dave Marton was left with no option but to lower the pegs to let him run on the pace. The pegs were dropped by 7mm and that resulting improvement in manoeuvrability turned Reynolds' season around.

From that point he was the man to beat, scoring a double at Mondello Park plus seven podiums in the final eight races of the year, including a first race win on the Brands Indy circuit.

Reynolds and the GSX-R1000 package was so strong he actually outscored the eventual champion over those last five rounds by 191 points to the 173 of Byrne but the MonsterMob Ducati rider's incredible first half to the season gave him the championship.

Byrne actually wrapped the title up winning the first race at Cadwell Park even though there were still five races to follow.

As he stood on the podium, at the Lincolnshire circuit, soaking up his title success after the first race, he said: "I've had a great season in BSB and by winning here I clinched the title just how I always dreamed of."

Yukio Kagayama had become the darling of the British crowds. He was the find of the series because the fun-loving Japanese star was such a great character. He had such a distinctive, unconventional riding style, but off the bike he embraced the British lifestyle and brought a refreshing brand of humour and humility to racing.

His results seemed to improve each race and after his Rockingham double he was also strong at Mondello Park with a third in race one. He was also battling Reynolds for the lead until be crashed out but the very next meeting he bounced back with a first and a second to Honda's Steve Plater at Oulton Park where, earlier in the year, he had struggled with what he called the "up and down and bump and jump" nature of the undulating Cheshire circuit.

Then it all went horribly wrong for Kagayama at Cadwell Park. He suffered an horrific crash that left him near to death with a smashed pelvis and serious internal injuries. Thankfully, he would later recover but only after enduring several lengthy operations and some touch and go situations that left everyone fearing the worst.

While he was fighting to overcome his injuries, it was business as usual in BSB. Reynolds and Emmett shared race wins while Byrne could only muster two thirds.

Emmett had to dodge bailiffs all weekend who had come to the track to serve him with a summons. He had been to the Renegade workshop and removed his old racebike as security against £50,000 wages, which he claimed was still owed to him. Emmett eventually returned the bike but never received the full amount of money he said was owing to him.

Byrne won the final two races of the year at Donington, taking his seasonal tally to 12 and he finished on the podium no less than 21 times in the 24 races.

Byrne had hoped to go to WSB with MonsterMob and said: "We gelled well as a team but I think both myself and the crew have reached a stage where we need a new challenge. I want to race in WSB for the next couple of years as a stepping stone to MotoGP. I know it's not going to be easy but I need to push myself and become a better rider.

"Winning BSB is just the first step. I've got to prove myself in WSB and if I can then race in MotoGP and beat someone like Rossi, only then will I start thinking that I've actually achieved something a bit special."

Winter turmoil over new WSB regulations and the imposition of a Pirelli control tyre rule left team boss Paul Bird (and many others) unimpressed and he opted to stay in the UK while 'Shakey' clinched a deal with Aprilia to go direct to MotoGP.

Reynolds finished second in the series, arguably with the Suzuki GSX-R1000 now the strongest bike in the championship.

Rutter faded to third with a bike that never matched Byrne's for speed or reliability. Rutter never spoke out publicly about the team's internal strife but that was more out of fear of losing his job and wages like Emmett did than to any real loyalty towards his team boss.

OTHER HIGHLIGHTS OF '03

- Neil Hodgson – the 2000 BSB Champion – wins the World Superbike title riding a Fila Ducati 999. Another Brit, James Toseland, is third riding a GSE Ducati 998 F02 and his team-mate Chris Walker is sixth overall
- Australian Chris Vermeulen dominates the World Supersport Championship riding a Ten Kate Honda
- Valentino Rossi wins the MotoGP title again
- British team Phase One Suzuki win the World Endurance series
- Other British Champions include: Karl Harris (Supersport) and Michael Wilcox (125). Andy Tinsley wins the National Superstock title and Tommy Hill earns a place in the Virgin Yamaha BSB team for 2004 after winning the Yamaha R6 Cup

OPPOSITE John Reynolds is unaware of the commotion behind him as Yukio Kagayama crashes out chasing his team-mate for the win

BELOW Francis Williamson was one of the leading competitors in the 'new' Privateer Cup on a hybrid R1-powered R7

ABOVE Cadwell victory lap with (left to right): Privateer Cup race winner Dennis Hobbs, race winner Steve Plater, newly crowned BSB champion Shane Byrne and the ever-popular John Reynolds

Griffiths often said Rutter had a job for life in his team if he wanted it but after the last race in October he was planning a WSB campaign, which Leon Haslam appeared to be a part of and he advised Rutter he should look for alternative employment.

Glen Richards finished fourth on the Hawk Kawasaki ZX7-RR – something that really should not have been possible with the ageing 750cc ZX-RR.

The likeable Aussie never won a race but got onto the podium with third places at Silverstone (twice), Thruxton and Mondello to secure fourth place in the championship ahead of a bunch of more well-equipped riders.

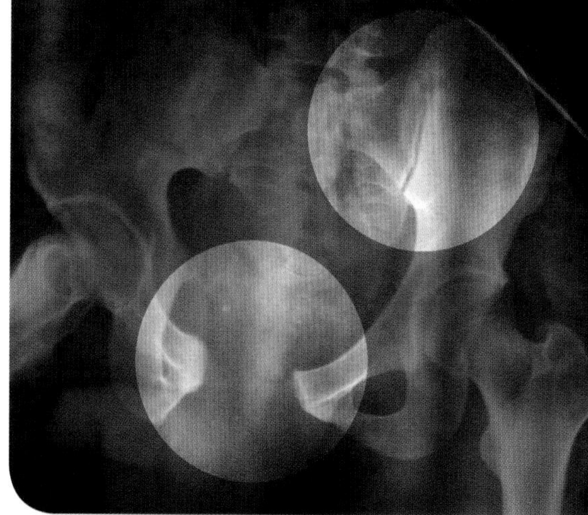

RIGHT Yuki's pelvis was separated (bottom) and broken (top right) which resulted in massive internal injuries

Sean Emmett was fifth overall after the most turbulent season of his career. He was a title contender in 2002 but the Ducati team he was riding for pulled out and he was forced to seek a ride elsewhere. This time he was sacked.

Getting a ride on the ETI Ducati after John Crawford had been sacked saved the day and he was straight on the pace at Mondello Park and gave the team its first-ever BSB win when he took the second race on the Brands Hatch Indy course.

Steve Plater found his form late in the season on the Honda and his job was even under threat early in the year when he was struggling to come to terms with a bike that had so much torque it pushed the front end in every corner at the merest whiff of the throttle.

Plater eventually won on it at Oulton Park and Cadwell Park and could even have celebrated a double at his Lincolnshire home circuit had it not been for the chain derailing after jumping the Mountain in race one.

Behind Kagayama in eighth overall was Gary Mason after a difficult season in the Virgin Yamaha camp. He signed as a number two but with the more experienced Hislop struggling, Mason shouldered more and more responsibilities in terms of development, carrying the team and achieving the results. He never quite managed to make the podium but did score four fourth places.

Suzuki had shown the 1,000cc fours could be made to work but whether they could outpace the Ducatis over a full season remained a burning question that we would have to wait until 2004 to answer.

2003 PRIVATEER CUP

Beyond the so called 'factory' teams the entry for the 2003 BSB series was thin, something that became very apparent at the first round at Silverstone when only 17 riders entered the first round, two were sidelined before racing commenced and just 11 finished the first race.

The idea of the 1,000cc fours introduced the previous year was to cut costs and make it possible for privateers to build competitive bikes but the only rider at Silverstone outside of the factory team loop was Paul Jones with his own GSX-R1000.

It was hoped that some of the smaller superbike teams like Russell Savory's MotoPower or supersport teams like Padgetts might embrace the class but the costs were still too prohibitive for them. Savory was unable to continue with the superbike programme he had started the previous year and teams like Padgetts opted not to switch classes. Privateers with superbikes preferred to run in the amateur MRO Powerbike series which was much more relaxed in atmosphere compared to the high-profile British Championship. The Powerbikes also ran under one day meeting formats to keep costs to an absolute minimum for the regular privateer riders.

However, BSB managed to woo them from the MRO by offering a lucrative cash incentive and the chance to race on the best circuits in the country.

Series boss Jos Foulston told *MCN*: "The superbike class has enough quality to rival a World Championship with factory bikes from five different manufacturers. But we recognise that the grid needs bolstering.

"We are working on a new Privateers' Cup initiative that will offer a well-promoted series for independent competitors." Foulston eventually launched the Cup series at the fourth BSB round at Oulton Park boosting the grid to an impressive 27 starters.

Before Oulton Park some privateers had already infiltrated the ranks. For the Snetterton round MRO Powerbike champion Sam Corke (24) on an old R1; 17-year-old Howie Mainwaring; Neil Cray with an ex-Rizla GSX-R1000 and Mike Walker joined the singleton Silverstone entrant Paul Jones.

The loosely-worded Cup regulations allowed virtually any 1,000cc four-strokes, so another MRO regular Francis Williamson was in the Thruxton line-up on his hybrid R1-powered R7, and the grid was bolstered further in the first official Cup round at Oulton with Corke, now on a GSX-R1000 plus Dave Wood, Alan Moreton and Jeremy Goodall. By season end 31 different riders had scored Privateer Cup points and BSB grid counts were by then very healthy.

Dave Wood won the series riding a GSX-R1000 Suzuki. The 35-year-old bike shop owner prepared an outstanding machine with ex-factory WP forks, radial AP brakes and a quick, reliable motor and scored six wins to clinch the title by 21 points from Dennis Hobbs.

Hobbs, 20 years old from Guisborough, was the find of the series, winning nine Privateer Cup races and taking four seconds in his 13 finishes. Going into the penultimate round Hobbs was just two points behind Wood but crashed heavily and sustained concussion which meant Wood could go to the final Donington Park round with the title virtually wrapped up.

LEFT David Wood came out top in the Privateer Cup series on his immaculately-prepared Suzuki GSX-R1000

Arai
HELMET
Q8 Oils
Q8 Oils
RIZLA+
SUZUKI
CRESCENT
Snap-on
NGK
SPARK PLUGS
www.rizla-suzuki.co.uk
EXPRESS

2004

JR gives GSX-R1000 its first BSB title

There were some significant changes to BSB for the 2004 season. Croft was allocated a championship round for the first time. The circuit near Darlington took over Rockingham's date, finally giving fans in the North East of the country their first chance of BSB on their doorstep.

Racing at Croft was good news for the BSB teams and riders too. They relished Rockingham's modern plush pit facilities and hospitality boxes but despaired at the wall-lined portion of the track, and its mickey-mouse infield section. Croft, on the other hand, had more quaint facilities harking back to its airfield roots, but the track itself offered some really challenging sections to the riders.

Besides, there was already a wealth of Midlands-based meetings. In addition to the Silverstone season-opener and the final round at Donington Park, Mallory Park made a return to the schedule after several safety-inspired changes to the course. There was a new chicane along the end of the back straight which made a much straighter run through the Esses, reducing the risk of highsides at a corner noted for its lack of run-off. The old control tower was gone too, which meant more run-off at the bottom of notorious Devil's Elbow. A brand new complex replaced the old buildings but there were still no new pit garages for the teams to work from.

The Brands Hatch owned group of circuits had changed hands in January with former Formula One competitor Dr Jonathan Palmer's MotorSport Vision company now in charge of Brands Hatch, Cadwell Park, Oulton Park and Snetterton.

At Cadwell Park, there was already a new chicane installed at Mansfield to reduce the risk of a repeat of the Yukio Kagayama crash at the left-hander just before the Mountain. Palmer also promised a rake of other improvements to his circuits for 2004 and true to his word there was more run-off created at the Cadwell Hairpin by the time the teams arrived in August. Not only that, Palmer ensured every single one of his circuits was given a good spring-clean and facelift to provide the fans with the kind of welcome he believes his customers should receive.

But the biggest change to BSB was behind the scenes with Spanish company Dorna signing a five-year deal to promote the series.

Dorna, are the promoters and rights holders of the World MotoGP Championship and their move was seen by some as a real slap in the face for FG Sport, the promoters of World Superbike. FG Sport had never had any hold on the British series but at a time when their own series was struggling for its very survival, Dorna's involvement in one of the most prestigious domestic superbike championships in the world was another cross for them to bear.

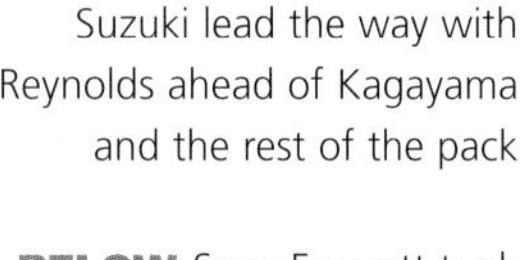

PREVIOUS PAGE Rizla Suzuki lead the way with Reynolds ahead of Kagayama and the rest of the pack

BELOW Sean Emmett took one hand off the bars to wave to the Thruxton crowd but instantly was in a massive slide at the final chicane blowing a certain victory. He made amends in race two with a win

Dorna's involvement in BSB immediately led to speculation that the series was about to spread its wings and move into Europe, a move strongly denied by all parties.

Robert Fearnall, the boss at Donington Park, had strong links with Dorna through the promotion of the British Grand Prix and helped broker the new BSB deal. He told *MCN*: "There is no intention to expand the series into other countries in Europe. BSB is the best (superbike) series in the world and we needed to guarantee its future. With Dorna we have stability for the first time and it will reach a much wider audience."

Having a five-year promotion deal was something of a first in BSB, allowing teams and sponsors to finally develop long-term business plans instead of one-year deals.

It also meant BSB could tap into the Spanish company's network of TV distribution and advertising contacts and their extensive marketing experience.

Plus there was the added bonus for British riders of having a much better chance of breaking into Grand Prix with all classes of BSB effectively acting as a feeder series.

Some people expected immediate changes but that was not how Dorna wanted to play it. Tony Partis, the Managing Director of Dorna UK, said: "You're not going to see any changes straight away. Our aim for 2004 is to take stock of the situation. We want to see how BSB works and then, if we need to, we can make improvements in the future."

Dorna arrived at the right time. The line up for the 2004 series could not have been any stronger. In fact it was much stronger than WSB, which was going though a period of turmoil.

The Motorcycle Sport Manufacturers Association (MSMA), representing the interests of all the major manufacturers involved in World Championship racing, had been unhappy with the lack in continuity of technical regulations in World Superbikes for some time and the switch to a Pirelli control tyre rule for 2004 by FG Sport finally encouraged the four Japanese companies to cancel their official support for the championship. It left Ducati as the only manufacturer directly involved in the World series.

ABOVE LEFT Michael Rutter gave himself and Honda a seasonal winning start at Silverstone

ABOVE New-boy Ryuichi Kiyonari listens as his crew chief Adrian Gorst explains a technical issue

HONDA'S FACTORY EFFORT

WSB's loss was BSB's gain as Honda needed somewhere to develop their new FireBlade superbike for the Suzuka Eight Hour. Normally they would have run a full-factory team in WSB but the MSMA's stance, plus the Pirelli tyre rule, meant they had to look elsewhere to race.

There was no point racing in the All Japan Superbike series because the quality of entry was also at a low ebb. American Honda ran their factory bikes on Dunlops in AMA Superbike, so if Honda wanted to develop the bike on Michelin tyres ready for the Eight Hour they had only one real choice of top international competition – BSB.

Honda's official racing arm, Honda Racing Corporation (HRC) did not spare any expense in its quest for the BSB title. There were four factory bikes and an army of Japanese technicians in addition to the British crew.

The team was based in the old Castrol Honda WSB headquarters on the outskirts of Louth, Lincolnshire and was managed by the former Castrol Honda boss Neil Tuxworth whose job it was to oversee the entire Honda Racing operation in Britain including Motocross, Touring Cars and Powerboats. Former Grand Prix star Tadayuki Okada also based himself in the UK, acting as link-man for the project between Louth and HRC in Japan.

The team also had top-level factory support from Michelin and Showa who both sent staff and the latest development equipment to every single test session and BSB race weekend.

Mirroring Suzuki's policy of sending Yukio Kagayama to the Rizla team to race in BSB, HRC also supplied a Japanese rider in Ryuichi Kiyonari. Unlike Kagayama, Kiyonari lacked real experience – even though he had raced in MotoGP in 2003.

Kiyonari had won the 2002 All Japan Supersport title but was thrust into MotoGP limelight after the untimely death of Daijiro Kato at the start of the 2003 campaign at Suzuka. It was a tough baptism on a production RCV211 as Kato's factory support went to the more experienced Sete Gibernau and, with no pre-season testing and a team who were still trying to come to terms with the death of their star rider, Kiyonari struggled.

Kiyonari's team-mate was Michael Rutter, one of the most experienced riders in BSB. Rutter's good understanding of technical matters and bike set-up would prove invaluable in this development year.

It was always going to be a demanding year. Honda Racing had competed in the 2003 BSB series using Colin Edwards' title-winning SP2 V-twin, on Dunlops (although the bike had been developed on Michelins) and it was difficult trying to adapt that bike to work on the tight British circuits.

For 2004 they were starting at ground zero with no data. Michelin were in a similar position, having last raced in the British series in 1999 with Red Bull Ducati.

SUZUKI'S IMPROVED PACKAGE

By comparison their main rivals Rizla Suzuki were into the third year with the GSX-R1000 and they had plenty of data to work from. John Reynolds and Suzuki had finished the 2003 season by far the strongest package.

ABOVE Tommy Hill hugs the Mallory Park Hairpin wall. He was the find of the year riding for Virgin Yamaha

OPPOSITE The normally reserved John Reynolds does a celebratory burn-out

The Rizla backed team enjoyed technical support from the factory and Yukio Kagayama's second season in Britain emphasised the level of commitment. Although they were supplied some factory parts, the bulk of the development was done at Crescent's workshop.

The team took early delivery of their 2004 GSX-R1000s and, using knowledge gained from two previous years with the model, transformed them into race bikes capable of winning the title.

For 2004 the engines now had factory pistons (which looked very similar in design and weight to those in the MotoGP GSV-R) and titanium con-rods. The combination offered a much lighter package than the Carillo rods and Yoshimura pistons they used the previous year.

While BSB rules still demanded stock cranks, the teams were allowed to fit lighter flywheels (on the end of the cranks) to reduce reciprocating weight for improved reliability and allow the engine to spin up faster.

The team continued to experiment with camshafts and cam timing all year, and there was a new twin-outlet Yoshimura tri-oval exhaust plus the latest generation Motec engine management system.

This allowed them to incorporate an air bleed system like HRC was reputed to have on the MotoGP RCV: sensors monitoring engine rpm, plus throttle and gear position relayed information to the on-board computer to tell the ECU when to allow more air into the inlet ports. By making the engine run leaner it reduced the amount of engine braking to assist the slipper clutch and make the bike smoother to ride into corners.

The team also had new Ohlins gas forks and the latest shock with remote adjusters for high and low-speed compression damping but Reynolds quickly ditched the gas forks he had tried in practice at Silverstone and went back to his conventional Ohlins he had used in 2003.

While Rizla Suzuki carried out their own development in-house with technical back-up and parts from the factory, Hawk Racing had virtually no help building their race bike from the brand new ZX10 road model.

HAWK'S NEW KAWASAKI

No one really thought the low budget, Leicestershire-based team would be seriously competitive, especially since there was no direct technical support or factory parts from Kawasaki Japan to speed development.

The bikes arrived late and, if the truth be known, they did not really have any technicians within the team with the kind of experience necessary to create a race bike from a production machine.

The retention of Scott Smart, for a second season, alongside Aussie Glen Richards, was their saving grace. Smart worked with the team's methodical engine builder John Trigger to speed development of the bikes.

The pair of them stayed in Smart's motorhome at famed engine tuner Frank Wrathall's workshop near Preston for several months preparing engines while the remainder of the Hawk technicians stayed back at base working on the rolling chassis.

Smart used his depth of electronics knowledge to build all the team's wiring looms and develop their engine management software. He also produced a lot of the team's carbon parts, including the airboxes and used his F1 contacts in making things like the special velocity stacks for the injection bodies to ensure they got the best possible performance from the engines. And he helped Trigger with a lot of the engine preparation and numerous dyno runs.

It meant his own pre-season training programme went out of the window but it ensured Hawk gave everyone a real kick up the backside from the very start of the year.

While their rivals struggled with the gas forks, Hawk persevered and made them work. They had to. Unlike other better-financed teams they did not have a pile of '03 conventional forks lying around to call upon.

Virgin Yamaha signed Steve Plater back from Honda to run alongside the promising Gary Mason and the 2003 R6 Cup champion Tommy Hill.

Yamaha also had a brand new bike and on paper, the team got the jump on their rivals by taking delivery of the R1 in November.

The apparently simple task of building on what they had learned from the 2003 model was not anything like as straightforward as it at first appeared, since the engine in the new bike had its cylinders slanted at 40-degrees instead of the 30 on the previous model, and the new frame and swing-arm were different in design to the previous model. In other words, the overall package was entirely different to what they had previously worked with. Thrown into the equation were new Ohlins gas forks and it is easy to understand why the team lost their way.

Instead of what looked like a simple programme of refining the engine power and delivery over the previous model, their season degenerated into a season-long battle to eradicate a series of handling problems.

Top-ranking Ducati opposition was thin on the ground in 2004, a dramatic turn around in fortunes compared to previous BSB seasons.

On paper Paul Bird's MonsterMob team offered the strongest opposition to the Japanese manufacturers. With a pair of factory F04 Ducati 999s that were virtually identical to Neil Hodgson's 2003 WSB title-winner bikes, new-signing Sean Emmett should have been a title contender. Instead he was only able to show his true potential in a handful of races all year.

The only other rider to be anything approaching a threat on a twin was Aussie Dean Thomas who rode in Enzo di Clementi's Sendo-backed team with a pair of well-proven ex-James Toseland F02 Ducati 998s at his disposal.

RUTTER DRAWS FIRST BLOOD

The series quickly developed into a straight shoot-out between John Reynolds and Michael Rutter – Suzuki and Honda.

HRC President Kyoji Nakajima had flown in from the Barcelona MotoGP pre-season test specially to see the debut of the Fireblade in the Silverstone opening round and he was rewarded when pole-sitter Rutter took the first win of the 2004 series.

The race started on a wet track and Rutter beat his young Japanese team-mate Ryuichi Kiyonari by just over two seconds. Kiyonari had crashed in practice but managed to qualify on the front row and impressed in both races.

Rutter struggled to get his bike off the line in race two but battled his way back through the field to hound Reynolds and Kiyonari but was not quite able to mount a challenge for the win.

In the next round at Brands Hatch Reynolds won the first race and looked set to claim the second until he got tangled with the backmarkers and had to be content with third. Rutter finished second to Emmett in a dash to the line.

Just eight months after nearly losing his life at Cadwell Park Yukio Kagayama scored an emotional victory in the first Snetterton race. Yukio held off his team-mate Reynolds to clinch the race by four tenths of a second but Reynolds bounced back to win the second race and edge into a 10-point championship lead as Rutter finished third and second at Snetterton. He was again hampered by bad starts.

Suzuki dominated Oulton Park but it was Kagayama on top, out-smarting Reynolds in race one and then controlling the second. Even so, JR edged further ahead – by 18-points – as Rutter finished third both times.

Thanks to a revamped clutch design Rutter was better away from the starting line, only to be swallowed up by the pack in the first corner of race one. His bike suffered an electrical problem just before race two, forcing him to start from the back of the grid on his spare bike.

Rutter set pole position at Mondello Park but crashed out while leading the first race. Unhurt, he bounced back to win the second but Reynolds, with two second places, left the Irish circuit 33 points clear of the Honda man.

Rutter inherited a lucky first race win at Thruxton and a second to MonsterMob's Sean Emmett in race two which put him firmly back in contention for the title. Reynolds sustained a fractured collar-bone in a second race crash after clashing with temporary team-mate Gregorio Lavilla.

Somehow Reynolds shook off the effects of the injury to score an incredible win in the first race at Brands Hatch just two weeks later and, even though Reynolds could only finish seventh in the second race, Rutter again failed to capitalise on his misfortune with tyre problems in the wet first race and a misfire in the second.

Things were worse for Honda at Knockhill when Rutter was ninth in race one. He had opted for a wet front and cut slick rear but the tyres did not reach working temperature quickly enough. His wet rear was spinning too much to get any traction in race two which meant he could do no better than fourth while Reynolds played it safe for the weekend with fourth and third places.

REYNOLDS' UPPER HAND

Rutter's mid-season lull continued at Mallory Park, a track he expected to win on. Struggling for rear grip in race one meant the rider who lives adjacent to the circuit could only finish sixth and then he crashed at high speed going into Gerards in race two when the front end broke away. Luckily he walked away unhurt.

The grim mid-season run saw him score just 43 points in six races while Reynolds' first and second places at the Leicestershire circuit contributed to a whopping 108 points in the same period. That gave the Suzuki man a 73-point cushion in the title race.

With only four rounds left Rutter managed to lift his spirits with a brilliant double at Croft after

BELOW Reynolds was always a threat on the Rizla Suzuki, but Sean Emmett (No.5) lacked consistency on the MonsterMob Ducati

BOTTOM RIGHT Reynolds had every reason to grimace, with an aggressive world-class rider like Gregorio Lavilla on the other side of the garage at Thruxton

ABOVE Smart just pips Reynolds at the line after a sensational last lap at Mondello Park

Reynolds struggled all weekend to have the bike working to his liking.

Rutter also won the next race at Cadwell Park after Reynolds uncharacteristically crashed out chasing the two Hondas.

Instead of backing it up with another win in race two to put Reynolds under serious pressure, Rutter made a really curious tyre choice opting for wets in the second race and as the track dried out he was forced to retire.

Rutter took the rap for the tyre choice but Kiyonari made the same decision suggesting that it was HRC or even Michelin calling the shots and not the riders. The truth was that Michelin simply didn't have a tyre to suit the conditions that particular weekend.

Ironically Reynolds also struggled with tyre problems in that race and could only finish eighth, which meant the title contenders were now 33 points apart.

With the pressure on after his below par Cadwell Park showing, Reynolds delivered a performance worthy of a champion, winning both races at Oulton Park to extend his title lead to 43 points going to the final round.

He did not have it easy, having to fight off Rutter and a highly-motivated Emmett in a hard-fought, rain-hit, two-part first race.

Reynolds also took control of race two from Rutter early on and the Honda rider was lucky to regain second on the last lap when Reynolds' team-mate Kagayama's rear tyre lost grip.

Reynolds needed just eight points at Donington in the final round to be assured of the title even if Michael Rutter won both races. He had to be content with third place in the first race but it was enough for Reynolds to clinch the title – the third superbike championship victory of his career.

Reynolds said: "This championship is no better or worse than the others. Every championship is hard. It's not one race it's a season-long grind.

"There's been times this year when it seemed like neither myself nor Michael wanted the title. Each weekend we seemed to do things to hand it to the other.

"So when I finally wrapped it up I had this feeling of total elation. Not just for me, for everyone in the team. In Rizla Suzuki everyone is rooting for you so much because they've all got the same goal. So I'm not just carrying my hopes when I'm out there I'm carrying the hopes of all my team. The passion here is immense but so is the pressure I put on myself to win for the team."

Rutter was gracious in defeat. He said: "Fair play to JR. He's ridden the perfect season. I know people will say he's had his ups and downs but we've all had those – especially in a championship this tough. We're all very determined but somehow JR always seems to put it together when it really matters."

Rutter's team-mate Kiyonari won both the Donington races to claim sixth overall in the points. His season started well enough with two seconds at Silverstone but he hit a mid-term lull and then bounced back with a series of strong results at the tail end of the year, culminating with the sensational Donington Park double, outclassing even his own team-mate.

ABOVE Yuki was body-slammed at the Snetterton chicane in practice and spent all weekend undergoing physio

BELOW Yuki in full flight. He became the darling of the British fans thanks to his aggressive riding and crazy personality!

KAGAYAMA'S EMOTIONAL SEASON

Kiyonari's fellow countryman Yukio Kagayama finished third overall in the championship in one of the most emotional seasons in BSB history.

The Japanese star was near to death after his horrific crash at Cadwell Park the previous August Bank Holiday Monday yet made a miraculous recovery to be ready for the start of the season.

He was still far from fit. His smashed pelvis was initially plated after the crash but was not done properly so he had to go undergo further surgery to have it re-plated. His massive internal injuries to his lower organs meant he had to endure months of misery with several operations and serious complications, including blood poisoning as a result of the injuries. He even raced all year with a colostomy bag – but he never once openly complained.

Despite all that trauma Yuki showed he had lost none of his desire or aggression and was competitive from the very first test in Valencia. He had difficulty walking and getting on and off his bike but still finished fourth in the first race of the year at Silverstone.

In late April he scored his first win of the year in the first race at Snetterton but even that was not without more agony.

He had highsided at Russells during Friday practice and landed with a mighty whack to the pelvis. Everyone thought the worst but no damage was done, apart from a severe dose of bruising that left medics questioning his intention of racing on Sunday.

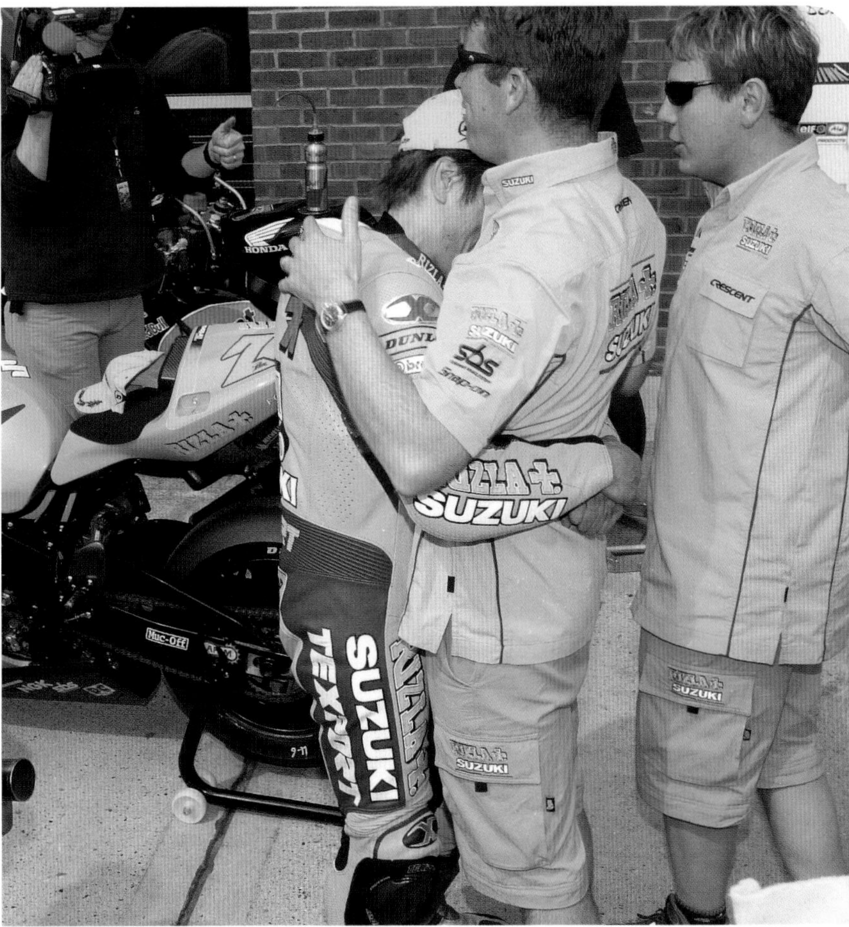

After intensive physiotherapy before he got on the bike each time he stunned everyone by winning the first race and backed it up with a double in the very next round at Oulton Park.

Kagayama said: "There were times in hospital when the pain was so much I thought I would go mad but as I recovered I thought I could win races again. I thought I would need longer, mid-season maybe so winning so early in the year is very special. It proves people can achieve impossible targets sometimes."

While Reynolds had been supportive when Kagayama won at Snetterton, he was not so happy at Oulton Park after Kagayama followed him all through the first race, only to pass him on the final lap.

Kagayama smashed his collarbone testing for the Suzuka Eight Hour race back in Japan. The crash was such that it bent a titanium plate holding a previous break in place. With another operation to remove the old plate and re-plate the new injury he was advised to miss the Thruxton round and wait until Brands Hatch to make his return in late June.

He finished fourth and third in the two races to set up an inspired run of form including two second places, three thirds and, of course, the unforgettable and emotional victory at Cadwell Park on 30 August – a year on from his crash.

Kagayama said: "Winning at Cadwell brought back so many memories, for many different reasons – but now they are all good ones. Cadwell is a very special circuit for me – I'm so happy to win here."

SMART – THE REVELATION

Scott Smart finished fourth in the table – the revelation of the series. He had won the 250cc British title as long ago as 1997 but a luckless two-year spell as a Grand Prix privateer effectively made him a forgotten talent.

It took three years in British Supersport racing to get his career back on track and then finishing runner-up in the 2002 series on his self-prepared Honda CBR600 finally earned him a BSB ride with Hawk Kawasaki, albeit on an 'obsolete' ZX-7RR.

Smart was fast and consistent on the new ZX10 for the start, racking up points in all of the first eight races, and outscoring his team-mate Glen Richards who had been the lead rider of the team only the previous year.

Smart's career-first superbike race win came in the fifth round at Mondello Park, and then in the most dramatic fashion.

Reynolds had what looked like a comfortable 1.3s lead over Smart going into the final lap but relaxed a little too much after a front wheel slide spooked him early in the lap.

Smart saw the gap coming down and decided to throw caution to the wind.

He was out of the saddle. He was pushing that hard. But as Reynolds cruised into the final hairpin for the final time, Smart stuffed his ZX10 underneath him and held off the GSX-R1000 in a drag race to the line by just 0.002s.

Smart said: "With three laps to go I'd given up hope of catching him, then going into the last lap I realised

ABOVE LEFT Yukio Kagayama after his emotional first win of the year at Snetterton

ABOVE Denning hugs Yuki after the win. The two had become very close after Yuki's long fight back to recovery from his Cadwell 2003 crash

there was a chance and went for it."Smart also won a rain-affected race at Knockhill and beat the opposition fair and square at Mallory Park after a pace-car session due to crashes.

In the winter he signed for Rizla Suzuki as Reynolds' team-mate after he had been courted by many of the top team bosses from WSB as well as BSB.

EMMETT SLATED

The popular opinion was that Sean Emmett should have been the title favourite, signing for the MonsterMob Ducati team, but it turned out to be a disastrous year for him and the team.

On more than one occasion he was slated by his team boss, Paul Bird for his lack of commitment to the job. It was true that Emmett still liked to have a beer and a cigarette, and that he did not exactly have as strict a training regime as his rivals but on his day he was simply unbeatable as he showed at Brands Hatch and Thruxton.

Emmett, however, did not have enough of those days in 2004 and ended up fifth in the points and looking for alternative employment for 2005.

After winning back-to-back titles with Steve Hislop in 2002 and Shane Byrne in 2003, Bird and the rest of the MonsterMob team expected continued success – but no one could have anticipated just how fickle the 999 would be on British tracks.

Neil Hodgson had won the WSB title in 2003 on a similar bike, but that did not mean it was problem free and the tighter BSB circuits seemed to amplify the unusual handling characteristics of the bike.

It was not just Emmett suffering. Italian Pierfrancesco Chili openly criticised his WSB 999 and reverted to an old 998 while Eric Bostrom could only win once all year on his 999 in the American national series.

On some circuits, with fast flowing sections, like Brands Hatch, Emmett would fly, but at other tracks with tighter corners or undulating surfaces he struggled to get the bike around corners.

While he claimed the bike was unridable, his team boss said he was not trying and the two parties quickly fell out.

Emmett won only twice all year. On his favourite Brands Hatch Indy circuit he was victorious in the day's second race after he had crashed heavily with Glen Richards in the first and been left with cuts and bruises.

Emmett said: "I got slated for not having any commitment but no one said it at Brands when I picked myself up after the first race crash and went out and won. The 999 was a fickle bike. It worked at some tracks and not at others. It was as simple as that."

His other win came at Thruxton – but it should have been two. He was in sensational form all weekend and had the first race wrapped up but for a moment of madness coming out of the final chicane. He took his left hand off the bars to wave to the crowd and was nearly highsided. By the time he recovered he had dropped to third. At least he made amends by winning the second race.

OTHER HIGHLIGHTS OF '04

- Valentino Rossi wins the MotoGP title after switching from Honda to Yamaha
- James Toseland clinches the WSB title in the final round in Magny Cours from Fila Ducati 999 team-mate Regis Laconi
- Aussie Mat Mladin claims a record-breaking fifth AMA Superbike title riding a Yoshimura Suzuki GSX-R1000
- 2003 BSB Champion Shane Byrne and 2003 WSB Champion (and 2002 BSB Champion) Neil Hodgson race in MotoGP for Aprilia and D'Antin Ducati respectively
- Other British Champions include: James Ellison (BSB Cup), Karl Harris (Supersport), Danny Beaumont (Superstock), Christian Elkin (125)
- Richard Wren wins the Virgin Mobile Yamaha R6 Cup to claim a place in the official Virgin Yamaha BSB team for 2005

Emmett completed the turbulent season with a third at Donington Park, his ninth visit to the podium but by then he had already agreed a deal to ride for the Virgin Yamaha team in 2005.

If Emmett's season was considered poor, then Virgin Yamaha's was a complete disaster. James Haydon's win at Knockhill gave Rob McElnea's Virgin Yamaha crew a little light relief in an otherwise appalling season.

Their promising pre-season test for Steve Plater and Gary Mason on the brand new R1s in Cartegena was not what it seemed and the team spent most of the year trying to sort out major handling problems. The team had topped the leaderboard at the Spanish track – but the opposition was very average. BSB proved a very different prospect.

Plater badly bust his wrist at Oulton Park so out of work James Haydon stepped in to help out but while everyone thought his Knockhill victory signalled an upturn in the team's fortunes it was not the case and they were still trying to fathom the bike in the final round at Donington Park.

The bright spot of the year was young Tommy Hill. After winning the R6 Cup in 2003 he earned a place on the Virgin Yamaha BSB and his youthful bravado meant he was prepared to push the unwieldy bike further than his more experienced team-mates.

OPPOSITE Yuki lays the ghost of his 2003 Cadwell crash to rest with a massive burn-out after an unforgettable race win a year later

BELOW Scott Smart worked wonders both on and off the track with the Hawk Kawasaki ZX10

ABOVE AND BELOW Rizla Suzuki plugged away developing the GSX-R1000, and by 2004 it was an awesome package

John Reynolds' title-winning 2004 Rizla Suzuki might have been a new machine but essentially it was an evolution of the bike he raced in 2003.

The engine was updated with factory titanium con-rods and slipper pistons from Suzuki. The weight of the rod and piston assembly was 140 grammes which represented a saving of half a kilo. The reduction in reciprocating weight gave an increase in reliability and performance.

Winter engine development yielded a gain of 6bhp. The team actually came up with more power the previous year but had to soften it off with the Motec engine management system to make the bike ridable.

Reynolds ran shorter gears than his team-mate Yukio Kagayama which allowed him to rev the engine out more, whereas Kagayama preferred to let the massive torque do the work.

Reynolds also used a road shift change – one down, the rest up – which led to problems in long-hanging lefts as JR could not put his foot under the lefts to change up. It meant at corners like the Devil's Elbow at Mallory Park his bike was geared taller so he could run third all through the corner.

To control the effect of engine braking on the rear tyre going into corners, Crescent used an updated version of their own ramp-style slipper clutch. The new Motec M8-80 system allowed them to refine the effect of engine braking to the rear wheel further by using an air bleed system.

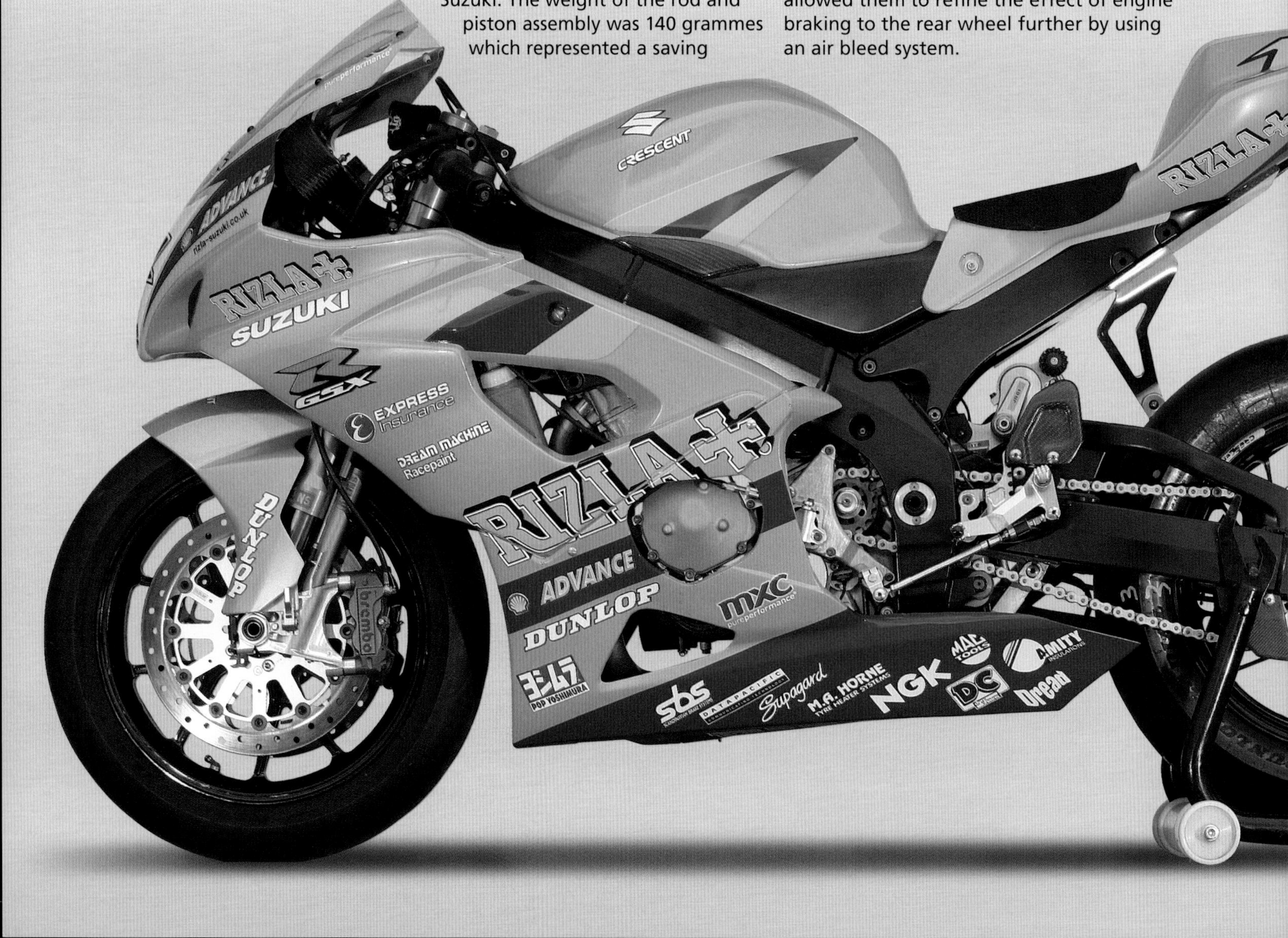

The GSX-R1000 was equipped with sensors to measure engine rpm, throttle position and gear position and that information allowed the computer to know when to tell solenoids to open and allow air into the inlet ports. Air introduced into the combustion chamber caused the engine to run lean which reduced the amount of resistance in the engine, and thus the amount of engine braking.

Reynolds said: "The bike was much smoother going into corners with the new system. It also softened the power on the way out of corners which was a boost in the low-speed corners."

The team's 2004 electrical system was a lot tidier on the latest bike thanks to a new wiring loom, incorporating a mix of military spec and F1 type connectors.

Rizla raced with new-style twin-outlet Yoshimura mufflers. This new design offered an increase in torque. The system gave a distinctive back-fire on the over-run but the noise it emitted on full throttle was nowhere near the new BSB limit of 107dba introduced for 2004 (it was 102 before).

The 2004 Ohlins shock came with a high and low compression external damping adjusters compared to just an external low speed adjuster in 2003. Previously, any high speed adjustment could only be made by stripping the shock and changing the internals.

Reynolds and Kagayama both briefly tried new gas Ohlins forks but ditched them before the first race and reverted to 2003 conventional Ohlins.

JR ran a lot less weight bias on the front of his bike than Kagayama, which meant his forks dived slower. He ran a higher front ride height than his team-mate by means of stepped triple clamps.

The team used the same radial-mount, two-pad Brembo brakes as they had used in 2003, Reynolds preferring twin 320mm discs compared to Kagayama's unique combination of 290mm and 320mm discs to give a little bite due to the higher front end bias he preferred.

2005

Lavilla provides Ducati upset

The big news for the 2005 British season was the return to racing of Darrell Healey's GSE Racing team. It had been mothballed after quitting the World series at the end of the 2003 season with only key staff like team manager Colin Wright and technician Dave Parkes retained but once Healey gave the nod the loyal troops were quickly reassembled.

With backing from Airwaves, a brand of Wrigleys chewing gum, GSE were back with 2004-spec factory Ducati 999 F04s for Leon Haslam and James Haydon yet in spite of the team's pedigree (two BSB titles and a reputation as the best-run privateer in WSB) and factory support, no one really considered they would be title contenders.

The main reason was how badly the 999 looked in BSB during 2004 when Sean Emmett rode for Paul Bird's MonsterMob team. After winning back-to-back titles in 2002/2003 (with Hislop and Byrne respectively) Emmett's season had been a disaster – a highly-publicised failure at that.

He constantly complained about the inability of the bike to change direction. Emmett also voiced concerns about the general lack of performance from what was fast being considered an uncompetitive V-twin against the allegedly superior 1,000cc four cylinders. Bird did not see it that way. He claimed there was nothing wrong with the bike and publicly lambasted his rider for his drinking habits and general lack of fitness. But the mud stuck – on both counts.

So with the 999 getting such a bad rap it looked like GSE's boys would be struggling, especially since defending champions Rizla Suzuki were expected to come into the season stronger than ever with a brand new bike that was thought to be a big step ahead of the old K4 model thanks largely to its smaller dimensions which Reynolds said he felt would suit him much more than the bike he won the title on the previous season.

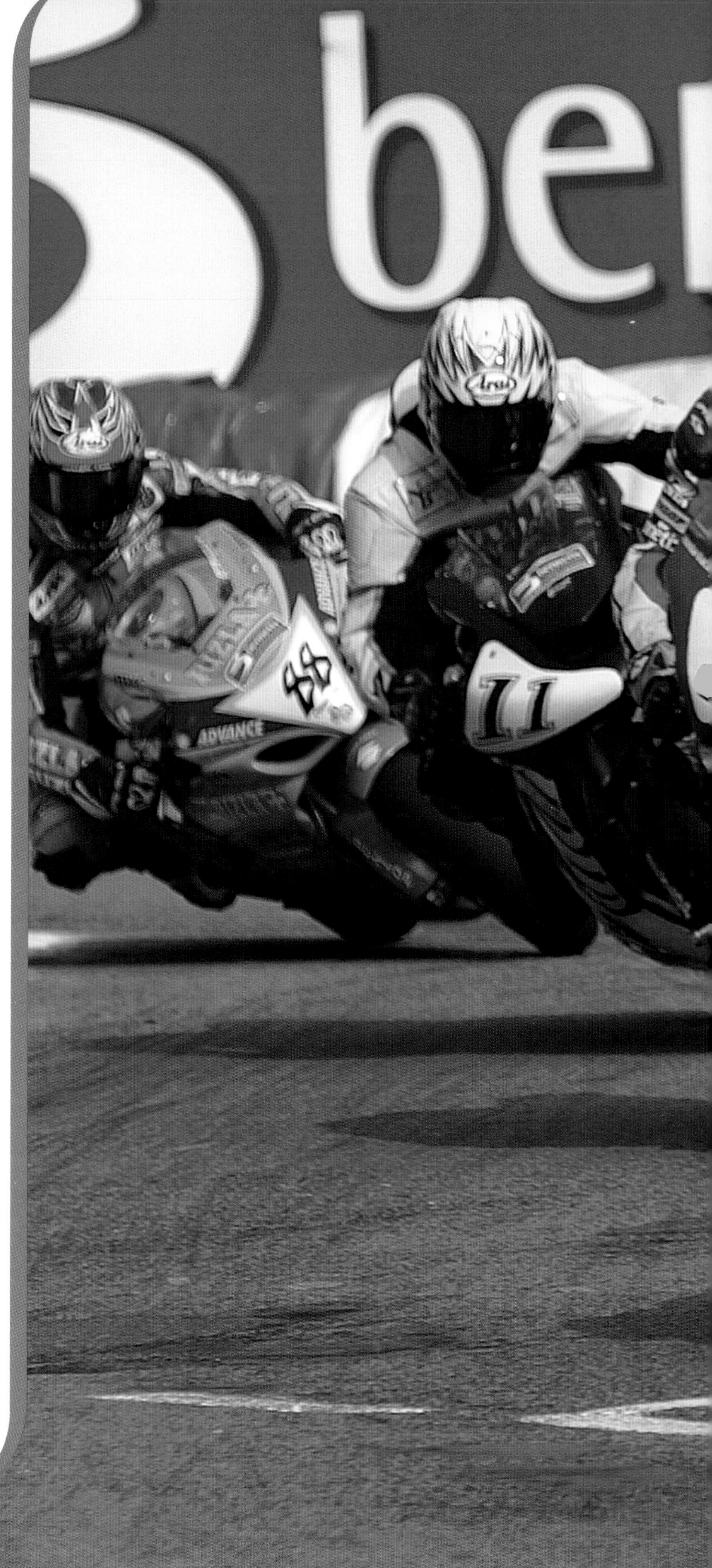

netts
SHOEI
SHARK
DUNLOP
Q8 Oils
HONDA
Airwaves
36
91
Arai

The team had lost crowd favourite Yukio Kagayama to the factory-backed Alstare Suzuki team in WSB, and Dave 'Oz' Marton, Reynolds' long-term crew chief, had opted to take a year out. Scott Smart, the emerging new hero of BSB after a blistering 2004 season on the Hawk Kawasaki, was signed to replace Yukio and top class engineer and tuner Stewart Johnstone took over as Reynolds' crew chief but also as the team's technical director – a role Marton had previously held.

In fact the Suzuki pit garage had a very different look to it for 2005. Team owner Paul Denning had been invited to run the MotoGP team so he took on former WSB marketing man South African Robert Wicks to look after the sponsorship and marketing side of the team, Niall Mackenzie was on hand at race weekends to liaise between riders and technical staff and Johnstone oversaw the technical development programme.

PREVIOUS PAGE Both Leon Haslam (No.91) and especially Gregorio Lavilla (No.36) proved the Ducati 999 to be a fearsomely competitive motorcycle

BELOW Haslam gets the jump on the four-cylinder bikes of Kawasaki's Glen Richards (No.75) and Suzuki's John Reynolds

TESTING TRAUMAS

Neither Airwaves Ducati nor Rizla Suzuki enjoyed much luck in pre-season testing. Airwaves' tests were plagued by bad weather in Spain and Haydon crashed twice at Almeria trying to run the pace of Haslam and then smashed his knuckle and broke two fingers at Albacete on the eve of the first round at Brands Hatch.

Suzuki's fortunes were even worse. In February Reynolds crashed on the morning of the very first shakedown test, breaking his leg in five places. While he was left fighting an incredibly tough personal battle to be fit enough for the first round, the team were faced with a development programme without the benefit of any input from the rider who could at least give comparisons between the new bike and the title-winning old one.

Instead they had to rely on Smart's feedback. All he wanted was a bike that stopped, turned, handled and felt like the ZX10 he had raced so successfully in 2004 but with a bit more get up and go from the engine. The problem was the team knew what did and did not work on the K4 and expected the K5 to respond in a similar way. The two factions went out and tried all manner of different set-ups but went into the first meeting without any real base setting.

Suzuki drafted in out-of-work Gregorio Lavilla to test the bike at Brands Hatch but Reynolds insisted he would be ready to race in the first round at the same track just two weeks later. The Spaniard had missed out on signing for Paul Bird's new-look Stobart Honda, ex-MotoGP man Jeremy McWilliams getting the ride instead, so Lavilla was facing a season in the wilderness when a very astute Colin Wright rang him to offer the Spaniard a ride at the Brands Hatch first round on the Ducati to replace the injured Haydon.

HONDA'S HECTIC PRE-SEASON

With everyone writing off the 999 Ducati and Reynolds seemingly out injured, the pre-season favourites had to be the HM Plant Honda team. Ryuichi Kiyonari had finished 2004 on a high note with a double at Donington and Michael Rutter seemed more motivated than at any time in his career.

The team had logged an incredible amount of pre-season testing, with Kiyonari clocking up the miles in Japan and then both he and Rutter working overtime in Europe helping with development of the latest Michelin rubber.

Their 2005 works FireBlade was billed as a 'kit bike' but it still had a full factory engine. It had Showa suspension, which had been built to look like the same kit that was available over the counter but in reality it was a factory spec system when examined internally.

The biggest visual change was the swing-arm, a production-looking component replacing the beefy Eight-Hour structure built for quick wheel changing that the team used for most of the 2004 season.

There was a massive increase in the amount of Honda riders on the grid for 2005. Conscious that Michelin and Showa might not continue to support one team in BSB, even if HRC was prepared to pay for the respective race service from each company, Louth-based Honda Racing developed their own FireBlades over the winter – the aim being to develop the bikes around Dunlop tyres and use WP suspension.

Karl Harris had two bikes, branded with honda-racing.co.uk logos in gaudy yellow, white and red colours hinting at heavy Dunlop investment while Jonathan Rea stepped up from Supersport with the Red Bull Rookies but only had a single machine at his disposal, also on Dunlops. The one-bike strategy was to encourage the youngster to learn to preserve his machinery and gradually build his speed. He went into each meeting knowing that one silly mistake in practice or a qualifying crash would really set him back for the weekend.

Shaun Muir's new and well-turned out Hydrex-backed team also had a pair of similar bikes for Kieran Clarke, another Supersport graduate.

After the disappointing 2004 season with the MonsterMob Ducati 999s, Paul Bird's team switched from MonsterMob livery to Stobart backing with a trio of Hondas for Jeremy McWilliams, Gary Mason and Michael Laverty.

Running three riders is a massive task for any team but their problems were compounded by late-arriving bikes, and their only winter testing at Knockhill being hampered by snow.

The team opted to run Magneti Marelli engine management in a bid to get one step ahead of the factory team, rather than follow it. The team had experience of the Italian equipment from working on Ducatis but the complex system took a lot longer to adapt to work on the Honda than they had expected.

On paper Hawk Kawasaki looked potential championship material after an impressive first season with the ZX10 but financial constraints of the low-budget team (in comparison with the massive Honda spend for example) led team boss Stuart Hicken to state that his aim was to finish the year with both riders in the top six.

Glen Richards was always a force to be reckoned with in 2004 as long as he was fit and now had an Aussie team-mate with Dean Thomas replacing Smart.

ABOVE Reynolds' hopes of successfully defending his number one plate took a big knock when he broke his leg in five places during pre-season testing

ABOVE The highlight of the season was the title scrap between Japanese Ryuichi Kiyonari and Spaniard Gregorio Lavilla. Some British domestic series!

Probably the most exciting technical development over the winter was Virgin Yamaha's so-called 'big-bang' version of the R1 with one pair of cylinders firing together and the other two independently to produce a flat, thundering bark rather than the familiar high-revving, smooth shriek of the four cylinders firing one after the other.

The aim was to overcome the harsh power delivery of the R1 that plagued the team all last year – and allow the rear tyre to cope better with the huge demands of 200-plus horsepower. The strict production-based regulations in the British Championship meant only the camshafts and new ignition maps could be altered to revise the firing order and the changes did not just reduce tyre spin, but also improved corner speed – dramatically.

Sean Emmett joined the team alongside Tommy Hill and 2004 R6 Cup Champion Richard Wren. Emmett said of the big-bang engine: "The conventional bike needed work to sort the chassis but the big-bang engine was so much easier to ride straight off. Immediately I knew it had bags more potential than a conventional engine."

KIYO STARTS WITH A DOUBLE

The season kicked off at Brands in a front of a massive 30,000 Easter Monday crowd and Kiyo demolished the opposition to take both race wins, shattering the lap record in the process. He won the first race by over 10 seconds and next time out finished five seconds ahead of team-mate Rutter.

Although Haslam set pole, Lavilla was pretty sensational on the Airwaves Ducati finishing second and third, fuelling suggestions that the team might run him as a third rider for the rest of the year.

Haslam all but highsided in race one coming out of Graham Hill Bend, knocking the kill switch off, but bounced back to fourth in race two.

Emmett was expected to be the man at his home circuit. In fairness he did challenge Kiyo for the lead early in race two but he only managed two fifth places. It was probably no surprise after suffering a massive crash in practice (his second get-off of the weekend) that left him nursing a badly bruised and gashed elbow.

Suzuki failed to shine which was not a big shock either. The fact that Reynolds rode at all was a miracle with his injured leg far from healed. Bone growth had been slow and at one time it looked like he may need another operation to re-pin his tibia. He was still unable to walk without crutches but managed to score two ninth places. Smart crashed in the first race and tweaked a long-term back injury. He was eighth in race two.

Kiyonari did the double again at Thruxton, even though he had damaged his ankle after a crash in qualifying on the Saturday. Rutter was second in the first race, underlining Honda's advantage but Lavilla took third in the first race, challenged Kiyo and then smashed the lap record before finishing second next time out.

Lavilla's efforts meant he got a massive reception from the 20,000 crowd and put GSE racing into a real predicament.

Clearly at this stage of the year, despite having had no pre-season testing, Lavilla was the only rider capable of taking the race to the Hondas. Even with 11 rounds left in the championship, he had a much better chance of taking the title than Haslam (who was fourth and seventh at Thruxton). Furthermore, no rider had ever won the BSB title after scoring nothing in the opening two rounds so it seemed unlikely Haydon could bounce back and be a contender, even if he was ready to race in round three.

Haydon had turned up at the Hampshire circuit and was telling anyone who would listen that he was fit to ride. He told *MCN*: "I've been passed by the circuit doctors and I'll definitely be back at Mallory."

However, his team boss did not see it that way. Wright was not prepared to take the word of the track medics and said: "The only decision whether James rides at Mallory will come when the specialist declares him fit." Wright also scotched any rumours of the team running three bikes, simply because there were not enough resources to do so.

HAYDON OUT, LAVILLA IN

The situation came to a head at Mallory Park. Haydon was indeed fit to race so GSE had to make a decision and Wright released him and signed Lavilla.

It was an agonising call for Wright to make but he explained by saying that to have dropped Lavilla would have handed the title to Honda.

Haydon talked about the decision being the right one for the team and towing the company line probably meant he received a good severance payout but after two soul-destroying years with Foggy Petronas and then rebuilding his career on the Virgin Yamaha in 2004, Haydon was devastated he never got a chance to race the 999.

He said: "There's no way my career is over. I'm 30 years old and I'm one of a very select few riders in BSB

ABOVE James Haydon wore shirts of many different team colours in 2005

BELOW Rutter congratulates Kiyonari after the Japanese rider beat him in the first race at Croft

SHARK
DUNLOP
Airwaves
ARLEN NESS
Q8 Oils
Q8 Oils
Airwaves
GSE RACING
bennetts
British Superbike Championship
36
DUNLOP
DUNLOP

who can win races. I proved in 2004 I can be a consistent finisher and I'm a more complete rider than ever before."

There was a glimmer of hope for Haydon though. Reynolds had a very bad time at Thruxton, spooked when another rider fell in front of him at high speed. The Suzuki rider struggled on the fast, bumpy track and things did not improve at Mallory Park. He was hampered by cramp in the first race and did not start the second. The suggestion was that Haydon could be a perfect stand-in for the next race. It did not look an easy or appealing task with the new K5 vastly under-performing. Scott Smart was struggling to dial in the bike to suit his riding style.

It was not just behind closed doors that fortunes were changing. On the track at the Leicestershire circuit there was real drama. Kiyonari's unbeaten run came to a nasty end when he crashed on the brakes going into Edwina's chicane in the first race. He and his bike speared off at a 45-degree angle to the track and as Kiyo slid along helplessly, his head clipped the tyre wall. He suffered concussion and missed race two but Honda still won both races thanks to Michael Rutter who also took the championship lead for the first time.

Lavilla suffered a strange crash in the middle of Gerrards in race one but was third in race two. Glen Richards had his best weekend of the season with a pair of second places on the Hawk Kawasaki.

HASLAM WINS AT OULTON

With Oulton Park only a week after the Mallory Park round Kiyo was sidelined when two scans revealed there were still some signs of swelling and bruising on his brain.

Rutter won the first race from Lavilla but the Spaniard had tyre problems in race two. It was then that Leon Haslam finally put a block on the Honda steamroller by winning the second race from Rutter. It meant the young Derbyshire racer was the first rider in eight races to beat the Hondas. Karl Harris had his best weekend of the season finishing third in both races.

Reynolds was withdrawn from the meeting by team boss Robert Wicks on health grounds and as expected Haydon was drafted in to replace him. The sport's super-sub of previous years worked the magic again, and scored an impressive fourth place in the second race. Rizla regular Smart continued to struggle, finishing ninth in race one before hitting tyre problems in race two.

Stobart Honda experiencing ongoing struggles to develop their Hondas also had the added problem of their top rider Jeremy McWilliams missing the Oulton Park round due to injury. In his round one crash at Brands Hatch he had damaged nerves in his arms and had lost the use of his bicep and a section of his shoulder muscle group. His absence at the Cheshire circuit led to all sorts of unsubstantiated rumours that he had been paid off by Bird after a string of poor results.

McWilliams was back in action at Mondello Park but still struggled with his arm injury and along with team-

ABOVE Tommy Hill scored the first BSB win of his career at Cadwell Park. Team boss Rob McElnea (standing way above everyone else on the pit wall) cannot conceal his emotions

OPPOSITE No job before the start of the year. No pre-season testing – not on a V-twin anyway. But Lavilla jumped onto the 999 Ducati and got the job done. It was simply a world-class performance

ABOVE Michael Laverty showed how competitive he and the Stobart Honda were mid-way through the year

BELOW Kiyo's crash at Mallory had a dramatic effect on his title bid

mate Gary Mason was put in the shade by 23-year-old Michael Laverty who was fourth in race two, proving that the 'Stobbies' were now well on the road to being competitive.

Kiyo was also back in action at Mondello and despite crashing in practice, was bang on the pace, beating Rutter by almost eight seconds in race one with Lavilla third. The Spaniard had asked his crew to knock the harsh edge off the power delivery of his 999 to suit the tight, bumpy track. He knew what he wanted and made it count. In the second race the Hondas had no answer to the Ducatis. Lavilla won from Haslam who beat off Kiyonari and then backed out of a last corner do-or-die overtake on his team-mate. He finished 0.018s behind Lavilla at the flag.

Rutter fifth in race two, still held the points lead though with 195, 45 clear of Lavilla and 54 ahead of Kiyo.

Haydon had crashed out of both races in Ireland and was now back out of a job with Reynolds coming back for Croft. Haydon, however, was given another reprieve with Sean Emmett now sidelined with the elbow injury sustained at Brands Hatch back in March. He finally discovered that his elbow was not just badly bruised and infected, rather it was in fact broken. That meant he missed Croft and Haydon pulled on his third different set of leathers of the year to ride the Virgin R1.

SMART OUT OF RIZLA, HAYDON IN

The Rizla team had a pretty dismal weekend with Reynolds and Smart qualifying on the fourth row of the grid – and Suzuki privateer James Buckingham adding to their ignominy by putting his 2003/2004 bike on the third row. Reynolds crashed in race one and was 12th in race two. Smart was 13th both times.

Haydon was not much better off. He struggled to get his head around the big-bang engine and finished eighth in race one then made a novice error in race two, touching the white line on the way to Turn One, destroying the bike in the process.

Kiyo and Rutter went 1–2 in the first Croft race with Lavilla third but the second encounter produced the race of the season with Lavilla slamming under Kiyo so hard in the Hairpin that the Honda rider had to lift his bike to avoid a clash. He blasted straight back, showing exactly how much power the HRC bike had by blowing the 999 into the weeds down the next straight. Then Kiyo made a mistake at Tower in the closing stages when light rain began to fall on the North Yorkshire circuit and that allowed Lavilla and Rutter by. The points gap was as before – 45. Rutter was on 235 points, Lavilla 190, Kiyonari 182.

A week after Croft, Smart was shown the door by Rizla Suzuki and replaced with Haydon. Smart struggled all year to get the GSX-R1000 to suit his high-corner speed style that relies heavily on having massive confidence in the front end. Smart never found that. Early in the year there appeared to be resistance from within the team to set-up the bike as he wanted. But even when he was giving a free-hand to run a WP shock (which went totally against the team's suspension backer Ohlins) and make other chassis changes he wanted, Smart never got to grips with the bike.

Neither had Haydon when he subbed for Reynolds, which suggested there was something more fundamentally wrong with the machine than the rider. The bottom line though was that by this stage of the season, neither Smart nor the team had confidence in each other, so a split was probably the best option for both parties.

Smart wasted no time securing a ride with Vivaldi Kawasaki, the team buying him the ex-AIM Racing ZX10s that John McGuinness used at Daytona in March. He pitched in to help rebuild the bike, along with the team, in time for the Scottish race.

Kiyo was untouchable at Knockhill. Not even Rutter could match his pace as the Japanese star set pole and won both races. Rutter was second in both races while Lavilla – even with the latest factory 42mm Ohlins TT25 forks installed – was only sixth in race one and third in the second. Rutter's points lead was now 43 ahead of Kiyo (275 points to 232) with Lavilla back to third on 216 points.

Knockhill was a great weekend for Michael Laverty, who claimed third place in race one – the 24-year-old enjoyed his first-ever BSB podium and that proved that his fourth places at Mondello and Croft were not fluke results. Laverty did it on old-style Dunlop 205-section tyres while his rivals were on the new 200s. His bike also lacked electronic controls to assist the STM slipper clutch into corners.

Laverty tested a new system at Croft then went to Snetterton and finished a brilliant second in race two after briefly leading the race. His first race ended with a broken wheel bearing.

Steve Plater's appalling season on the Sendo Kawaski had ended when the mobile phone-based company hit major financial problems just before Knockhill. Plater sat

BELOW LEFT Scott Smart wondering where it all went so wrong

BELOW Haslam matured as the season progressed into a class act. Even Lavilla could not beat him in the final Brands Hatch race

ABOVE Lavilla shows how much he wants it by carving inside Kiyonari at Croft

BELOW Tommy Hill lived up to the promise shown in 2004. It was a difficult year, having to adapt to the new 'big-bang' R1

out the Scottish race but clinched a deal with Shaun Muir's Hydrex Honda team to ride a freshly-built bike at Snetterton, alongside the team's regular rider Kieran Clarke who had been struggling all season. Muir, already plotting his 2006 team plans, saw having Plater on board as a great chance to impress potential backers. He was therefore delighted when his new rider scored seventh and fifth places on the FireBlade.

While Laverty was fast-emerging as BSB's new hero and Plater was back in the ballpark, the championship contenders were thrashing it out at the front of the field with Kiyonari and Lavilla both winning a race each – and both crashing in the other.

Rutter also crashed in Saturday morning practice and broke his right collarbone and displaced his left shoulder. Luckily the broken bone did not displace so Rutter was able to race, albeit in some considerable discomfort. Ironically, his fifth and third place finishes meant he actually edged two points further ahead of Kiyo and Lavilla in the championship.

After a six-week lay-off Silverstone brought a massive shift of fortunes for several riders – mainly the main championship contenders.

The first to suffer was Laverty. He crashed going into Copse in the first race when his bike blew out coolant. He was absolutely unhurt and just sitting up after coming to rest on the so-called high-abrasion run-off area but the fluids from his bike also caused two other bikes to crash and Karl Harris's Honda slid across the track at high speed and slammed into Laverty's midriff.

Incredibly he suffered no serious injuries but the massive bruising the impact caused would affect his riding right up to the last race of the year.

In the first race Rutter crashed at the chicane, one lap away from a podium finish when he tucked the front. He salvaged 15th place despite having to ride the last lap with no left-hand clip on. Lacking confidence in his front tyre meant he could only finish fourth in race two.

Kiyo also crashed in the first race – much earlier on, at the same spot where Rutter later came to grief

OPPOSITE Michael Rutter's highside at Cadwell Park was the start of the downward trend in his season's fortunes

– and remounted to claim eighth place and eight vital championship points. Lavilla won the race and followed Kiyo across the line in race two so the championship table now read: Rutter 316, Kiyonari 290, Lavilla 286.

RUTTER'S LOST CAUSE

Rutter finally lost his championship lead completely after another dismal performance at Cadwell Park. He only finished eighth in race one and then crashed out of the second. Kiyo was also off the pace with fifth and third places so Lavilla took control of the championship for the first time in the year.

His two second places gave him a two-point lead over Rutter. It could have been even more but for an extraordinary mistake by Haslam in the first race.

The Airwaves Ducatis had the race under control but Haslam desperately wanted the race win and made an audacious out-braking bid up the inside going into Park on the final lap.

Lavilla tried to turn in but had nowhere to go and took to the grass to avoid a crash. By then Haslam was far too late on the brakes and also had to run wide onto the grass to avoid falling off.

Incredibly both riders survived and managed to get back on track but by then Tommy Hill had taken the lead and went on to clinch the first BSB win of his career.

Hill had been the one to watch for several races. He had won the non-championship superbike race at Castle Combe and while his BSB results had not been exactly stunning (seventh in race two at Snetterton being the best), his lap times had been. What hampered him was his inability to get up to speed during Friday practice so he could set a good grid time Saturday. Invariably, he was still trying to establish a race set-up in final qualifying and that meant starting races too far down the grid.

The good thing was that McElnea had at least instilled a new-found confidence in the 20-year-old who had finally learned to get the best from the very different power characteristics and handling of the big-bang R1.

Haslam came out determined to make amends for his first-race faux pas and won race two from Lavilla. Kiyonari could only finish third so Lavilla still clung to a two-point lead over Rutter with Kiyo third just nine points adrift of the leader.

Rutter's title chances finally disappeared as the championship returned for a second visit to Oulton Park. He finished a dismal 10th in race one thanks to a seized back brake and then crashed yet again in race two.

Kiyo clinched a sensational second race victory there, beating Lavilla by just four thousandths of a second. It was the kind of result that typified the closely-fought title battle. Kiyo had already won the first race, again from Lavilla, and his double meant that he now held the championship lead – by a solitary point.

John Reynolds, finally back to some semblance of fitness, finished third in both races on the Rizla Suzuki. It was his best weekend of the year with results that virtually guaranteed him keeping his job for 2006.

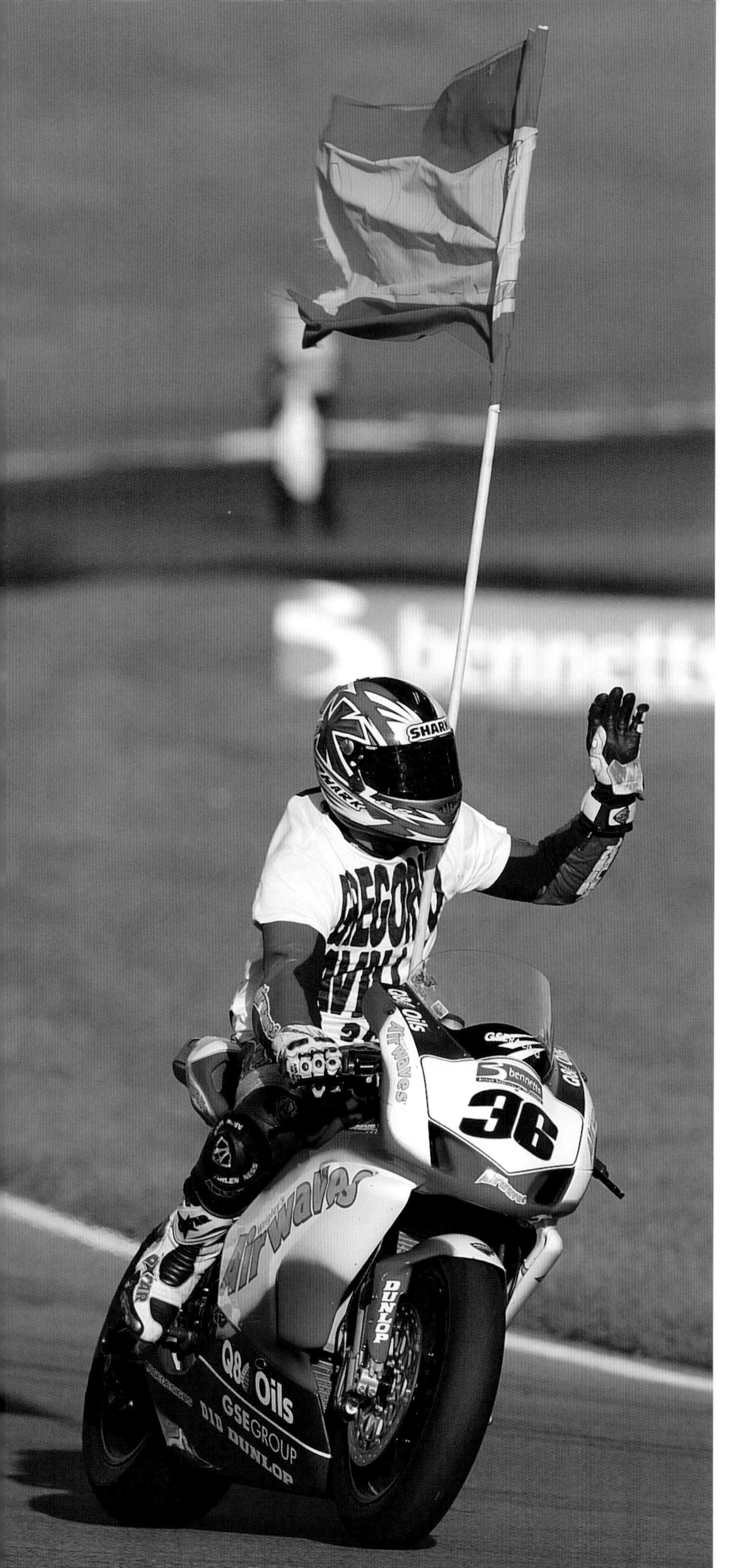

LAVILLA'S DONINGTON DOUBLE

Michelin's massive tyre development programme with HRC had given them the edge early in the year but from Snetterton onwards they seemed to be losing their grip on the tyre war.

Rutter had been more and more vociferous in his criticism of the front Michelin which he said might suit Kiyonari's point and squirt riding, but certainly did not suit his style which relied massively on front tyre confidence.

Dunlop had come on in leaps and bounds with their 200 rear. They had produced a tyre that many riders described as having the grip of a qualifier but with the ability to go race distance.

Dunlop were not aiming to lose the title having come so close and for Donington Park (and the Brands Hatch finale) mounted a massive programme bringing a wider range of product and recruiting top technicians from their WSB and AMA Superbike programmes. The Airwaves Ducati team received the very best they could hope for at a circuit where everyone expected Michelin to really dominate, just as they had done in 2004.

Lavilla won both races and his team-mate Leon Haslam did a perfect job, beating Kiyonari back to third place in the second which meant Lavilla would go to the final Brands round with a 13-point lead.

The build up to the final round was bizarre. On the Tuesday before the meeting, Rutter was told that he no longer figured in Honda's plans for 2006 and Harris, after a solid but far from stunning season, was suddenly given a factory bike for Brands Hatch. Honda said it was to reward him for his sterling work for the company over the past three seasons (back-to-back British Supersport titles in 2003/2004) but the aim was to try and help Kiyonari. What it did do though was alienate WP staff who had worked with Harris all year only to be told the factory bike had to run Showa kit so they switched their spare capacity to Steve Plater. Since his impressive Snetterton debut on the Hydrex Honda he had struggled to get the best from the bike during practice/qualifying and subsequently always had to come from a poor grid place.

Practice had only just started on Friday when it was red-flagged after John Reynolds had slammed into the barrier coming down the hill from Druids Hairpin. He suffered four broken ribs, a punctured lung, a broken left collarbone and two damaged vertebrae. By Sunday night Reynolds had announced his retirement from racing.

Speaking from his hospital bed on Sunday night after the dust was settling over the final round, Reynolds admitted his career was finally over.

He said: "As soon as I hit the barrier I knew that was it. It was the biggest impact of my career and lying there with the medics all around I knew it was one more warning I could not ignore. I told my wife Shelley and my father I'm finished."

JR was always well known as one of the most determined, gritty characters on the track, but a real gentleman off it. He won the British Supersport title for Kawasaki in 1990 and then the British Superbike title in 1991, still with Team Green.

He then spent two seasons in World Championship 500cc Grand Prix and another two years in World Superbikes , initially with Reve Kawasaki and then on a factory Suzuki GSX-R750.

From 1997 until 2000 JR was never outside the top four in the British Superbike Championship. He won the title again in 2001 riding a Red Bull Ducati, and then once more in 2004 on the Rizla Suzuki.

After his latest accident, though, the 42-year-old was left facing his second lengthy rehabilitation period of the year, having broken his leg in five places in pre-season testing.

In a sad twist of irony, JR had only just returned to his true potential on the race track in the previous round at Donington Park, so much so that team owner Paul Denning told him on the Wednesday before Brands Hatch that his place in the Rizla Suzuki team was confirmed for 2006.

Denning said: "Obviously I feel for John but I'm just so pleased that we'd already agreed that he'd ride for us. At least John was able retire because he wanted to, knowing he was at the top of his game and there was a place for him in our team.

"In early September he also had a meeting with Suzuki to discuss the future of our team in BSB and we agreed there that we didn't want John ever riding for anyone else because we wanted to retain him as a marketing ambassador for Suzuki. So John will continue to be very much part of the Rizla Suzuki

OTHER HIGHLIGHTS OF '05

- Valentino Rossi wins the MotoGP title yet again, winning 11 of the 17 races on his Gauloises Yamaha M1. Spaniard Dani Pedrosa is the GP250 champion for Honda, and Swiss Thomas Luthi wins the GP125 class on a Honda by five points from KTM rider Mika Kallio
- Troy Corser wins the WSB series on an Alstare Suzuki, with fellow Aussie Chris Vermeulen runner-up on a Ten Kate Honda. Yet another Australian, Mat Mladin continues to dominate the AMA Superbike championship on his Yoshimura Suzuki GSX-R1000
- Leon Camier wins the British Supersport title riding a Padgetts Honda. Lee Jackson takes the Superstock title on an R1 and Christian Elkin is the 125 British Champion for the second year running. James Buckingham is the BSB Privateer Cup winner
- Aussie Billy McConnell claims the Virgin Mobile Yamaha R6 Cup title and wins himself a place in the Virgin Yamaha BSB team for 2006

OPPOSITE Lavilla flies the Spanish flag over Brands Hatch after clinching the title

BELOW John Reynolds never had the chance to have a proper crack at defending his title

ABOVE Gregorio Lavilla – BSB Champion. Who would have thought it at the start of the year?

team and the Suzuki brand in general for a long time to come."

Reynolds added: "It's good to know that Paul supported me and believed in me enough to offer me the ride for next year. That meant a lot to me.

"But it was my decision to quit and it was good to know I have a career to look forward to when I'm over the medical hurdles I'm facing. I'll be working as hard as ever to regain my fitness so I can be in the BSB paddock for the start of next season."

In spite of Reynolds's misfortune, Haydon, his team-mate, put his Rizla Suzuki on pole for the first time all year and then claimed third place, pushing Kiyonari back to fourth with some typically aggressive but fair riding.

That was the last thing Kiyo needed, with the added pressure of a small army of HRC top brass, including boss Saturo Horike, flown in to watch the final round.

With the two Airwaves Ducatis dominating the race, Lavilla taking the victory ahead of Haslam, it meant the Spanish rider needed just one point from the final race to secure his first ever major crown.

Haslam was let loose now to run his own race after shadowing his team-mate in race one, and Lavilla finished second. The pair of them went on a lap-record smashing spree mid-race as they celebrated with speed and style.

Kiyonari endured even more embarrassment when Plater beat him to third place on a privateer Honda. That was a cruel way to rub Kiyo's and HRC's noses in defeat.

The season quite simply belonged to Lavilla, a rider who did not even have a full time job at the start of the season. He told *MCN*: "It's been an amazing year, especially the way I arrived with no testing and no experience of this championship. But the team has been perfect for me.

"Everyone said the Ducati was finished but we have worked on the bike, learned the tracks and, thanks to the team, the whole combination has been perfect. It meant I could go to every race thinking anything is possible.

"I feel really happy that I've done a good job and proved to many people who forgot about me how competitive I am."

Two weeks later Lavilla was confirmed, alongside Haslam, for another season of BSB with the Airwaves Ducati team on 2006 Ducati factory 999s. That established the exciting prospect of a re-match against Ryuichi Kiyonari and the HRC factory team.

So advanced was the 2006 F06 Ducati that the factory Ducati Corse team decided to send an electronics technician to look after the traction control and launch control systems on the V-twin. The Airwaves team was the only outfit outside the factory WSB teams to get such machinery.

Similarly, HM Plant were the only team in the world, including WSB, to get such a highly sophisticated factory FireBlade – with specially built Showa suspension that even the might of Honda America didn't have for the AMA series.

The HM Plant team signed two-times British Supersport Champion (2003/2004) Karl Harris alongside HRC's favourite son Kiyonari to replace Rutter, but also agreed, after a request from Honda Racing in Louth, to supply a third factory bike for Red Bull-backed Jonathan Rea. Rea's bike though would run on Dunlops, while the HM Plant bikes would continue to receive the sole attention of Michelin.

Rutter – with a lot to prove after being dumped by Honda before the 2005 season had finished – switched to ride for Paul Bird's privately run Stobart Honda team along with Laverty. Even after initial testing Rutter said the bike was better than his HRC Blade in some areas, and that the Dunlops suited much better the way he liked to push the front end into corners.

Shaun Muir's emerging Hydrex Honda team pulled off something of a coup, signing Glen Richards as his number-one rider – and then added Gary Mason as a strong number two.

Without Richards, Hawk Kawasaki brought in former Australian Superbike Champion Craig Coxhell alongside fellow countryman Dean Thomas.

Virgin Yamaha announced the biggest shock of the winter, switching to Pirelli tyres to add spice to the already intense Dunlop/Michelin tyre war. Rob McElnea's team also announced they would ditch the 'big-bang' engine and return to conventional firing-order 'screamer' R1 engines for Tommy Hill, Keiran Clarke and R6 Cup champion Billy McConnell.

But the most exciting announcement of the off-season came from Rizla Suzuki. With Reynolds retiring from racing to take an advisory role with his old crew, team boss Paul Denning signed 2003 BSB champion Shane Byrne – arguably one of the most charismatic BSB stars in recent history.

Even crashing out twice on the very first day of testing with the team in Spain failed to dampen Shakey's enthusiasm for a season of BSB, after two years of frustration running around at the back end of the MotoGP field on uncompetitive bikes.

He said: "I'm really, really happy to be back in BSB. I feel like I'm back amongst friends. I know I'm here to do a job and we've got to win, but there's nothing wrong with having a giggle, is there?

"But I've got no doubts or worries about the job either. And the reason is that I know every last person in the team wants me. Support like that means so much to me, plus the knowledge I can go to the grid when the season starts knowing I've got a chance to win races."

So, incredible as it might seem after such an amazing 2005 season, the prospects for 2006 looked even better – with more factory bikes on the grid, a bigger tyre war and an even bigger-name star-studded line-up than any other superbike championship in the world.

The thought of Byrne battling with Lavilla, Haslam, Kiyonari and Rutter for the title, with all the races screened live in an exciting new ITV deal was one to savour. And what better way to continue the colourful history of British Superbike racing?

BELOW Honda riders Kiyonari and Rutter lead the field at an unusually sun-kissed Knockhill, but the title went to Lavilla and Ducati. Who would come out on top in 2006?

RESULTS

All the scores, all the races

RESEARCHED AND COMPILED BY DAVE FERN

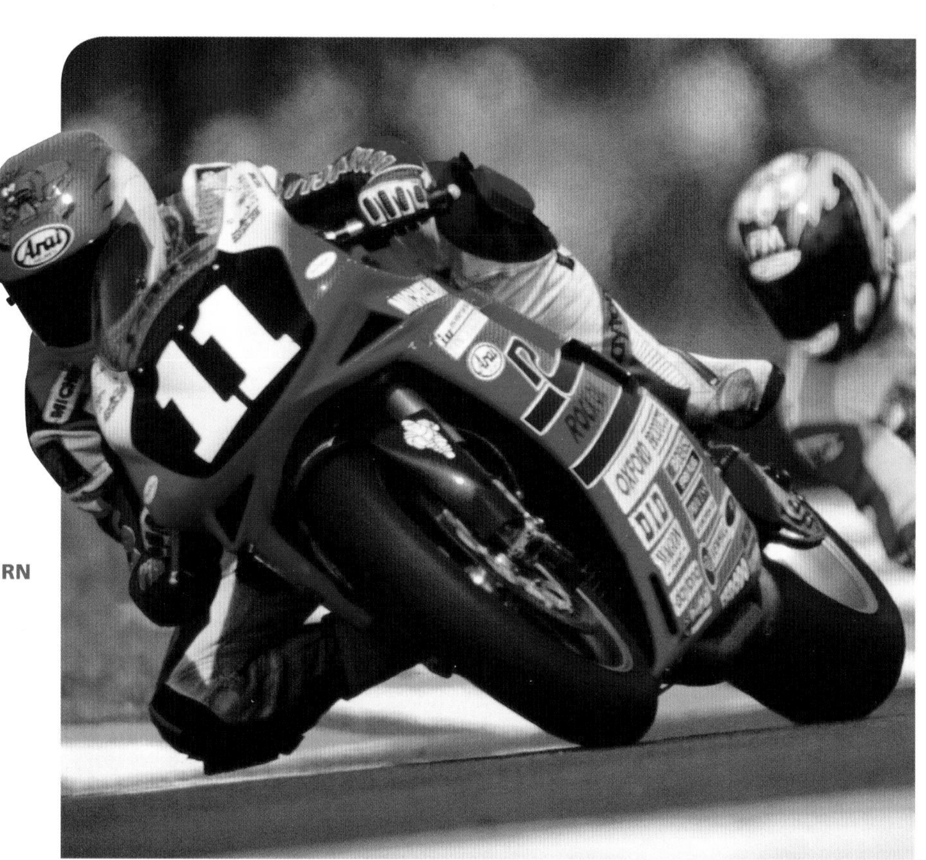

1995 SEASON SUPERCUP BRITISH CHAMPIONSHIP

DONINGTON PARK
ROUND 1 – APRIL 17

RACE 1		
1	Michael Rutter	Ducati
2	Ian Simpson	Honda
3	John Reynolds	Kawasaki
4	Steve Hislop	Ducati
5	Jim Moodie	Honda
6	Dave Jefferies	Kawasaki
7	Paul Brown	Honda
8	Alex Buckingham	Yamaha
9	Andy Ward	Kawasaki
10	Simon Beck	Ducati
11	Dean Ashton	Ducati
12	Lee Pullan	Kawasaki
13	Michael Brown	Kawasaki
14	Nigel Nottingham	Yamaha
15	Jason Griffiths	Kawasaki

RACE 2		
1	James Whitham	Ducati
2	John Reynolds	Kawasaki
3	Steve Hislop	Ducati
4	Michael Rutter	Ducati
5	Matt Llewellyn	Ducati
6	Ian Simpson	Honda
7	Ray Stringer	Ducati
8	David Jefferies	Kawasaki
9	Iain Duffus	Ducati
10	Paul Brown	Honda
11	Alex Buckingham	Yamaha
12	Dean Ashton	Ducati
13	Lee Pullan	Kawasaki
14	Simon Beck	Ducati
15	Peter Graves	Yamaha

STANDINGS

Rutter 23, Reynolds 22, Hislop 18, Simpson 17, Whitham 15, Jefferies 8

MALLORY PARK
ROUND 2 – APRIL 30

RACE 1		
1	James Whitham	Ducati
2	Steve Hislop	Ducati
3	Michael Rutter	Ducati
4	Matt Llewellyn	Ducati
5	Ian Simpson	Honda
6	Jim Moodie	Honda
7	Phil Borley	Honda
8	Paul Brown	Honda
9	Dean Ashton	Ducati
10	Andrew Corbett	Yamaha
11	Alex Buckingham	Yamaha
12	Brett Sampson	Kawasaki
13	Michael Brown	Kawasaki
14	Dave Heal	Yamaha
15	Jason Griffiths	Kawasaki

RACE 2		
1	James Whitham	Ducati
2	Steve Hislop	Ducati
3	Matt Llewellyn	Ducati
4	Michael Rutter	Ducati
5	Jim Moodie	Honda
6	Ian Simpson	Honda
7	Phil Borley	Honda
8	Dean Ashton	Ducati
9	Ray Stringer	Ducati
10	Paul Brown	Honda
11	Shaun Muir	Kawasaki
12	Andrew Corbett	Yamaha
13	Brett Sampson	Kawasaki
14	Jason Emmett	Ducati
15	Peter Graves	Yamaha

STANDINGS

Whitham 45, Hislop 42, Rutter 41, Simpson 28, Llewellyn 24, Reynolds 22

OULTON PARK
ROUND 3 – MAY 8

RACE 1		
1	James Whitham	Ducati
2	Steve Hislop	Ducati
3	Matt Llewellyn	Ducati
4	Ray Stringer	Ducati
5	Phil Borley	Honda
6	Shaun Muir	Kawasaki
7	Jim Moodie	Honda
8	Ian Simpson	Honda
9	Jason Emmett	Ducati
10	Graham Ward	Kawasaki
11	Dave Heal	Yamaha
12	Brett Sampson	Kawasaki
13	Andrew Corbett	Yamaha
14	Nigel Nottingham	Yamaha
15	Peter Graves	Yamaha

RACE 2		
1	Steve Hislop	Ducati
2	Matt Llewellyn	Ducati
3	Ian Simpson	Honda
4	Phil Borley	Honda
5	Shaun Muir	Kawasaki
6	Paul Brown	Honda
7	Dean Ashton	Ducati
8	Michael Rutter	Ducati
9	Alex Buckingham	Yamaha
10	Jason Emmett	Ducati
11	Nigel Nottingham	Yamaha
12	Ian Harrison	Kawasaki
13	N Manning-Norton	Kawasaki
14	Stuart Nicholson	Yamaha
15	Steve Gordon	Kawasaki

STANDINGS

Hislop 69, Whitham 60, Llewellyn 46, Rutter 44, Simpson 41, Borley & Reynolds 22

SNETTERTON
ROUND 4 – JUNE 25

RACE 1		
1	James Whitham	Ducati
2	Michael Rutter	Ducati
3	Matt Llewellyn	Ducati
4	Steve Hislop	Ducati
5	Iain Duffus	Ducati
6	Jason Emmett	Ducati
7	Peter Graves	Yamaha
8	Lee Pullan	Kawasaki
9	Alex Buckingham	Yamaha
10	Brett Sampson	Kawasaki
11	Nigel Nottingham	Yamaha
12	Phil Borley	Honda
13	Tom Knight	Ducati
14	Steve Gordon	Kawasaki
15	Brian Morrison	Honda

RACE 2		
1=	Steve Hislop	Ducati
1=	James Whitham	Ducati
3	Matt Llewellyn	Ducati
4	Phil Borley	Honda
5	Iain Duffus	Ducati
6	Jason Emmett	Ducati
7	Lee Pullan	Kawasaki
8	Peter Graves	Yamaha
9	Brett Sampson	Kawasaki
10	Alex Buckingham	Yamaha
11	Nigel Nottingham	Yamaha
12	Tom Knight	Ducati

STANDINGS

Hislop 90.5, Whitham 88.5, Llewellyn 66, Rutter 56, Simpson 41, Borley 30

1995 SEASON SHELL ADVANCE INTERNATIONAL SUPERBIKE TROPHY

KNOCKHILL
ROUND 5 – JULY 9

RACE 1

1	Steve Hislop	Ducati
2	James Whitham	Ducati
3	Matt Llewellyn	Ducati
4	Michael Rutter	Ducati
5	Phil Borley	Honda
6	Ray Stringer	Ducati
7	Iain Duffus	Ducati
8	Dean Ashton	Ducati
9	Paul Brown	Honda
10	Jim Moodie	Honda
11	Robert Holden	Ducati
12	Roger Bennett	Kawasaki
13	Andy Hatton	Ducati
14	Karl Wilson	Kawasaki
15	Carl Marsden	Kawasaki

RACE 2

1	James Whitham	Ducati
2	Steve Hislop	Ducati
3	Matt Llewellyn	Ducati
4	Ray Stringer	Ducati
5	Michael Rutter	Ducati
6	Jim Moodie	Honda
7	Phil Borley	Honda
8	Iain Duffus	Ducati
9	Paul Brown	Honda
10	Dean Ashton	Ducati
11	Robert Holden	Ducati
12	Andy Hatton	Ducati
13	Carl Marsden	Kawasaki
14	Dennis Irvine	Honda
15	Karl Wilson	Kawasaki

STANDINGS

Hislop 117.5, Whitham 115.5, Llewellyn 86, Rutter 70 Simpson 41, Borley 40

CADWELL PARK
ROUND 6 – 28 AUGUST

RACE 1

1	Steve Hislop	Ducati
2	Ray Stringer	Ducati
3	Matt Llewellyn	Ducati
4	Terry Rymer	Honda
5	Dean Ashton	Ducati
6	Paul Brown	Honda
7	Andy Hatton	Ducati
8	Brett Sampson	Kawasaki
9	Jason Griffiths	Kawasaki
10	Andy Ward	Kawasaki
11	Jason Emmett	Ducati
12	Stuart Nicholson	Yamaha
13	Steve Gordon	Kawasaki
14	David Higgins	Yamaha

RACE 2

1	Steve Hislop	Ducati
2	Matt Llewellyn	Ducati
3	Ray Stringer	Ducati
4	Terry Rymer	Honda
5	Dean Ashton	Ducati
6	Michael Rutter	Ducati
7	Paul Brown	Honda
8	Ron Haslam	Honda
9	Brett Sampson	Kawasaki
10	Peter Graves	Yamaha
11	Graham Ward	Kawasaki
12	Jason Griffiths	Kawasaki
13	Steve Ellis	Kawasaki
14	Andy Ward	Kawasaki
15	Stuart Nicholson	Yamaha

STANDINGS

Hislop 147.5, Whitham 115.5, Llewellyn 108, Rutter 75, Stringer 49, Simpson 41

BRANDS HATCH INDY
ROUND 7 – SEPTEMBER 3

RACE 1

1	Steve Hislop	Ducati
2	Terry Rymer	Honda
3	Matt Llewellyn	Ducati
4	Paul Brown	Honda
5	Ray Stringer	Ducati
6	Alex Buckingham	Yamaha
7	Ron Haslam	Honda
8	Steve Ellis	Kawasaki
9	Brett Sampson	Kawasaki
10	Andy Hatton	Ducati
11	Graeme Ritchie	Ducati
12	James Bunton	Yamaha

RACE 2

1	Steve Hislop	Ducati
2	Terry Rymer	Honda
3	Matt Llewellyn	Ducati
4	Michael Rutter	Ducati
5	Paul Brown	Honda
6	Dean Ashton	Ducati
7	Ron Haslam	Honda
8	Alex Buckingham	Yamaha
9	Brett Sampson	Kawasaki
10	Steve Ellis	Kawasaki
11	Andy Hatton	Ducati
12	Dave Redgate	Yamaha
13	Steve Marks	Kawasaki
14	Graeme Ritchie	Ducati
15	James Bunton	Kawasaki

FINAL STANDINGS

Hislop 177.5, Llewellyn 128, Whitham 115.5, Rutter 83, Stringer 55, Brown and Borley 41

SCORING

In 1995 BSB points were scored 15–12–10–8–6–5–4–3–2–1 from first through to tenth place, but from 1996 the series adopted the same FIM point scoring system as WSB: 25–20–16–13–11–10–9–8–7–6–5–4–3–2–1 from first through to 15th place.

OPPOSITE Steve Hislop leads James Whitham. The season was all about these two Ducati stars until Whitham got sick. Hizzy was just leading the points chase at the time

BELOW Hizzy had plenty to celebrate once he wrapped up the '95 BSB series

BRANDS HATCH
ROUND 1 – MAY 14

RACE 1

1	James Whitham	Ducati
2	Steve Hislop	Ducati
3	Matt Llewellyn	Ducati

RACE 2

1	James Whitham	Ducati
2	Steve Hislop	Ducati
3	Matt Llewellyn	Ducati

STANDINGS

Whitham 30, Hislop 24, Llewellyn 20

OULTON PARK
ROUND 2 – JUNE 18

RACE 1

1	James Whitham	Ducati
2	Matt Llewellyn	Ducati
3	Steve Hislop	Ducati

RACE 2

1	Steve Hislop	Ducati
2	Matt Llewellyn	Ducati
3	Michael Rutter	Ducati

STANDINGS

Hislop 49, Whitham 45, Llewellyn 44

DONINGTON PARK
ROUND 3 – SEPTEMBER 23

RACE 1

1	Aaron Slight	Honda
2	Simon Crafar	Honda
3	Chris Walker	Ducati

RACE 2

1	Aaron Slight	Honda
2	Simon Crafar	Honda
3	Michael Rutter	Ducati

FINAL STANDINGS

Llewellyn 58, Hislop 49, Whitham 45

SHELL ADVANCE INTERNATIONAL SUPERBIKE TROPHY

In 1995 the separate televised Shell Advance International Superbike Trophy was run over just three rounds, introduced to appease the BBC who were keen to cover bike racing but could not accommodate a seven-round SuperCup British series in their schedules.

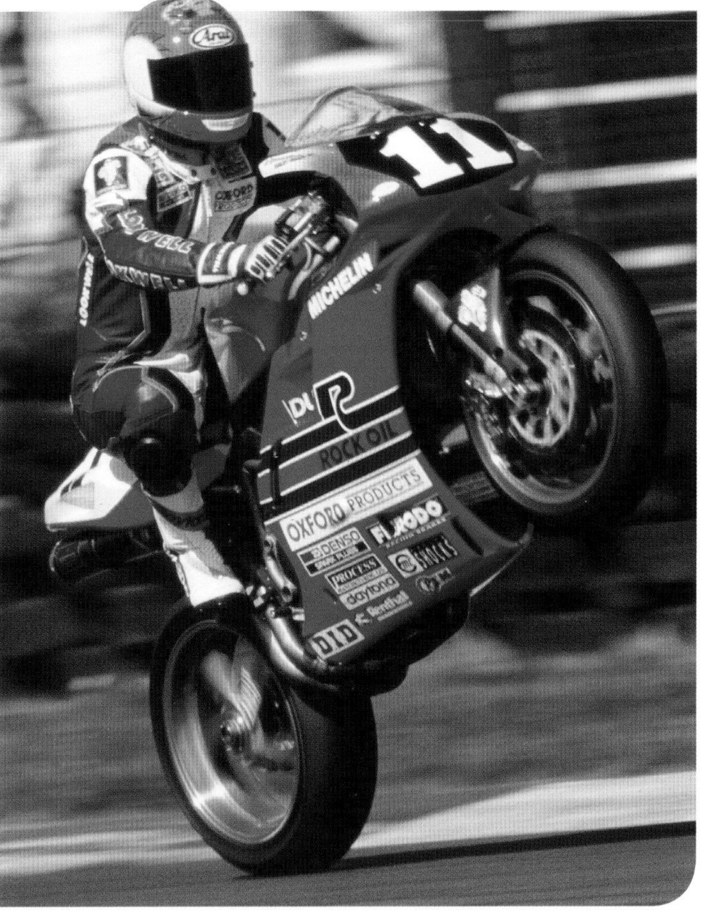

1996 SEASON *MCN* BRITISH SUPERBIKE CHAMPIONSHIP

DONINGTON PARK
ROUND 1 – MARCH 31

RACE 1

1	Niall Mackenzie	Yamaha
2	Steve Hislop	Kawasaki
3	Ian Simpson	Ducati
4	Chris Walker	Ducati
5	Dean Ashton	Ducati
6	Jim Moodie	Ducati
7	Matt Llewellyn	Kawasaki
8	Ray Stringer	Kawasaki
9	Michael Rutter	Ducati
10	Shaun Muir	Kawasaki
11	Graham Ward	Ducati
12	Mike Edwards	Honda
13	Alex Buckingham	Yamaha
14	Andy Ward	Ducati
15	Jim Hodson	Kawasaki

RACE 2

1	Terry Rymer	Ducati
2	Niall Mackenzie	Yamaha
3	Ian Simpson	Ducati
4	Jim Moodie	Ducati
5	Graham Ward	Ducati
6	Michael Rutter	Ducati
7	Ray Stringer	Kawasaki
8	David Jefferies	Honda
9	Brett Sampson	Kawasaki
10	Alex Buckingham	Yamaha
11	Alexander Kvintas	Kawasaki
12	Andy Ward	Ducati
13	Jim Hodson	Kawasaki
14	James Bunton	Yamaha
15	Paul Jones	Yamaha

STANDINGS

Mackenzie 45, Simpson 32, Rymer 25, Moodie 23, Hislop 20, Rutter & Stringer 17

THRUXTON
ROUND 2 – APRIL 8

RACE 1

1	Terry Rymer	Ducati
2	James Whitham	Yamaha
3	Niall Mackenzie	Yamaha
4	Jim Moodie	Ducati
5	Ian Simpson	Ducati
6	Steve Hislop	Kawasaki
7	Graham Ward	Ducati
8	Michael Rutter	Ducati
9	Matt Llewellyn	Kawasaki
10	Dave Jefferies	Honda
11	Brett Sampson	Kawasaki
12	Alex Buckingham	Yamaha
13	Tom Knight	Ducati
14	Shaun Muir	Kawasaki
15	Ian Cobby	Suzuki

RACE 2

1	Niall Mackenzie	Yamaha
2	James Whitham	Yamaha
3	Ray Stringer	Kawasaki
4	Michael Rutter	Ducati
5	Jim Moodie	Ducati
6	Steve Hislop	Kawasaki
7	Ian Simpson	Ducati
8	Chris Walker	Ducati
9	Dave Jefferies	Honda
10	Graham Ward	Ducati
11	Tom Knight	Ducati
12	Alex Buckingham	Yamaha
13	Matt Llewellyn	Kawasaki
14	Shaun Muir	Kawasaki
15	Jim Hodson	Kawasaki

STANDINGS

Mackenzie 86, Simpson 52, Rymer 50, Moodie 47, Hislop & Whitham 40

OULTON PARK
ROUND 3 – MAY 6

RACE 1

1	James Whitham	Yamaha
2	Niall Mackenzie	Yamaha
3	Michael Rutter	Ducati
4	Chris Walker	Ducati
5	Dave Jefferies	Honda
6	Graham Ward	Ducati
7	Shaun Muir	Kawasaki
8	Ray Stringer	Kawasaki
9	Alex Buckingham	Yamaha
10	Peter Graves	Ducati
11	Andy Hatton	Ducati
12	Tom Knight	Ducati
13	Jim Hodson	Kawasaki
14	Nigel Nottingham	Yamaha
15	Brett Sampson	Kawasaki

RACE 2

1	Terry Rymer	Ducati
2	James Whitham	Yamaha
3	Niall Mackenzie	Yamaha
4	Michael Rutter	Ducati
5	Steve Hislop	Kawasaki
6	Dave Jefferies	Honda
7	Matt Llewellyn	Kawasaki
8	Ray Stringer	Kawasaki
9	Jim Moodie	Ducati
10	Peter Graves	Ducati
11	Brett Sampson	Kawasaki
12	Jim Hodson	Kawasaki
13	James Bunton	Yamaha
14	Ian Cobby	Suzuki
15	Colin Hipwell	Kawasaki

STANDINGS

Mackenzie 122, Whitham 85, Rymer 75, Rutter 67, Moodie 54, Hislop 51

SNETTERTON
ROUND 4 – MAY 12

RACE 1

1	James Whitham	Yamaha
2	Chris Walker	Ducati
3	Niall Mackenzie	Yamaha
4	Terry Rymer	Ducati
5	Michael Rutter	Ducati
6	Jim Moodie	Ducati
7	Matt Llewellyn	Kawasaki
8	Ray Stringer	Kawasaki
9	Graham Ward	Ducati
10	Steve Hislop	Kawasaki
11	Peter Graves	Ducati
12	Andy Hatton	Ducati
13	Steve Marks	Kawasaki
14	Nigel Nottingham	Yamaha
15	Ian Cobby	Suzuki

RACE 2

1	James Whitham	Yamaha
2	Niall Mackenzie	Yamaha
3	Michael Rutter	Ducati
4	Terry Rymer	Ducati
5	Ian Simpson	Ducati
6	Jim Moodie	Ducati
7	Matt Llewellyn	Kawasaki
8	Ray Stringer	Kawasaki
9	Steve Hislop	Kawasaki
10	Brett Sampson	Kawasaki
11	Andy Hatton	Ducati
12	Paul Denning	Suzuki
13	Steve Marks	Kawasaki
14	Ian Cobby	Suzuki
15	Richard Defago	Kawasaki

STANDINGS

Mackenzie 158, Whitham 135, Rymer 101, Rutter 94, Moodie 74, Stringer 65

BRANDS HATCH INDY
ROUND 5 – JUNE 23

RACE 1

1	James Whitham	Yamaha
2	Terry Rymer	Ducati
3	Niall Mackenzie	Yamaha
4	Michael Rutter	Ducati
5	Matt Llewellyn	Kawasaki
6	Ray Stringer	Kawasaki
7	Jim Moodie	Ducati
8	Chris Walker	Ducati
9	Dave Jefferies	Honda
10	Peter Graves	Ducati
11	Alex Buckingham	Yamaha
12	Dean Ashton	Ducati
13	Tom Knight	Ducati
14	Steve Marks	Kawasaki
15	Richard Defago	Kawasaki

RACE 2

1	James Whitham	Yamaha
2	Terry Rymer	Ducati
3	Niall Mackenzie	Yamaha
4	Michael Rutter	Ducati
5	Ray Stringer	Kawasaki
6	Chris Walker	Ducati
7	Ian Simpson	Ducati
8	Jim Moodie	Ducati
9	Alex Buckingham	Yamaha
10	Tom Knight	Ducati
11	Brett Sampson	Kawasaki
12	Peter Graves	Ducati
13	Shaun Muir	Kawasaki
14	Ian Cobby	Suzuki
15	Richard Defago	Kawasaki

STANDINGS

Mackenzie 190, Whitham 185, Rymer 141, Rutter 120, Moodie 91, Stringer 86

KNOCKHILL
ROUND 6 – AUGUST 18

RACE 1

1	Niall Mackenzie	Yamaha
2	James Whitham	Yamaha
3	Steve Hislop	Kawasaki
4	Michael Rutter	Ducati
5	Ian Simpson	Ducati
6	Jim Moodie	Ducati
7	Scott Smart	Ducati
8	Dave Jefferies	Honda
9	Ray Stringer	Kawasaki
10	Roger McCurdy	Kawasaki
11	Peter Graves	Ducati
12	Ian Cobby	Suzuki
13	Simon Beck	Kawasaki

RACE 2

1	Niall Mackenzie	Yamaha
2	James Whitham	Yamaha
3	Steve Hislop	Kawasaki
4	Jim Moodie	Ducati
5	Scott Smart	Ducati
6	Ray Stringer	Kawasaki
7	Dave Jefferies	Honda
8	Graham Ward	Ducati
9	Peter Graves	Ducati
10	Simon Beck	Kawasaki
11	Roger Bennett	Kawasaki
12	Ian Cobby	Suzuki
13	Paul Denning	Suzuki
14	Jim Hodson	Kawasaki

STANDINGS

Mackenzie 240, Whitham 225, Rymer 141, Rutter 133, Moodie 114, Stringer 103

LEFT Chris Walker quit the Old spice Ducati team to go GP500 racing

OPPOSITE David Jefferies broke into BSB with a Medd Honda

CADWELL PARK
ROUND 7 – AUGUST 26

RACE 1		
1	James Whitham	Yamaha
2	Niall Mackenzie	Yamaha
3	Steve Hislop	Kawasaki
4	Dave Jefferies	Honda
5	Matt Llewellyn	Ducati
6	Jim Moodie	Suzuki
7	Ray Stringer	Kawasaki
8	Dean Ashton	Ducati
9	Michael Rutter	Ducati
10	Andy Hatton	Ducati
11	Tom Knight	Ducati
12	Ian Simpson	Ducati
13	Richard Defago	Kawasaki
14	Jim Hodson	Kawasaki
15	Colin Hipwell	Kawasaki

RACE 2		
1	James Whitham	Yamaha
2	Niall Mackenzie	Yamaha
3	Michael Rutter	Ducati
4	Terry Rymer	Ducati
5	Steve Hislop	Kawasaki
6	Ian Simpson	Ducati
7	Dean Ashton	Ducati
8	Matt Llewellyn	Ducati
9	Ray Stringer	Kawasaki
10	Jim Moodie	Suzuki
11	Andy Hatton	Ducati
12	Tom Knight	Ducati
13	Simon Beck	Kawasaki
14	Colin Hipwell	Kawasaki
15	James Bunton	Yamaha

STANDINGS

Mackenzie 280, Whitham 275, Rutter 156, Rymer 154, Moodie 130, Hislop 123

MALLORY PARK
ROUND 8 – SEPTEMBER 15

RACE 1		
1	James Whitham	Yamaha
2	Steve Hislop	Kawasaki
3	Niall Mackenzie	Yamaha
4	Dave Jefferies	Honda
5	Michael Rutter	Ducati
6	Jim Moodie	Suzuki
7	Ian Simpson	Ducati
8	Ray Stringer	Kawasaki
9	Peter Graves	Ducati
10	Brett Sampson	Kawasaki
11	Steve Marks	Kawasaki
12	Andy Ward	Ducati
13	Tom Knight	Ducati
14	Colin Hipwell	Kawasaki
15	James Bunton	Yamaha

RACE 2		
1	James Whitham	Yamaha
2	Niall Mackenzie	Yamaha
3	Steve Hislop	Kawasaki
4	Terry Rymer	Ducati
5	Jim Moodie	Suzuki
6	Michael Rutter	Ducati
7	Dave Jefferies	Honda
8	Peter Graves	Ducati
9	Brett Sampson	Kawasaki
10	Dean Ashton	Ducati
11	Andy Ward	Ducati
12	Steve Marks	Kawasaki
13	Tom Knight	Ducati
14	David Higgins	Yamaha
15	James Bunton	Yamaha

STANDINGS

Whitham 325, Mackenzie 316, Rutter 177, Rymer 167, Hislop 159, Moodie 151

BRANDS HATCH INDY
ROUND 9 – SEPTEMBER 29

RACE 1		
1	Terry Rymer	Ducati
2	Niall Mackenzie	Yamaha
3	Michael Rutter	Ducati
4	James Whitham	Yamaha
5	Andy Ward	Ducati
6	Ian Simpson	Ducati
7	Dave Jefferies	Honda
8	Steve Marks	Kawasaki
9	Ray Stringer	Kawasaki
10	Brett Sampson	Kawasaki
11	Phil Borley	Ducati
12	James Bunton	Yamaha
13	Paul Jones	Yamaha
14	Nigel Nottingham	Yamaha
15		

RACE 2		
1	Terry Rymer	Ducati
2	Dave Jefferies	Honda
3	Andy Ward	Ducati
4	Niall Mackenzie	Yamaha
5	James Whitham	Yamaha
6	Ian Simpson	Ducati
7	Steve Hislop	Kawasaki
8	Brett Sampson	Kawasaki
9	Andrew Stroud	Suzuki
10	Steve Marks	Kawasaki
11	Andy Hatton	Ducati
12	Alex Buckingham	Yamaha
13	Paul Jones	Yamaha
14	Nigel Nottingham	Yamaha
15		

STANDINGS

Mackenzie & Whitham 349, Rymer 217, Rutter 193, Hislop 168, Moodie 151

DONINGTON PARK
ROUND 10 – OCTOBER 13

RACE 1		
1	Niall Mackenzie	Yamaha
2	Sean Emmett	Ducati
3	James Whitham	Yamaha
4	Steve Hislop	Kawasaki
5	Michael Rutter	Ducati
6	Terry Rymer	Ducati
7	Jim Moodie	Suzuki
8	Ian Simpson	Ducati
9	Ray Stringer	Kawasaki
10	Peter Graves	Ducati
11	Dean Ashton	Ducati
12	Alex Buckingham	Yamaha
13	Andy Hatton	Ducati
14	Andy Ward	Ducati
15	Brett Sampson	Kawasaki

RACE 2		
1	James Whitham	Yamaha
2	Niall Mackenzie	Yamaha
3	Steve Hislop	Kawasaki
4	Sean Emmett	Ducati
5	Michael Rutter	Ducati
6	Jim Moodie	Suzuki
7	Ian Simpson	Ducati
8	Ray Stringer	Kawasaki
9	Scott Smart	Ducati
10	Peter Graves	Ducati
11	Brett Sampson	Kawasaki
12	Andy Ward	Ducati
13	Alex Buckingham	Yamaha
14	Nigel Nottingham	Yamaha
15	Richard Defago	Kawasaki

FINAL STANDINGS

Mackenzie 394, Whitham 390, Rymer 227, Rutter 215, Hislop 197, Moodie 170

1997 SEASON *MCN* BRITISH SUPERBIKE CHAMPIONSHIP

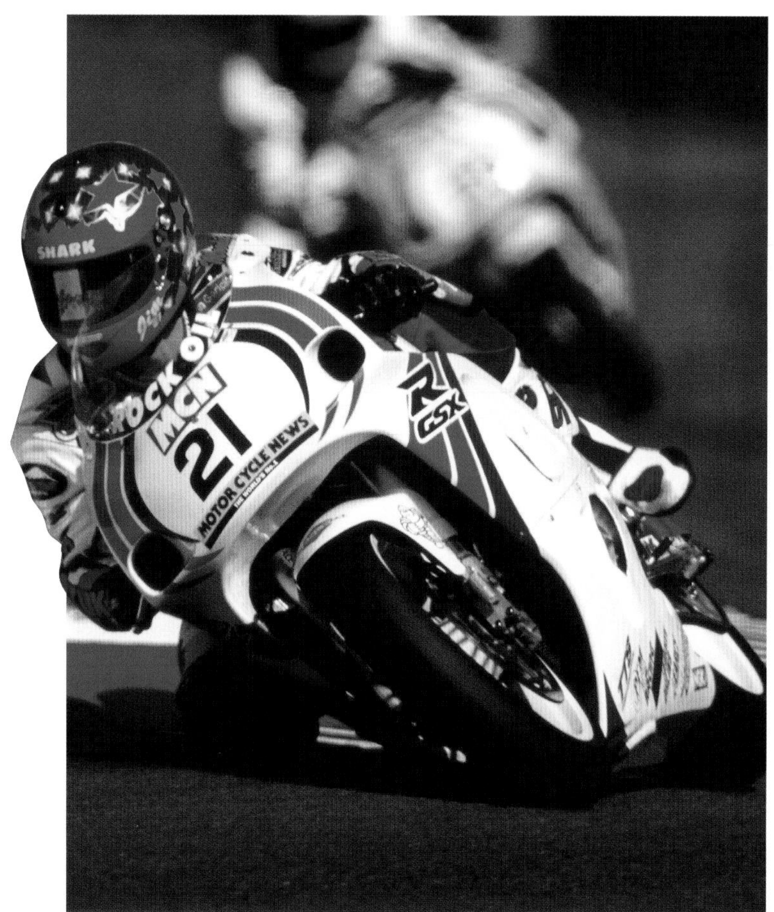

DONINGTON PARK GP
ROUND 1 – APRIL 13

RACE 1

1	Niall Mackenzie	Yamaha
2	John Reynolds	Ducati
3	Steve Hislop	Ducati
4	Chris Walker	Yamaha
5	Jim Moodie	Suzuki
6	Terry Rymer	Kawasaki
7	Sean Emmett	Ducati
8	Iain MacPherson	Kawasaki
9	Michael Rutter	Honda
10	Ray Stringer	Kawasaki
11	Andy Hatton	Ducati
12	Dean Ashton	Ducati
13	Andrew Ward	Ducati
14	Roger Bennett	Kawasaki
15	Darren Dixon	Kawasaki

RACE 2

1	Niall Mackenzie	Yamaha
2	Chris Walker	Yamaha
3	Sean Emmett	Ducati
4	Terry Rymer	Kawasaki
5	Jim Moodie	Suzuki
6	Michael Rutter	Honda
7	Matt Llewellyn	Suzuki
8	Dean Ashton	Ducati
9	Ray Stringer	Kawasaki
10	Andrew Ward	Ducati
11	Brett Sampson	Kawasaki
12	Graham Ward	Kawasaki
13	Colin Hipwell	Kawasaki
14	Nigel Nottingham	Yamaha
15	Jon Ward	Ducati

STANDINGS

Mackenzie 50, Walker 33, Emmett 25, Rymer 23, Moodie 22, Reynolds 20

OULTON PARK
ROUND 2 – APRIL 27

RACE 1

1	Chris Walker	Yamaha
2	John Reynolds	Ducati
3	Terry Rymer	Kawasaki
4	Sean Emmett	Ducati
5	Niall Mackenzie	Yamaha
6	Matt Llewellyn	Suzuki
7	Jim Moodie	Suzuki
8	Michael Rutter	Honda
9	Iain MacPherson	Kawasaki
10	Ray Stringer	Kawasaki
11	Andy Hatton	Ducati
12	Graham Ward	Kawasaki
13	Brett Sampson	Kawasaki
14	Andrew Ward	Ducati
15	Roger Bennett	Kawasaki

RACE 2

1	John Reynolds	Ducati
2	Terry Rymer	Kawasaki
3	Niall Mackenzie	Yamaha
4	Steve Hislop	Ducati
5	Sean Emmett	Ducati
6	Matt Llewellyn	Suzuki
7	Jim Moodie	Suzuki
8	Iain MacPherson	Kawasaki
9	Ray Stringer	Kawasaki
10	Brett Sampson	Kawasaki
11	Andy Hatton	Ducati
12	Dean Ashton	Ducati
13	Graham Ward	Kawasaki
14	Darren Dixon	Kawasaki
15	Nigel Nottingham	Yamaha

STANDINGS

Mackenzie 77, Reynolds 65, Rymer 59, Walker 58, Emmett 49, Moodie 40

SNETTERTON
ROUND 3 – MAY 11

RACE 1

1	Niall Mackenzie	Yamaha
2	Chris Walker	Yamaha
3	Michael Rutter	Honda
4	Matt Llewellyn	Suzuki
5	Jim Moodie	Suzuki
6	Brian Morrison	Kawasaki
7	Sean Emmett	Ducati
8	John Reynolds	Ducati
9	Andy Hatton	Ducati
10	Lee Dickinson	Kawasaki
11	Ray Stringer	Kawasaki
12	Andrew Ward	Ducati
13	Steve Hislop	Ducati
14	Dean Ashton	Ducati
15	Neil Cray	Kawasaki

RACE 2

1	Chris Walker	Yamaha
2	Niall Mackenzie	Yamaha
3	Matt Llewellyn	Suzuki
4	Jim Moodie	Suzuki
5	Sean Emmett	Ducati
6	Brian Morrison	Kawasaki
7	Andy Hatton	Ducati
8	Ray Stringer	Kawasaki
9	Michael Rutter	Honda
10	Tom Knight	Ducati
11	Darren Dixon	Kawasaki
12	Dean Ashton	Ducati
13	Colin Hipwell	Kawasaki
14	David Higgins	Suzuki

STANDINGS

Mackenzie 122, Walker 103, Reynolds 73, Emmett 69, Moodie 64, Rymer 59

BRANDS HATCH INDY
ROUND 4 – JUNE 22

RACE 1

1	Sean Emmett	Ducati
2	Chris Walker	Yamaha
3	Terry Rymer	Kawasaki
4	Michael Rutter	Honda
5	Iain MacPherson	Kawasaki
6	Dean Ashton	Ducati
7	Andrew Ward	Ducati
8	Niall Mackenzie	Yamaha
9	Darren Dixon	Kawasaki
10	Matt Llewellyn	Suzuki
11	Steve Hislop	Ducati
12	Brett Sampson	Kawasaki
13	Andy Hatton	Ducati
14	Steve Marks	Kawasaki
15	David Higgins	Suzuki

RACE 2

1	John Reynolds	Ducati
2	Michael Rutter	Honda
3	Iain MacPherson	Kawasaki
4	Niall Mackenzie	Yamaha
5	Chris Walker	Yamaha
6	Sean Emmett	Ducati
7	Steve Hislop	Ducati
8	Jim Moodie	Suzuki
9	Darren Dixon	Kawasaki
10	Brett Sampson	Kawasaki
11	Andrew Ward	Ducati
12	Dean Ashton	Ducati
13	Matt Llewellyn	Suzuki
14	Ray Stringer	Kawasaki
15	Graham Ward	Kawasaki

STANDINGS

Mackenzie 143, Walker 134, Emmett 104, Reynolds 96, Rutter 81, Rymer 75

THRUXTON
ROUND 5 – JULY 6

RACE 1

1	Niall Mackenzie	Yamaha
2	Terry Rymer	Ducati
3	Chris Walker	Yamaha
4	Iain MacPherson	Kawasaki
5	John Reynolds	Ducati
6	Jim Moodie	Suzuki
7	Michael Rutter	Honda
8	Matt Llewellyn	Suzuki
9	Ray Stringer	Kawasaki
10	Brett Sampson	Kawasaki
11	Graham Ward	Kawasaki
12	Steve Hislop	Ducati
13	Peter Graves	Ducati
14	Andrew Ward	Ducati
15	Tom Knight	Ducati

RACE 2

1	Niall Mackenzie	Yamaha
2	Terry Rymer	Kawasaki
3	John Reynolds	Ducati
4	Iain MacPherson	Kawasaki
5	Chris Walker	Yamaha
6	Jim Moodie	Suzuki
7	Sean Emmett	Ducati
8	Matt Llewellyn	Suzuki
9	Ray Stringer	Kawasaki
10	Michael Rutter	Honda
11	Graham Ward	Kawasaki
12	Brett Sampson	Kawasaki
13	Jim Hodson	Kawasaki
14	Andrew Ward	Ducati
15	Dean Ashton	Ducati

STANDINGS

Mackenzie 193, Walker 161, Reynolds 125, Rymer 115, Emmett 113, Rutter 96

OULTON PARK
ROUND 6 – JULY 20

RACE 1

1	Niall Mackenzie	Yamaha
2	John Reynolds	Ducati
3	Chris Walker	Yamaha
4	Michael Rutter	Honda
5	Matt Llewellyn	Suzuki
6	Jim Moodie	Suzuki
7	Ray Stringer	Kawasaki
8	Ian Simpson	Ducati
9	Brett Sampson	Kawasaki
10	Graham Ward	Kawasaki
11	Peter Graves	Ducati
12	Darren Dixon	Kawasaki
13	Andrew Ward	Ducati
14	Jim Hodson	Kawasaki
15	Colin Hipwell	Kawasaki

RACE 2

1	Niall Mackenzie	Yamaha
2	John Reynolds	Ducati
3	Chris Walker	Yamaha
4	Michael Rutter	Honda
5	Iain MacPherson	Kawasaki
6	Sean Emmett	Ducati
7	Jim Moodie	Suzuki
8	Matt Llewellyn	Suzuki
9	Ray Stringer	Kawasaki
10	Brett Sampson	Kawasaki
11	Peter Graves	Ducati
12	Andrew Ward	Ducati
13	Darren Dixon	Kawasaki
14	Lee Dickinson	Kawasaki
15	James Bunton	Yamaha

STANDINGS

Mackenzie 243, Walker 193, Reynolds 165, Emmett 123, Rutter 122, Rymer 115

MALLORY PARK
ROUND 7 – JULY 27

RACE 1

1	Niall Mackenzie	Yamaha
2	Iain MacPherson	Kawasaki
3	Steve Hislop	Kawasaki
4	Sean Emmett	Ducati
5	Jim Moodie	Suzuki
6	Chris Walker	Yamaha
7	Ray Stringer	Kawasaki
8	Michael Rutter	Honda
9	Ian Simpson	Ducati
10	Dean Ashton	Ducati
11	Graham Ward	Kawasaki
12	Lee Dickinson	Kawasaki
13	Darren Dixon	Kawasaki
14	Peter Graves	Ducati
15	Steve Marks	Kawasaki

RACE 2

1	Niall Mackenzie	Yamaha
2	Steve Hislop	Kawasaki
3	Chris Walker	Yamaha
4	Michael Rutter	Honda
5	Jim Moodie	Suzuki
6	Ray Stringer	Kawasaki
7	Ian Simpson	Ducati
8	Brett Sampson	Kawasaki
9	Dean Ashton	Ducati
10	Lee Dickinson	Kawasaki
11	Andrew Ward	Ducati
12	Peter Graves	Ducati
13	Steve Marks	Kawasaki
14	Darren Dixon	Kawasaki
15	Colin Hipwell	Kawasaki

STANDINGS

Mackenzie 293, Walker 219, Reynolds 165, Rutter 143, Emmett 136, Moodie 133

MALLORY PARK
ROUND 8 – AUGUST 10

RACE 1

1	Iain MacPherson	Kawasaki
2	Steve Hislop	Kawasaki
3	Michael Rutter	Honda
4	Chris Walker	Yamaha
5	Terry Rymer	Kawasaki
6	Ian Simpson	Ducati
7	Dave Jefferies	Ducati
8	Ray Stringer	Kawasaki
9	Andrew Ward	Ducati
10	Brett Sampson	Kawasaki
11	Nigel Nottingham	Yamaha
12	Colin Hipwell	Kawasaki

RACE 2

1	Niall Mackenzie	Yamaha
2	Chris Walker	Yamaha
3	Iain MacPherson	Kawasaki
4	Steve Hislop	Kawasaki
5	Matt Llewellyn	Suzuki
6	Terry Rymer	Kawasaki
7	Jim Moodie	Suzuki
8	Ian Simpson	Ducati
9	Ray Stringer	Kawasaki
10	Dave Jefferies	Ducati
11	Andrew Ward	Ducati
12	Brett Sampson	Kawasaki
13	Roger Bennett	Kawasaki
14	Colin Hipwell	Kawasaki

STANDINGS

Mackenzie 318, Walker 252, Reynolds 165, Rutter 159, MacPherson 148, Moodie 142

CADWELL PARK
ROUND 9 – AUGUST 25

RACE 1

1	Ian Simpson	Ducati
2	Michael Rutter	Honda
3	Terry Rymer	Kawasaki
4	Iain MacPherson	Kawasaki
5	Chris Walker	Yamaha
6	Sean Emmett	Ducati
7	Niall Mackenzie	Yamaha
8	Jim Moodie	Suzuki
9	Andrew Ward	Ducati
10	Ray Stringer	Kawasaki
11	Matt Llewellyn	Suzuki
12	Dean Ashton	Ducati
13	Brett Sampson	Kawasaki
14	Jim Hodson	Kawasaki
15	Scott Hanney	Suzuki

RACE 2

1	Michael Rutter	Honda
2	Chris Walker	Yamaha
3	Sean Emmett	Ducati
4	Iain MacPherson	Kawasaki
5	Ian Simpson	Ducati
6	Dave Jefferies	Ducati
7	Andrew Ward	Ducati
8	Brett Sampson	Kawasaki
9	Matt Llewellyn	Suzuki
10	Ray Stringer	Kawasaki
11	Colin Hipwell	Kawasaki
12	Steve Hislop	Kawasaki

STANDINGS

Mackenzie 327, Walker 283, Rutter 204, MacPherson 174, Reynolds 165, Emmett 162

BRANDS HATCH GP
ROUND 10 – SEPTEMBER 14

RACE 1

1	Niall Mackenzie	Yamaha
2	John Reynolds	Ducati
3	Sean Emmett	Ducati
4	Michael Rutter	Honda
5	Terry Rymer	Kawasaki
6	Jim Moodie	Suzuki
7	Iain MacPherson	Kawasaki
8	Steve Hislop	Kawasaki
9	Ray Stringer	Kawasaki
10	Ian Simpson	Ducati
11	Chris Walker	Yamaha
12	David Heal	Honda
13	Dave Jefferies	Ducati
14	Brett Sampson	Kawasaki
15	Pete Jennings	Kawasaki

RACE 2

1	Niall Mackenzie	Yamaha
2	Sean Emmett	Ducati
3	Chris Walker	Yamaha
4	John Reynolds	Ducati
5	Terry Rymer	Kawasaki
6	Michael Rutter	Honda
7	Steve Hislop	Kawasaki
8	Ray Stringer	Kawasaki
9	Ian Simpson	Ducati
10	David Heal	Honda
11	Dave Jefferies	Ducati
12	Brett Sampson	Kawasaki
13	Graham Ward	Kawasaki
14	Andrew Ward	Ducati
15	Steve Marks	Kawasaki

STANDINGS

Mackenzie 377, Walker 304, Rutter 227, Emmett & Reynolds 198, MacPherson 183

DONINGTON PARK NAT
ROUND 11 – SEPTEMBER 28

RACE 1

1	Niall Mackenzie	Yamaha
2	John Reynolds	Ducati
3	Chris Walker	Yamaha
4	Terry Rymer	Kawasaki
5	Iain MacPherson	Kawasaki
6	Matt Llewellyn	Suzuki
7	Michael Rutter	Honda
8	Steve Hislop	Kawasaki
9	Dave Heal	Honda
10	Dean Thomas	Honda
11	Dean Ashton	Ducati
12	Brett Sampson	Kawasaki
13	Graham Ward	Kawasaki
14	Andrew Ward	Ducati
15	Roger Bennett	Kawasaki

RACE 2

1	Chris Walker	Yamaha
2	Sean Emmett	Ducati
3	Terry Rymer	Kawasaki
4	Iain MacPherson	Kawasaki
5	Matt Llewellyn	Suzuki
6	Michael Rutter	Honda
7	John Reynolds	Ducati
8	Dean Thomas	Honda
9	Ray Stringer	Kawasaki
10	Dave Heal	Honda
11	Brett Sampson	Kawasaki
12	Andrew Ward	Ducati
13	Graham Ward	Kawasaki
14	Juha Berner	Kawasaki
15	Roger Bennett	Kawasaki

FINAL STANDINGS

Mackenzie 402, Walker 345, Rutter 246, Reynolds 227, Emmett 218, MacPherson 207

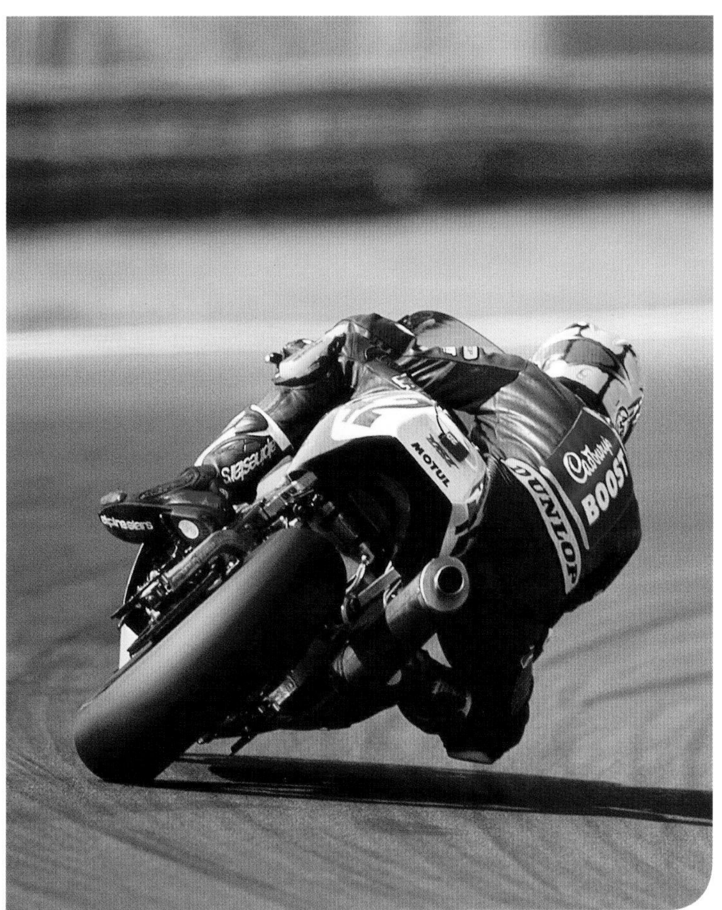

LEFT While Mackenzie was always stylish to watch, Walker was simply sensational

OPPOSITE Jim Moodie became a full-time Suzuki rider in 1997

1998 SEASON *MCN* BRITISH SUPERBIKE CHAMPIONSHIP

BRANDS HATCH INDY
ROUND 1 – MARCH 29

RACE 1

Pos	Rider	Make
1	Chris Walker	Kawasaki
2	Sean Emmett	Ducati
3	James Haydon	Suzuki
4	Troy Bayliss	Ducati
5	Terry Rymer	Suzuki
6	Niall Mackenzie	Yamaha
7	Steve Hislop	Yamaha
8	Iain MacPherson	Kawasaki
9	John Reynolds	Ducati
10	Michael Rutter	Honda
11	Peter Graves	Ducati
12	Phil Giles	Kawasaki
13	Jamie Robinson	Ducati
14	Max Vincent	Kawasaki
15	Dave Heal	Honda

RACE 2

Pos	Rider	Make
1	Niall Mackenzie	Yamaha
2	Steve Hislop	Yamaha
3	Chris Walker	Kawasaki
4	Sean Emmett	Ducati
5	Troy Bayliss	Ducati
6	Terry Rymer	Suzuki
7	Iain MacPherson	Kawasaki
8	James Haydon	Suzuki
9	Michael Rutter	Honda
10	John Reynolds	Ducati
11	Ian Simpson	Honda
12	Phil Giles	Kawasaki
13	Jamie Robinson	Ducati
14	Brett Sampson	Kawasaki
15	Max Vincent	Kawasaki

STANDINGS
Walker 41, Mackenzie 35, Emmett 33, Hislop 29, Bayliss & Haydon 24

OULTON PARK
ROUND 2 – APRIL 26

RACE 1

Pos	Rider	Make
1	Michael Rutter	Honda
2	Terry Rymer	Suzuki
3	Chris Walker	Kawasaki
4	Niall Mackenzie	Yamaha
5	James Haydon	Suzuki
6	Ian Simpson	Honda
7	Troy Bayliss	Ducati
8	Matt Llewellyn	Ducati
9	Steve Hislop	Yamaha
10	Iain MacPherson	Kawasaki
11	Jamie Robinson	Ducati
12	Brett Sampson	Kawasaki
13	Nigel Nottingham	Yamaha
14	Ray Stringer	Kawasaki
15	Dave Heal	Honda

RACE 2

Pos	Rider	Make
1	Steve Hislop	Yamaha
2	Niall Mackenzie	Yamaha
3	Chris Walker	Kawasaki
4	James Haydon	Suzuki
5	Troy Bayliss	Ducati
6	Ian Simpson	Honda
7	Ray Stringer	Kawasaki
8	Jamie Robinson	Ducati
9	Phil Giles	Kawasaki
10	Brett Sampson	Ducati
11	Dave Heal	Honda
12	Colin Hipwell	Suzuki
13	Jim Hodson	Kawasaki
14	Nigel Nottingham	Yamaha

STANDINGS
Walker 73, Mackenzie 68, Hislop 61, Haydon 48, Bayliss 44, Rymer 41

THRUXTON
ROUND 3 – MAY 4

RACE 1

Pos	Rider	Make
1	Niall Mackenzie	Yamaha
2	Terry Rymer	Suzuki
3	Steve Hislop	Yamaha
4	James Haydon	Suzuki
5	Chris Walker	Kawasaki
6	Michael Rutter	Honda
7	Ray Stringer	Kawasaki
8	Troy Bayliss	Ducati
9	Ian Simpson	Honda
10	Phil Giles	Kawasaki
11	Peter Graves	Ducati
12	John Reynolds	Ducati
13	Jamie Robinson	Ducati
14	Max Vincent	Kawasaki
15	Jim Hodson	Kawasaki

RACE 2

Pos	Rider	Make
1	Niall Mackenzie	Yamaha
2	Steve Hislop	Yamaha
3	Iain MacPherson	Kawasaki
4	Terry Rymer	Suzuki
5	James Haydon	Suzuki
6	Ian Simpson	Honda
7	Ray Stringer	Kawasaki
8	Phil Giles	Kawasaki
9	John Reynolds	Ducati
10	Peter Graves	Ducati
11	Michael Rutter	Honda
12	Dave Heal	Honda
13	Jim Hodson	Kawasaki
14	Steve Marks	Kawasaki
15	Nigel Nottingham	Yamaha

STANDINGS
Mackenzie 118, Hislop 97, Walker 84, Rymer 74, Haydon 72, Rutter 53

SNETTERTON
ROUND 4 – MAY 10

RACE 1

Pos	Rider	Make
1	Steve Hislop	Yamaha
2	Niall Mackenzie	Yamaha
3	Chris Walker	Kawasaki
4	James Haydon	Suzuki
5	Troy Bayliss	Ducati
6	Terry Rymer	Suzuki
7	Matt Llewellyn	Ducati
8	John Reynolds	Ducati
9	Ian Simpson	Honda
10	Michael Rutter	Honda
11	Jamie Robinson	Ducati
12	Peter Graves	Ducati
13	Max Vincent	Kawasaki
14	Brett Sampson	Kawasaki
15	Phil Giles	Kawasaki

RACE 2

Pos	Rider	Make
1	Terry Rymer	Suzuki
2	Chris Walker	Kawasaki
3	Steve Hislop	Yamaha
4	Niall Mackenzie	Yamaha
5	Troy Bayliss	Ducati
6	Matt Llewellyn	Ducati
7	Michael Rutter	Honda
8	John Reynolds	Ducati
9	Iain MacPherson	Kawasaki
10	Peter Graves	Ducati
11	Max Vincent	Kawasak
12	Jamie Robinson	Ducati
13	Ian Simpson	Honda
14	Warwick Nowland	Kawasaki
15	Brett Sampson	Kawasaki

STANDINGS
Mackenzie 151, Hislop 138, Walker 120, Rymer 109, Haydon 85, Bayliss 74

DONINGTON PARK NAT
ROUND 5 – JUNE 21

RACE 1

Pos	Rider	Make
1	Steve Hislop	Yamaha
2	James Haydon	Suzuki
3	Chris Walker	Kawasaki
4	Troy Bayliss	Ducati
5	Terry Rymer	Suzuki
6	Iain MacPherson	Kawasaki
7	Sean Emmett	Ducati
8	John Reynolds	Ducati
9	Ian Simpson	Honda
10	Jamie Robinson	Ducati
11	Dave Heal	Honda
12	Max Vincent	Kawasaki
13	Brett Sampson	Kawasaki
14	Nigel Nottingham	Yamaha
15	John Pugh	Kawasaki

RACE 2

Pos	Rider	Make
1	Niall Mackenzie	Yamaha
2	Steve Hislop	Yamaha
3	James Haydon	Suzuki
4	Chris Walker	Kawasaki
5	Terry Rymer	Suzuki
6	John Reynolds	Ducati
7	Michael Rutter	Honda
8	Iain MacPherson	Kawasaki
9	Ian Simpson	Honda
10	Sean Emmett	Ducati
11	Dave Heal	Honda
12	Peter Graves	Ducati
13	Max Vincent	Kawasaki
14	Brett Sampson	Kawasaki
15	Steve Marks	Kawasaki

STANDINGS
Hislop 183, Mackenzie 176, Walker 149, Rymer 131, Haydon 121, Bayliss 87

OULTON PARK
ROUND 6 – JULY 19

RACE 1

Pos	Rider	Make
1	Troy Bayliss	Ducati
2	Niall Mackenzie	Yamaha
3	Steve Hislop	Yamaha
4	John Reynolds	Ducati
5	Terry Rymer	Suzuki
6	James Haydon	Suzuki
7	Sean Emmett	Ducati
8	Peter Graves	Ducati
9	Phil Giles	Kawasaki
10	Dave Heal	Honda
11	Iain MacPherson	Kawasaki
12	Colin Hipwell	Suzuki
13	John Pugh	Kawasaki

RACE 2

Pos	Rider	Make
1	Sean Emmett	Ducati
2	Niall Mackenzie	Yamaha
3	Steve Hislop	Yamaha
4	James Haydon	Suzuki
5	John Reynolds	Ducati
6	Iain MacPherson	Kawasaki
7	Chris Walker	Kawasaki
8	Matt Llewellyn	Ducati
9	Brett Sampson	Kawasaki
10	Terry Rymer	Suzuki
11	Phil Giles	Kawasaki
12	Colin Hipwell	Suzuki
13	Peter Graves	Ducati
14	Roger Smith	Yamaha

STANDINGS
Mackenzie 216, Hislop 215, Walker 158, Rymer 148, Haydon 144, Bayliss 112

KNOCKHILL
ROUND 7 – AUGUST 9

RACE 1

Pos	Rider	Make
1	Niall Mackenzie	Yamaha
2	Chris Walker	Kawasaki
3	John Reynolds	Ducati
4	Matt Llewellyn	Ducati
5	Troy Bayliss	Ducati
6	Sean Emmett	Ducati
7	Terry Rymer	Suzuki
8	Phil Giles	Kawasaki
9	Max Vincent	Kawasaki
10	Brett Sampson	Kawasaki
11	Nigel Nottingham	Yamaha
12	Colin Hipwell	Suzuki

RACE 2

Pos	Rider	Make
1	Niall Mackenzie	Yamaha
2	Steve Hislop	Yamaha
3	Troy Bayliss	Ducati
4	Chris Walker	Kawasaki
5	Michael Rutter	Honda
6	Terry Rymer	Suzuki
7	Matt Llewellyn	Ducati
8	James Haydon	Suzuki
9	John Reynolds	Ducati
10	Sean Emmett	Ducati
11	Max Vincent	Kawasaki
12	Phil Giles	Kawasaki
13	Brett Sampson	Kawasaki
14	Nigel Nottingham	Yamaha
15	Colin Hipwell	Suzuki

STANDINGS
Mackenzie 266, Hislop 235, Walker 191, Rymer 167, Haydon 152, Bayliss 139

MALLORY PARK
ROUND 8 – AUGUST 16

RACE 1

Pos	Rider	Make
1	Matt Llewellyn	Ducati
2	John Reynolds	Ducati
3	Michael Rutter	Honda
4	Terry Rymer	Suzuki
5	Sean Emmett	Ducati
6	Steve Hislop	Yamaha
7	Niall Mackenzie	Yamaha
8	Max Vincent	Kawasaki
9	Phil Giles	Kawasaki
10	James Haydon	Suzuki
11	Ray Stringer	Kawasaki
12	Troy Bayliss	Ducati
13	Brett Sampson	Kawasaki
14	Peter Graves	Ducati
15	Dave Heal	Honda

RACE 2

Pos	Rider	Make
1	Chris Walker	Kawasaki
2	Niall Mackenzie	Yamaha
3	Michael Rutter	Honda
4	Terry Rymer	Suzuki
5	John Reynolds	Ducati
6	Matt Llewellyn	Ducati
7	Steve Hislop	Yamaha
8	Sean Emmett	Ducati
9	Ray Stringer	Kawasaki
10	Phil Giles	Kawasaki
11	Max Vincent	Kawasaki
12	James Haydon	Suzuki
13	Peter Graves	Ducati
14	Dave Heal	Honda
15	Colin Hipwell	Suzuki

STANDINGS
Mackenzie 295, Hislop 254, Walker 216, Rymer 193, Haydon 162, Bayliss 143

LEFT Rutter was brilliant in the wet as usual, winning the first race of round two at Oulton

CADWELL PARK
ROUND 9 – AUGUST 31

RACE 1

1	Chris Walker	Kawasaki
2	John Reynolds	Ducati
3	Iain MacPherson	Kawasaki
4	Matt Llewellyn	Ducati
5	Niall Mackenzie	Yamaha
6	Terry Rymer	Suzuki
7	Sean Emmett	Ducati
8	Max Vincent	Kawasaki
9	Colin Hipwell	Suzuki
10	Nigel Nottingham	Yamaha
11	Roger Smith	Yamaha

RACE 2

1	Chris Walker	Kawasaki
2	Michael Rutter	Honda
3	Troy Bayliss	Ducati
4	Iain MacPherson	Kawasaki
5	Matt Llewellyn	Ducati
6	John Reynolds	Ducati
7	Niall Mackenzie	Yamaha
8	Terry Rymer	Suzuki
9	Max Vincent	Kawasaki
10	Phil Giles	Kawasaki
11	Peter Graves	Ducati
12	Brett Sampson	Kawasaki
13	Sean Emmett	Ducati
14	Roger Smith	Yamaha
15	Nigel Nottingham	Yamaha

STANDINGS

Mackenzie 315, Walker 266, Hislop 254, Rymer 211, Reynolds 166, Haydon 162

SILVERSTONE
ROUND 10 – SEPTEMBER 6

RACE 1

1	James Haydon	Suzuki
2	Niall Mackenzie	Yamaha
3	Michael Rutter	Honda
4	John Reynolds	Ducati
5	Sean Emmett	Ducati
6	Ian Simpson	Honda
7	Max Vincent	Kawasaki
8	Phil Giles	Kawasaki
9	Troy Bayliss	Ducati
10	Peter Graves	Ducati
11	Brett Sampson	Kawasaki
12	Dave Heal	Honda
13	Colin Hipwell	Suzuki
14	Chris Walker	Kawasaki
15	Roger Smith	Yamaha

RACE 2

1	Troy Bayliss	Ducati
2	Chris Walker	Kawasaki
3	Michael Rutter	Honda
4	John Reynolds	Ducati
5	James Haydon	Suzuki
6	Niall Mackenzie	Yamaha
7	Iain MacPherson	Kawasaki
8	Terry Rymer	Suzuki
9	Matt Llewellyn	Ducati
10	Ian Simpson	Honda
11	Sean Emmett	Ducati
12	Phil Giles	Kawasaki
13	Peter Graves	Ducati
14	Max Vincent	Kawasaki
15	Brett Sampson	Kawasaki

STANDINGS

Mackenzie 345, Walker 248, Hislop 254, Rymer 219, Haydon 198, Reynolds 192

BRANDS HATCH GP
ROUND 11 – SEPTEMBER 20

RACE 1

1	Steve Hislop	Yamaha
2	John Reynolds	Ducati
3	Chris Walker	Kawasaki
4	Niall Mackenzie	Yamaha
5	Matt Llewellyn	Ducati
6	Michael Rutter	Honda
7	Iain MacPherson	Kawasaki
8	Sean Emmett	Ducati
9	Terry Rymer	Suzuki
10	Ian Simpson	Honda
11	Peter Graves	Ducati
12	Max Vincent	Kawasaki
13	Phil Giles	Kawasaki
14	Brett Sampson	Kawasaki
15	Colin Hipwell	Suzuki

RACE 2

1	John Reynolds	Ducati
2	Chris Walker	Kawasaki
3	Niall Mackenzie	Yamaha
4	Iain MacPherson	Kawasaki
5	Steve Hislop	Yamaha
6	Sean Emmett	Ducati
7	Ian Simpson	Honda
8	Michael Rutter	Honda
9	Matt Llewellyn	Ducati
10	James Haydon	Suzuki
11	Peter Graves	Ducati
12	Max Vincent	Kawasaki
13	Phil Giles	Kawasaki
14	David Wood	Kawasaki
15	Colin Hipwell	Suzuki

STANDINGS

Mackenzie 374, Walker 324, Hislop 290, Reynolds 237, Rymer 226, Haydon 204

DONINGTON PARK GP
ROUND 12 – SEPTEMBER 27

RACE 1

1	Chris Walker	Kawasaki
2	Michael Rutter	Honda
3	Iain MacPherson	Kawasaki
4	Niall Mackenzie	Yamaha
5	James Haydon	Suzuki
6	Troy Bayliss	Ducati
7	Matt Llewellyn	Ducati
8	Ian Simpson	Honda
9	Sean Emmett	Ducati
10	John Reynolds	Ducati
11	Steve Hislop	Yamaha
12	David Wood	Kawasaki
13	Phil Giles	Kawasaki
14	Pete Graves	Ducati
15	Brett Sampson	Kawasaki

RACE 2

1	Michael Rutter	Honda
2	Matt Llewellyn	Ducati
3	Terry Rymer	Suzuki
4	James Haydon	Suzuki
5	Chris Walker	Kawasaki
6	David Wood	Kawasaki
7	John Reynolds	Ducati
8	Phil Giles	Kawasaki
9	Colin Hipwell	Suzuki
10	Nigel Nottingham	Yamaha
11	Francis Williamson	Yamaha
12	Dave Redgate	Kawasaki

FINAL STANDINGS

Mackenzie 387, Walker 360, Hislop 295, Reynolds 252, Rymer 242, Rutter 236

1999 SEASON *MCN* BRITISH SUPERBIKE CHAMPIONSHIP

BRANDS HATCH INDY
ROUND 1 – MARCH 28

RACE 1

1	Neil Hodgson	Ducati
2	Chris Walker	Kawasaki
3	John Reynolds	Ducati
4	Troy Bayliss	Ducati
5	James Haydon	Suzuki
6	Sean Emmett	Ducati
7	Niall Mackenzie	Yamaha
8	Steve Hislop	Kawasaki
9	Paul Young	Yamaha
10	Dave Heal	Kawasaki
11	Dave Wood	Kawasaki
12	Marty Craggill	Suzuki
13	Phil Giles	Kawasaki
14	Dean Ashton	Yamaha
15	Damion Bailey	Suzuki

RACE 2

1	James Haydon	Suzuki
2	Chris Walker	Kawasaki
3	Neil Hodgson	Ducati
4	John Reynolds	Ducati
5	Sean Emmett	Ducati
6	Steve Hislop	Kawasaki
7	Troy Bayliss	Ducati
8	Paul Young	Yamaha
9	Dave Heal	Kawasaki
10	Marty Craggill	Suzuki
11	Dave Wood	Kawasaki
12	Phil Giles	Kawasaki
13	Dean Ashton	Yamaha
14	Roger Smith	Yamaha
15	Nigel Nottingham	Yamaha

STANDINGS

Hodgson 41, Walker 40, Haydon 36, Reynolds 29, Bayliss 22, Emmett 21

THRUXTON
ROUND 2 – APRIL 5

RACE 1

1	Troy Bayliss	Ducati
2	James Haydon	Suzuki
3	Chris Walker	Kawasaki
4	Steve Hislop	Kawasaki
5	John Reynolds	Ducati
6	Sean Emmett	Ducati
7	Paul Young	Yamaha
8	Dave Wood	Kawasaki
9	Marty Craggill	Suzuki
10	John Crockford	Kawasaki
11	Brett Sampson	Yamaha
12	Jim Hodson	Kawasaki
13	Paul Jones	Kawasaki
14	Nigel Nottingham	Yamaha
15	Colin Hipwell	Suzuki

RACE 2

1	James Haydon	Suzuki
2	Chris Walker	Kawasaki
3	Troy Bayliss	Ducati
4	Steve Hislop	Kawasaki
5	Neil Hodgson	Ducati
6	Niall Mackenzie	Yamaha
7	Paul Young	Yamaha
8	Dave Wood	Kawasaki
9	Marty Craggill	Suzuki
10	Brett Sampson	Yamaha
11	Phil Giles	Kawasaki
12	Paul Jones	Kawasaki
13	Roger Smith	Yamaha
14	Jim Hodson	Kawasaki
15	Dan Harris	Yamaha

STANDINGS

Haydon 81, Walker 76, Bayliss 63, Hodgson 52, Hislop 44, Reynolds 40

OULTON PARK
ROUND 3 – APRIL 25

RACE 1

1	Troy Bayliss	Ducati
2	Sean Emmett	Ducati
3	Chris Walker	Kawasaki
4	Neil Hodgson	Ducati
5	Niall Mackenzie	Yamaha
6	Marty Craggill	Suzuki
7	Steve Hislop	Kawasaki
8	Paul Young	Yamaha
9	Phil Giles	Kawasaki
10	Dave Wood	Kawasaki
11	David Heal	Kawasaki
12	Brett Sampson	Yamaha
13	Dean Ashton	Yamaha
14	Nigel Nottingham	Yamaha
15	Jim Hodson	Kawasaki

RACE 2

1	Troy Bayliss	Ducati
2	James Haydon	Suzuki
3	John Reynolds	Ducati
4	Chris Walker	Kawasaki
5	Neil Hodgson	Ducati
6	Niall Mackenzie	Yamaha
7	Marty Craggill	Suzuki
8	Paul Young	Yamaha
9	Phil Giles	Kawasaki
10	Steve Hislop	Kawasaki
11	Dave Heal	Kawasaki
12	Dave Wood	Kawasaki
13	Sean Emmett	Ducati
14	Nigel Nottingham	Yamaha
15	Roger Smith	Yamaha

STANDINGS

Bayliss 113, Walker 105, Haydon 101, Hodgson 76, Hislop 59, Reynolds 56

SNETTERTON
ROUND 4 – MAY 9

RACE 1

1	John Reynolds	Ducati
2	Troy Bayliss	Ducati
3	Neil Hodgson	Ducati
4	Chris Walker	Kawasaki
5	Steve Hislop	Kawasaki
6	Niall Mackenzie	Yamaha
7	James Haydon	Suzuki
8	Marty Craggill	Suzuki
9	Sean Emmett	Ducati
10	Phil Giles	Kawasaki
11	Paul Young	Yamaha
12	Dave Heal	Kawasaki
13	Nigel Nottingham	Yamaha
14	Dean Ashton	Yamaha
15	Dan Harris	Yamaha

RACE 2

1	Troy Bayliss	Ducati
2	John Reynolds	Ducati
3	Chris Walker	Kawasaki
4	Neil Hodgson	Ducati
5	Steve Hislop	Kawasaki
6	Sean Emmett	Ducati
7	Niall Mackenzie	Yamaha
8	James Haydon	Suzuki
9	Marty Craggill	Suzuki
10	Phil Giles	Kawasaki
11	Paul Young	Yamaha
12	Dave Heal	Kawasaki
13	Dave Wood	Kawasaki
14	Dean Ashton	Yamaha
15	Nigel Nottingham	Yamaha

STANDINGS

Bayliss 158, Walker 134, Haydon 118, Hodgson 105, Reynolds 101, Hislop 81

RIGHT INS Ducati duo Neil Hodgson and Troy Bayliss were the ones to beat in 1999

DONINGTON PARK NAT
ROUND 5 – MAY 31

RACE 1

1	James Haydon	Suzuki
2	Chris Walker	Kawasaki
3	Neil Hodgson	Ducati
4	Sean Emmett	Ducati
5	Marty Craggill	Suzuki
6	Dave Heal	Kawasaki
7	Brett Sampson	Yamaha
8	Nigel Nottingham	Yamaha
9	Dave Wood	Kawasaki
10	Ray Stringer	Yamaha
11	Dean Ashton	Yamaha
12	Dan Harris	Yamaha
13	Roger Smith	Yamaha
14	Paul Jones	Kawasaki
15	Dave Redgate	Kawasaki

RACE 2

1	John Reynolds	Ducati
2	James Haydon	Suzuki
3	Neil Hodgson	Ducati
4	Chris Walker	Kawasaki
5	Niall Mackenzie	Yamaha
6	Troy Bayliss	Ducati
7	Marty Craggill	Suzuki
8	Sean Emmett	Ducati
9	Steve Hislop	Kawasaki
10	Paul Young	Yamaha
11	Dave Heal	Kawasaki
12	Ray Stringer	Yamaha
13	Dave Redgate	Kawasaki
14	Brett Sampson	Yamaha
15	Nigel Nottingham	Yamaha

STANDINGS

Bayliss 168, Walker 167, Haydon 163, Hodgson 137, Reynolds 126, Emmett 92

SILVERSTONE
ROUND 6 – JUNE 20

RACE 1

1	Troy Bayliss	Ducati
2	John Reynolds	Ducati
3	Neil Hodgson	Ducati
4	Sean Emmett	Ducati
5	Niall Mackenzie	Yamaha
6	Marty Craggill	Suzuki
7	Shane Byrne	Kawasaki
8	Steve Hislop	Kawasaki
9	Dave Heal	Kawasaki
10	Dave Wood	Kawasaki
11	Brett Sampson	Yamaha
12	Nigel Nottingham	Yamaha
13	Paul Jones	Kawasaki
14	Dan Harris	Yamaha
15	Steven Marks	Yamaha

RACE 2

1	Troy Bayliss	Ducati
2	Chris Walker	Kawasaki
3	John Reynolds	Ducati
4	Neil Hodgson	Ducati
5	Niall Mackenzie	Yamaha
6	Marty Craggill	Suzuki
7	Sean Emmett	Ducati
8	Shane Byrne	Kawasaki
9	Paul Young	Yamaha
10	Steve Hislop	Kawasaki
11	Brett Sampson	Yamaha
12	Dave Wood	Kawasaki
13	Dave Redgate	Kawasaki
14	Dan Harris	Yamaha
15	Nigel Nottingham	Yamaha

STANDINGS

Bayliss 218, Walker 187, Hodgson 166, Haydon 163, Reynolds 162, Emmett 114

OULTON PARK
ROUND 7 – JULY 18

RACE 1

1	John Reynolds	Ducati
2	Sean Emmett	Ducati
3	Neil Hodgson	Ducati
4	James Haydon	Suzuki
5	Troy Bayliss	Ducati
6	Paul Young	Yamaha
7	Shane Byrne	Kawasaki
8	Marty Craggill	Suzuki
9	Dave Heal	Kawasaki
10	Max Vincent	Kawasaki
11	Phil Giles	Kawasaki
12	Dave Wood	Kawasaki
13	Nigel Nottingham	Yamaha
14	Brett Sampson	Yamaha
15	Dan Harris	Yamaha

RACE 2

1	Sean Emmett	Ducati
2	Troy Bayliss	Ducati
3	John Reynolds	Ducati
4	Neil Hodgson	Ducati
5	James Haydon	Suzuki
6	Chris Walker	Kawasaki
7	Marty Craggill	Suzuki
8	Shane Byrne	Kawasaki
9	Max Vincent	Kawasaki
10	Phil Giles	Kawasaki
11	Dave Wood	Kawasaki
12	Brett Sampson	Yamaha
13	Nigel Nottingham	Yamaha
14	Steven Marks	Yamaha
15	Jim Hodson	Kawasaki

STANDINGS

Bayliss 249, Reynolds 203, Walker 197, Hodgson 195, Haydon 187, Emmett 159

KNOCKHILL
ROUND 8 – AUGUST 8

RACE 1

1	Sean Emmett	Ducati
2	Chris Walker	Kawasaki
3	James Haydon	Suzuki
4	Niall Mackenzie	Yamaha
5	John Reynolds	Ducati
6	Marty Craggill	Suzuki
7	Phil Giles	Kawasaki
8	Troy Bayliss	Ducati
9	Dave Heal	Kawasaki
10	Dave Wood	Kawasaki
11	Max Vincent	Kawasaki
12	Brett Sampson	Yamaha
13	Paul Young	Yamaha
14	Nigel Nottingham	Yamaha
15	Dan Harris	Yamaha

RACE 2

1	John Reynolds	Ducati
2	Niall Mackenzie	Yamaha
3	Chris Walker	Kawasaki
4	Sean Emmett	Ducati
5	Phil Giles	Kawasaki
6	Paul Young	Yamaha
7	Marty Craggill	Suzuki
8	Dave Heal	Kawasaki
9	Brett Sampson	Yamaha
10	Gordon Blackley	Kawasaki
11	Roger Bennett	Kawasaki
12	Jim Hodson	Kawasaki
13	Nigel Nottingham	Yamaha
14	Kris Wilson	Honda

STANDINGS

Bayliss 257, Reynolds 239, Walker 233, Haydon 203, Emmett 197, Hodgson 196

MALLORY PARK
ROUND 9 – AUGUST 15

RACE 1

1	James Haydon	Suzuki
2	Sean Emmett	Ducati
3	Chris Walker	Kawasaki
4	Troy Bayliss	Ducati
5	Neil Hodgson	Ducati
6	John Reynolds	Ducati
7	Niall Mackenzie	Yamaha
8	Phil Giles	Kawasaki
9	Marty Craggill	Suzuki
10	Dave Heal	Kawasaki
11	Gordon Blackley	Kawasaki
12	Paul Young	Yamaha
13	Dave Wood	Kawasaki
14	Brett Sampson	Yamaha
15	Nigel Nottingham	Yamaha

RACE 2

1	John Reynolds	Ducati
2	Troy Bayliss	Ducati
3	Chris Walker	Kawasaki
4	Sean Emmett	Ducati
5	James Haydon	Suzuki
6	Neil Hodgson	Ducati
7	Niall Mackenzie	Yamaha
8	Paul Young	Yamaha
9	Marty Craggill	Suzuki
10	Phil Giles	Kawasaki
11	Matt Llewellyn	Kawasaki
12	Gordon Blackley	Kawasaki
13	Nigel Nottingham	Yamaha
14	Brett Sampson	Yamaha
15	Dave Wood	Kawasaki

STANDINGS

Bayliss 290, Reynolds 274, Walker 265, Haydon 239, Emmett 230, Hodgson 216

CADWELL PARK
ROUND 10 – AUGUST 30

RACE 1

1	Chris Walker	Kawasaki
2	Neil Hodgson	Ducati
3	John Reynolds	Ducati
4	Troy Bayliss	Ducati
5	Steve Hislop	Yamaha
6	Sean Emmett	Ducati
7	James Haydon	Suzuki
8	Marty Craggill	Suzuki
9	Niall Mackenzie	Yamaha
10	Phil Giles	Kawasaki
11	Dave Heal	Kawasaki
12	Brett Sampson	Yamaha
13	Gordon Blackley	Kawasaki
14	Dan Harris	Yamaha
15	Jim Hodson	Kawasaki

RACE 2

1	Troy Bayliss	Ducati
2	Chris Walker	Kawasaki
3	John Reynolds	Ducati
4	Steve Hislop	Yamaha
5	Neil Hodgson	Ducati
6	Sean Emmett	Ducati
7	Niall Mackenzie	Yamaha
8	Marty Craggill	Suzuki
9	James Haydon	Suzuki
10	Matt Llewellyn	Kawasaki
11	Dave Heal	Kawasaki
12	Brett Sampson	Yamaha
13	Phil Giles	Kawasaki
14	Dean Ashton	Yamaha
15	Jim Hodson	Kawasaki

STANDINGS

Bayliss 328, Walker 310, Reynolds 306, Haydon 265, Emmett 250, Hodgson 240

BRANDS HATCH GP
ROUND 11 – SEPTEMBER 19

RACE 1

1	Chris Walker	Kawasaki
2	Troy Bayliss	Ducati
3	Neil Hodgson	Ducati
4	Steve Hislop	Yamaha
5	Niall Mackenzie	Yamaha
6	John Reynolds	Ducati
7	James Haydon	Suzuki
8	Marty Craggill	Suzuki
9	Matt Llewellyn	Kawasaki
10	Dave Heal	Kawasaki
11	Shane Byrne	Kawasaki
12	Phil Giles	Kawasaki
13	Gordon Blackley	Kawasaki
14	Dean Ashton	Yamaha
15	Steven Marks	Yamaha

RACE 2

1	John Reynolds	Ducati
2	Sean Emmett	Ducati
3	Troy Bayliss	Ducati
4	Neil Hodgson	Ducati
5	Niall Mackenzie	Yamaha
6	Steve Hislop	Yamaha
7	Marty Craggill	Suzuki
8	James Haydon	Suzuki
9	Shane Byrne	Kawasaki
10	Dave Heal	Kawasaki
11	Phil Giles	Kawasaki
12	Paul Young	Yamaha
13	Brett Sampson	Yamaha
14	Gordon Blackley	Kawasaki
15	Dean Ashton	Yamaha

STANDINGS

Bayliss 364, Reynolds 341, Walker 335, Hodgson 276, Haydon 272, Emmett 270

DONINGTON PARK GP
ROUND 12 – SEPTEMBER 26

RACE 1

1	Chris Walker	Kawasaki
2	Niall Mackenzie	Yamaha
3	John Reynolds	Ducati
4	Steve Hislop	Yamaha
5	Shane Byrne	Kawasaki
6	Troy Bayliss	Ducati
7	James Haydon	Suzuki
8	Paul Young	Yamaha
9	Dave Heal	Kawasaki
10	Marty Craggill	Suzuki
11	Steven Marks	Yamaha
12	Jim Hodson	Kawasaki
13	Juha Berner	Kawasaki
14	John Crockford	Suzuki
15	Gus Scott	Honda

RACE 2

1	Neil Hodgson	Ducati
2	Troy Bayliss	Ducati
3	Sean Emmett	Ducati
4	Marty Craggill	Suzuki
5	Steve Hislop	Yamaha
6	Shane Byrne	Kawasaki
7	Niall Mackenzie	Yamaha
8	James Haydon	Suzuki
9	Phil Giles	Kawasaki
10	Chris Walker	Kawasaki
11	Dave Heal	Kawasaki
12	Paul Young	Yamaha
13	Gordon Blackley	Kawasaki
14	Dave Redgate	Kawasaki
15	Gus Scott	Honda

FINAL STANDINGS

Bayliss 394, Walker 366, Reynolds 357, Hodgson 301, Haydon 289, Emmett 286

2000 SEASON MB4U.COM BRITISH SUPERBIKE CHAMPIONSHIP

BRANDS HATCH INDY
ROUND 1 – MARCH 26

RACE 1

Pos	Rider	Make
1	John Reynolds	Ducati
2	Chris Walker	Suzuki
3	Steve Hislop	Yamaha
4	Neil Hodgson	Ducati
5	James Haydon	Ducati
6	Niall Mackenzie	Ducati
7	Shane Byrne	Honda
8	Paul Brown	Yamaha
9	Steve Plater	Kawasaki
10	John Crawford	Suzuki
11	James Toseland	Honda
12	Sean Emmett	Honda
13	Paul Young	Yamaha
14	John Crockford	Suzuki
15	Gordon Blackley	Kawasaki

RACE 2

Pos	Rider	Make
1	James Haydon	Ducati
2	Steve Hislop	Yamaha
3	Neil Hodgson	Ducati
4	John Reynolds	Ducati
5	Chris Walker	Suzuki
6	John Crawford	Suzuki
7	Paul Brown	Yamaha
8	Sean Emmett	Honda
9	James Toseland	Honda
10	Michael Rutter	Yamaha
11	Paul Young	Yamaha
12	Gordon Blackley	Kawasaki
13	Dave Wood	Yamaha
14	Dave Heal	Honda
15	Steven Marks	Yamaha

STANDINGS
Reynolds 38, Haydon & Hislop 36, Walker 31, Hodgson 29, Brown 17

DONINGTON PARK GP
ROUND 2 – APRIL 9

RACE 1

Pos	Rider	Make
1	John Reynolds	Ducati
2	Neil Hodgson	Ducati
3	James Haydon	Ducati
4	Niall Mackenzie	Ducati
5	Steve Plater	Kawasaki
6	Sean Emmett	Honda
7	Peter Goddard	Kawasaki
8	James Toseland	Honda
9	John Crawford	Suzuki
10	Shane Byrne	Honda
11	Paul Brown	Yamaha
12	John Crockford	Suzuki
13	Gordon Blackley	Kawasaki
14	Paul Young	Yamaha
15	Dave Wood	Yamaha

RACE 2

Pos	Rider	Make
1	Chris Walker	Suzuki
2	John Reynolds	Ducati
3	Neil Hodgson	Ducati
4	Steve Hislop	Yamaha
5	Niall Mackenzie	Ducati
6	Steve Plater	Kawasaki
7	James Toseland	Honda
8	Shane Byrne	Honda
9	Michael Rutter	Yamaha
10	Paul Young	Yamaha
11	Paul Brown	Yamaha
12	John Crockford	Suzuki
13	Gordon Blackley	Kawasaki
14	Francis Williamson	Yamaha
15	Dave Heal	Honda

STANDINGS
Reynolds 83, Hodgson 65, Walker 56, Haydon 52, Hislop 49, Mackenzie 34

THRUXTON
ROUND 3 – APRIL 24

RACE 1

Pos	Rider	Make
1	James Haydon	Ducati
2	Chris Walker	Suzuki
3	Neil Hodgson	Ducati
4	John Reynolds	Ducati
5	Steve Hislop	Yamaha
6	Steve Plater	Kawasaki
7	Niall Mackenzie	Ducati
8	John Crawford	Suzuki
9	Peter Goddard	Kawasaki
10	Paul Young	Yamaha
11	Sean Emmett	Honda
12	Michael Rutter	Yamaha
13	John Crockford	Suzuki
14	Francis Williamson	Yamaha
15	Nigel Nottingham	Yamaha

RACE 2

Pos	Rider	Make
1	Neil Hodgson	Ducati
2	Steve Hislop	Yamaha
3	John Reynolds	Ducati
4	James Haydon	Ducati
5	Chris Walker	Suzuki
6	Paul Brown	Yamaha
7	Steve Plater	Kawasaki
8	Peter Goddard	Kawasaki
9	John Crockford	Suzuki
10	James Toseland	Honda
11	Paul Young	Yamaha
12	John Crawford	Suzuki
13	Sean Emmett	Honda
14	Gordon Blackley	Kawasaki
15	Steven Marks	Yamaha

STANDINGS
Reynolds 112, Hodgson 106, Haydon 90, Walker 87, Hislop 80, Plater 47

OULTON PARK
ROUND 4 – MAY 21

RACE 1

Pos	Rider	Make
1	Neil Hodgson	Ducati
2	Chris Walker	Suzuki
3	John Reynolds	Ducati
4	James Haydon	Ducati
5	Steve Hislop	Yamaha
6	Steve Plater	Kawasaki
7	James Toseland	Honda
8	John Crawford	Suzuki
9	Shane Byrne	Honda
10	Peter Goddard	Kawasaki
11	Paul Brown	Yamaha
12	Michael Rutter	Yamaha
13	Paul Young	Yamaha
14	Dave Heal	Honda
15	Dave Wood	Yamaha

RACE 2

Pos	Rider	Make
1	John Reynolds	Ducati
2	James Haydon	Ducati
3	Niall Mackenzie	Ducati
4	Neil Hodgson	Ducati
5	Steve Hislop	Yamaha
6	James Toseland	Honda
7	Steve Plater	Kawasaki
8	John Crawford	Suzuki
9	Peter Goddard	Kawasaki
10	Shane Byrne	Honda
11	Michael Rutter	Yamaha
12	Paul Brown	Yamaha
13	Paul Young	Yamaha
14	Chris Walker	Suzuki
15	John Crockford	Suzuki

STANDINGS
Reynolds 153, Hodgson 144, Haydon 123, Walker 109, Hislop 102, Plater 66

SNETTERTON
ROUND 5 – MAY 31

RACE 1

Pos	Rider	Make
1	Chris Walker	Suzuki
2	Neil Hodgson	Ducati
3	John Reynolds	Ducati
4	James Haydon	Ducati
5	Niall Mackenzie	Ducati
6	John Crawford	Suzuki
7	Marty Craggill	Kawasaki
8	Steve Hislop	Yamaha
9	James Toseland	Honda
10	Michael Rutter	Yamaha
11	Paul Brown	Yamaha
12	Sean Emmett	Honda
13	John Crockford	Suzuki
14	Francis Williamson	Yamaha
15	Dave Heal	Kawasaki

RACE 2

Pos	Rider	Make
1	John Reynolds	Ducati
2	Neil Hodgson	Ducati
3	Chris Walker	Suzuki
4	James Haydon	Ducati
5	Niall Mackenzie	Ducati
6	John Crawford	Suzuki
7	Michael Rutter	Yamaha
8	Paul Brown	Yamaha
9	James Toseland	Honda
10	Steve Hislop	Yamaha
11	Francis Williamson	Yamaha
12	Nigel Nottingham	Yamaha
13	Dean Ellison	Honda
14	Dave Redgate	Kawasaki
15	Gordon Blackley	Kawasaki

STANDINGS
Reynolds 194, Hodgson 184, Walker 150, Haydon 149, Hislop 116, Mackenzie 81

SILVERSTONE
ROUND 6 – JULY 2

RACE 1

Pos	Rider	Make
1	Neil Hodgson	Ducati
2	Chris Walker	Suzuki
3	John Reynolds	Ducati
4	James Haydon	Ducati
5	Steve Plater	Kawasaki
6	Niall Mackenzie	Ducati
7	Steve Hislop	Yamaha
8	Paul Young	Yamaha
9	Sean Emmett	Honda
10	James Toseland	Honda
11	Paul Brown	Yamaha
12	Dave Heal	Kawasaki
13	John Crawford	Suzuki
14	Gordon Blackley	Kawasaki
15	John Crockford	Suzuki

RACE 2

Pos	Rider	Make
1	Chris Walker	Suzuki
2	James Haydon	Ducati
3	Steve Hislop	Yamaha
4	Niall Mackenzie	Ducati
5	John Reynolds	Ducati
6	Steve Plater	Kawasaki
7	John Crawford	Suzuki
8	James Toseland	Honda
9	Sean Emmett	Honda
10	Paul Young	Yamaha
11	Marty Craggill	Kawasaki
12	Paul Brown	Yamaha
13	Rob Frost	Honda
14	Dave Heal	Kawasaki
15	John Crockford	Suzuki

STANDINGS
Reynolds 221, Hodgson 209, Walker 195, Haydon 182, Hislop 141, Mackenzie 104

OULTON PARK
ROUND 7 – JULY 16

RACE 1

Pos	Rider	Make
1	Neil Hodgson	Ducati
2	James Haydon	Ducati
3	Steve Hislop	Yamaha
4	Chris Walker	Suzuki
5	John Reynolds	Ducati
6	Niall Mackenzie	Ducati
7	James Toseland	Honda
8	John Crawford	Suzuki
9	Paul Young	Yamaha
10	Marty Craggill	Kawasaki
11	Sean Emmett	Honda
12	Paul Brown	Yamaha
13	Dave Heal	Kawasaki
14	Gordon Blackley	Kawasaki
15	Carl Rennie	Kawasaki

RACE 2

Pos	Rider	Make
1	Chris Walker	Suzuki
2	Neil Hodgson	Ducati
3	John Reynolds	Ducati
4	James Haydon	Ducati
5	Steve Hislop	Yamaha
6	James Toseland	Honda
7	John Crawford	Suzuki
8	Paul Young	Yamaha
9	Sean Emmett	Honda
10	Michael Rutter	Yamaha
11	Paul Brown	Yamaha
12	Dave Heal	Kawasaki
13	Francis Williamson	Yamaha
14	Dave Wood	Yamaha
15	Nigel Nottingham	Yamaha

STANDINGS
Hodgson 254, Reynolds 248, Walker 233, Haydon 215, Hislop 168, Mackenzie 114

KNOCKHILL
ROUND 8 – AUGUST 13

RACE 1

Pos	Rider	Make
1	Chris Walker	Suzuki
2	Michael Rutter	Yamaha
3	Paul Young	Yamaha
4	Niall Mackenzie	Ducati
5	John Reynolds	Ducati
6	Neil Hodgson	Ducati
7	Steve Plater	Kawasaki
8	Tom Kipp	Honda
9	Sean Emmett	Honda
10	Dean Ellison	Honda
11	John Crockford	Suzuki
12	Gordon Blackley	Kawasaki
13	Steven Marks	Yamaha
14	Paul Jones	Kawasaki
15	Colin Hipwell	Suzuki

RACE 2

Pos	Rider	Make
1	Chris Walker	Suzuki
2	Neil Hodgson	Ducati
3	James Haydon	Ducati
4	John Reynolds	Ducati
5	John Crawford	Suzuki
6	Michael Rutter	Yamaha
7	Paul Young	Yamaha
8	Sean Emmett	Honda
9	Steve Plater	Kawasaki
10	Paul Brown	Yamaha
11	John Crockford	Suzuki
12	Dave Heal	Kawasaki
13	Gordon Blackley	Kawasaki
14	Tom Kipp	Honda
15	Dean Ellison	Honda

STANDINGS
Hodgson 284, Walker 283, Reynolds 272, Haydon 231, Hislop 168, Mackenzie 127,

CADWELL PARK
ROUND 9 – AUGUST 28

RACE 1

Pos	Rider	Make
1	Neil Hodgson	Ducati
2	Chris Walker	Suzuki
3	John Reynolds	Ducati
4	Niall Mackenzie	Ducati
5	John Crawford	Suzuki
6	Sean Emmett	Honda
7	Shane Byrne	Honda
8	Paul Young	Yamaha
9	Dave Jefferies	Yamaha
10	Steve Plater	Kawasaki
11	Michael Rutter	Yamaha
12	Gordon Blackley	Kawasaki
13	Dave Heal	Kawasaki
14	Tom Kipp	Honda
15	Dave Wood	Yamaha

RACE 2

Pos	Rider	Make
1	Chris Walker	Suzuki
2	Neil Hodgson	Ducati
3	James Haydon	Ducati
4	John Reynolds	Ducati
5	Steve Plater	Kawasaki
6	Sean Emmett	Honda
7	Michael Rutter	Yamaha
8	Paul Young	Yamaha
9	Shane Byrne	Honda
10	Dave Jefferies	Yamaha
11	Dave Wood	Yamaha
12	Dave Heal	Kawasaki
13	Tom Kipp	Honda
14	Gordon Blackley	Kawasaki
15	Nigel Nottingham	Yamaha

STANDINGS

Hodgson 329, Walker 328, Reynolds 301, Haydon 247, Hislop 168, Mackenzie 140

MALLORY PARK
ROUND 10 – SEPTEMBER 17

RACE 1

Pos	Rider	Make
1	Neil Hodgson	Ducati
2	Chris Walker	Suzuki
3	John Reynolds	Ducati
4	Steve Plater	Kawasaki
5	James Haydon	Ducati
6	John Crawford	Suzuki
7	Dave Jefferies	Yamaha
8	Sean Emmett	Honda
9	Niall Mackenzie	Ducati
10	Michael Rutter	Yamaha
11	Paul Young	Yamaha
12	Marty Craggill	Kawasaki
13	Anthony Gobert	Yamaha
14	Dave Heal	Kawasaki
15	Gordon Blackley	Kawasaki

RACE 2

Pos	Rider	Make
1	Chris Walker	Suzuki
2	John Reynolds	Ducati
3	James Haydon	Ducati
4	Neil Hodgson	Ducati
5	Steve Plater	Kawasaki
6	John Crawford	Suzuki
7	Niall Mackenzie	Ducati
8	Michael Rutter	Yamaha
9	Sean Emmett	Honda
10	Shane Byrne	Honda
11	Dave Jefferies	Yamaha
12	Tom Kipp	Honda
13	Paul Young	Yamaha
14	Dave Heal	Kawasaki
15	Dave Wood	Yamaha

STANDINGS

Walker 373, Hodgson 367, Reynolds 337, Haydon 274, Hislop 168, Mackenzie 156

BRANDS HATCH INDY
ROUND 11 – SEPTEMBER 24

RACE 1

Pos	Rider	Make
1	Michael Rutter	Yamaha
2	James Haydon	Ducati
3	John Reynolds	Ducati
4	Anthony Gobert	Yamaha
5	Sean Emmett	Honda
6	Neil Hodgson	Ducati
7	Dave Jefferies	Yamaha
8	Niall Mackenzie	Ducati
9	Shane Byrne	Honda
10	Paul Young	Yamaha
11	Tom Kipp	Honda
12	Karl Harris	Suzuki
13	Dean Ellison	Honda
14	Francis Williamson	Yamaha
15	Gordon Blackley	Kawasaki

RACE 2

Pos	Rider	Make
1	Chris Walker	Suzuki
2	Michael Rutter	Yamaha
3	John Reynolds	Ducati
4	Niall Mackenzie	Ducati
5	Shane Byrne	Honda
6	Steve Plater	Kawasaki
7	James Haydon	Ducati
8	Dean Ellison	Honda
9	Karl Harris	Suzuki
10	John Crawford	Suzuki
11	Gordon Blackley	Kawasaki
12	Steven Marks	Yamaha
13	Dave Wood	Yamaha
14	Nigel Nottingham	Yamaha
15	Dave Redgate	Kawasaki

STANDINGS

Walker 398, Hodgson 377, Reynolds 369, Haydon 303, Mackenzie 177, Hislop 168

DONINGTON PARK
ROUND 12 – OCTOBER 8

RACE 1

Pos	Rider	Make
1	Neil Hodgson	Ducati
2	John Reynolds	Ducati
3	Chris Walker	Suzuki
4	James Haydon	Ducati
5	Steve Plater	Kawasaki
6	Niall Mackenzie	Ducati
7	John Crawford	Suzuki
8	Sean Emmett	Honda
9	Dave Jefferies	Yamaha
10	Anthony Gobert	Yamaha
11	John Crockford	Suzuki
12	Tom Kipp	Honda
13	Gordon Blackley	Kawasaki
14	Dave Wood	Yamaha
15	Francis Williamson	Yamaha

RACE 2

Pos	Rider	Make
1	James Haydon	Ducati
2	Neil Hodgson	Ducati
3	John Reynolds	Ducati
4	Niall Mackenzie	Ducati
5	Steve Plater	Kawasaki
6	Anthony Gobert	Yamaha
7	John Crawford	Suzuki
8	Alesandro Gramigni	Kawasaki
9	Michael Rutter	Yamaha
10	Sean Emmett	Honda
11	Tom Kipp	Honda
12	Shane Byrne	Honda
13	Gordon Blackley	Kawasaki
14	Dave Heal	Kawasaki
15	Dean Ellison	Honda

FINAL STANDINGS

Hodgson 422, Walker 414, Reynolds 405, Haydon 341, Mackenzie 200, Plater 176

LEFT Walker was always value for money on the Crescent Suzuki GSX-R750

2001 SEASON BRITISH SUPERBIKE CHAMPIONSHIP

DONINGTON PARK GP
ROUND 1 – APRIL 1

RACE 1

1	John Reynolds	Ducati
2	Steve Hislop	Ducati
3	John Crawford	Suzuki
4	Steve Plater	Kawasaki
5	Michael Rutter	Kawasaki
6	Paul Brown	Ducati
7	Shane Byrne	Suzuki
8	James Haydon	Yamaha
9	Dean Ellison	Honda
10	Francis Williamson	Yamaha
11	Jason Davis	Honda
12	Nigel Nottingham	Yamaha
13	Gordon Blackley	Kawasaki
14	Lee Jackson	Yamaha
15	Paul Jones	Kawasaki

RACE 2

1	John Reynolds	Ducati
2	James Haydon	Yamaha
3	John Crawford	Suzuki
4	Steve Hislop	Ducati
5	Michael Rutter	Kawasaki
6	Sean Emmett	Ducati
7	Paul Brown	Ducati
8	Shane Byrne	Suzuki
9	Jamie Robinson	Yamaha
10	Francis Williamson	Yamaha
11	Lee Jackson	Yamaha
12	Jason Davis	Honda
13	Gordon Blackley	Kawasaki
14	Steven Marks	Yamaha
15	Paul Jones	Kawasaki

STANDINGS

Reynolds 50, Hislop 33, Crawford 32, Haydon 28, Rutter 22, Brown 19

SILVERSTONE
ROUND 2 – APRIL 16

RACE 1

1	John Reynolds	Ducati
2	Steve Hislop	Ducati
3	John Crawford	Suzuki
4	James Haydon	Yamaha
5	Sean Emmett	Ducati
6	Michael Rutter	Kawasaki
7	Paul Brown	Ducati
8	Jamie Robinson	Yamaha
9	Shane Byrne	Suzuki
10	Gordon Blackley	Kawasaki
11	Lee Jackson	Yamaha
12	Nigel Nottingham	Yamaha
13	Dave Wood	Kawasaki
14	Steven Marks	Yamaha
15	Paul Jones*	Honda

RACE 2

1	Steve Hislop	Ducati
2	John Reynolds	Ducati
3	James Haydon	Yamaha
4	Sean Emmett	Ducati
5	John Crawford	Suzuki
6	Michael Rutter	Kawasaki
7	Jamie Robinson	Yamaha
8	Paul Brown	Ducati
9	Shane Byrne	Suzuki
10	Dean Ellison	Honda
11	Lee Jackson	Yamaha
12	Mark Burr	Kawasaki
13	Nigel Nottingham	Yamaha
14	Dave Wood	Kawasaki
15	Steven Marks	Yamaha

STANDINGS

Reynolds 95, Hislop 78, Crawford 59, Haydon 57, Rutter 42, Brown 36

SNETTERTON
ROUND 3 – MAY 7

RACE 1

1	John Reynolds	Ducati
2	Steve Hislop	Ducati
3	James Haydon	Yamaha
4	Sean Emmett	Ducati
5	Paul Brown	Ducati
6	Shane Byrne	Suzuki
7	John Crawford	Suzuki
8	Paul Jones*	Honda
9	Lee Jackson	Yamaha
10	Dave Wood	Kawasaki
11	Mark Burr	Kawasaki
12	Gordon Blackley	Kawasaki
13	Nigel Nottingham	Yamaha
14	Dean Ellison	Honda
15	Steven Marks	Yamaha

RACE 2

1	John Reynolds	Ducati
2	Steve Hislop	Ducati
3	James Haydon	Yamaha
4	Sean Emmett	Ducati
5	Paul Brown	Ducati
6	Shane Byrne	Suzuki
7	John Crawford	Suzuki
8	Jamie Robinson	Yamaha
9	Paul Jones*	Honda
10	Lee Jackson	Yamaha
11	Dave Wood	Kawasaki
12	Mark Burr	Kawasaki
13	Nigel Nottingham	Yamaha
14	Gordon Blackley	Kawasaki
15	Steven Marks	Yamaha

STANDINGS

Reynolds 145, Hislop 118, Haydon 89, Crawford 77, Emmett 50, Brown 58

OULTON PARK
ROUND 4 – MAY 13

RACE 1

1	Steve Hislop	Ducati
2	John Reynolds	Ducati
3	Sean Emmett	Ducati
4	Shane Byrne	Suzuki
5	Paul Brown	Ducati
6	Michael Rutter	Kawasaki
7	Jamie Morley	Kawasaki
8	Jamie Robinson	Yamaha
9	Dave Wood	Kawasaki
10	Nigel Nottingham	Yamaha
11	Paul Jones*	Honda
12	Jason Davis	Honda
13	Gordon Blackley	Kawasaki
14	Mark Burr	Kawasaki
15	Francis Williamson	Yamaha

RACE 2

1	Steve Hislop	Ducati
2	John Reynolds	Ducati
3	James Haydon	Yamaha
4	John Crawford	Suzuki
5	Michael Rutter	Kawasaki
6	Sean Emmett	Ducati
7	Paul Brown	Ducati
8	Shane Byrne	Suzuki
9	Lee Jackson	Yamaha
10	Paul Jones*	Honda
11	Dave Wood	Kawasaki
12	Gordon Blackley	Kawasaki
13	Nigel Nottingham	Yamaha
14	Jason Davis	Honda
15	Mark Burr	Kawasaki

STANDINGS

Reynolds 185, Hislop 168, Haydon 105, Crawford 90, Emmett 86, Brown 78

RIGHT Hislop at one of his favourite tracks – Cadwell

*Signifies Paul Jones of Liverpool, as opposed to Paul Jones of Cardiff

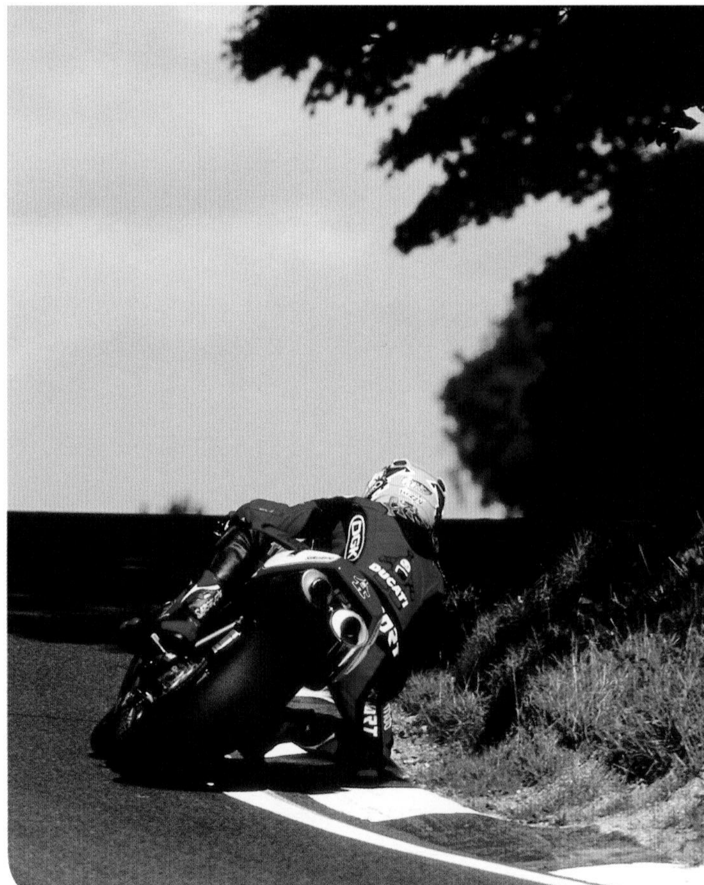

BRANDS HATCH GP
ROUND 5 – JUNE 17

RACE 1

1	Steve Hislop	Ducati
2	John Reynolds	Ducati
3	Steve Plater	Kawasaki
4	Michael Rutter	Kawasaki
5	Shane Byrne	Suzuki
6	Jamie Robinson	Yamaha
7	Dave Wood	Kawasaki
8	Lee Jackson	Yamaha
9	Jason Davis	Honda
10	Dean Ellison	Honda
11	Gordon Blackley	Kawasaki
12	Nigel Nottingham	Yamaha
13	Dave Redgate	Kawasaki
14	Peter Berwick	Honda
15	Mark Burr	Kawasaki

RACE 2

1	Steve Hislop	Ducati
2	Michael Rutter	Kawasaki
3	James Haydon	Yamaha
4	Shane Byrne	Suzuki
5	Steve Plater	Kawasaki
6	John Crawford	Suzuki
7	Paul Brown	Ducati
8	Lee Jackson	Yamaha
9	Nigel Nottingham	Yamaha
10	Jason Davis	Honda
11	Steve Marks	Yamaha
12	Dave Redgate	Kawasaki
13	Dean Ellison	Honda
14	Gordon Blackley	Kawasaki
15	Peter Berwick	Honda

STANDINGS

Hislop 218, Reynolds 205, Haydon 121, Crawford 100, Byrne & Rutter 96

THRUXTON
ROUND 6 – JULY 1

RACE 1		
1	Steve Hislop	Ducati
2	Steve Plater	Kawasaki
3	Sean Emmett	Ducati
4	John Reynolds	Ducati
5	James Haydon	Yamaha
6	Paul Brown	Ducati
7	Michael Rutter	Kawasaki
8	Shane Byrne	Suzuki
9	John Crawford	Suzuki
10	Lee Jackson	Yamaha
11	Jamie Robinson	Yamaha
12	Paul Jones*	Honda
13	Gordon Blackley	Kawasaki
14	Steven Marks	Yamaha
15	Mark Burr	Kawasaki

RACE 2		
1	John Reynolds	Ducati
2	James Haydon	Yamaha
3	Michael Rutter	Kawasaki
4	Sean Emmett	Ducati
5	Shane Byrne	Suzuki
6	Steve Hislop	Ducati
7	Paul Brown	Ducati
8	John Crawford	Suzuki
9	Jamie Robinson	Yamaha
10	Lee Jackson	Yamaha
11	Mark Burr	Kawasaki
12	Jason Davis	Honda
13	Nigel Nottingham	Yamaha
14	Paul Jones*	Honda
15	Dean Ellison	Honda

STANDINGS

Hislop 253, Reynolds 243, Haydon 152, Rutter 121, Byrne, Crawford & Emmett 115

OULTON PARK
ROUND 7 – JULY 22

RACE 1		
1	Steve Hislop	Ducati
2	John Reynolds	Ducati
3	James Haydon	Yamaha
4	Sean Emmett	Ducati
5	John Crawford	Suzuki
6	Paul Brown	Ducati
7	Jamie Robinson	Yamaha
8	Dean Ellison	Honda
9	Dave Wood	Kawasaki
10	Lee Jackson	Yamaha
11	Nigel Nottingham	Yamaha
12	Gordon Blackley	Kawasaki
13	Dave Redgate	Kawasaki
14	Peter Berwick	Honda
15	Steven Marks	Yamaha

RACE 2		
1	Steve Hislop	Ducati
2	John Reynolds	Ducati
3	James Haydon	Yamaha
4	Sean Emmett	Ducati
5	Paul Brown	Ducati
6	Michael Rutter	Kawasaki
7	Jamie Robinson	Yamaha
8	Shane Byrne	Suzuki
9	Dave Wood	Kawasaki
10	Dean Ellison	Honda
11	Lee Jackson	Yamaha
12	Nigel Nottingham	Yamaha
13	Jason Davis	Honda
14	Gordon Blackley	Kawasaki
15	Brett Sampson	Yamaha

STANDINGS

Hislop 303, Reynolds 283, Haydon 184, Emmett 141, Rutter 131, Brown 127

KNOCKHILL
ROUND 8 – AUGUST 12

RACE 1		
1	John Reynolds	Ducati
2	Sean Emmett	Ducati
3	Steve Hislop	Ducati
4	James Haydon	Yamaha
5	Niall Mackenzie	Suzuki
6	John Crawford	Suzuki
7	Paul Brown	Ducati
8	Shane Byrne	Suzuki
9	Jamie Robinson	Yamaha
10	Dean Ellison	Honda
11	Gordon Blackley	Kawasaki
12	Nigel Nottingham	Yamaha
13	Michael Rutter	Kawasaki
14	Mark Burr	Kawasaki

RACE 2		
1	John Reynolds	Ducati
2	Steve Hislop	Ducati
3	Sean Emmett	Ducati
4	Niall Mackenzie	Suzuki
5	Michael Rutter	Kawasaki
6	Shane Byrne	Suzuki
7	Paul Brown	Ducati
8	Jamie Robinson	Yamaha
9	Mark Burr	Kawasaki
10	Gordon Blackley	Kawasaki
11	Nigel Nottingham	Yamaha

STANDINGS

Hislop 339, Reynolds 333, Haydon 197, Emmett 177, Brown & Rutter 145

CADWELL PARK
ROUND 9 – AUGUST 27

RACE 1		
1	Steve Hislop	Ducati
2	James Haydon	Yamaha
3	John Reynolds	Ducati
4	Sean Emmett	Ducati
5	John Crawford	Suzuki
6	Michael Rutter	Kawasaki
7	Shane Byrne	Suzuki
8	Steve Plater	Yamaha
9	Lee Jackson	Yamaha
10	Dave Wood	Kawasaki
11	Dean Ellison	Honda
12	Mark Burr	Kawasaki
13	Gordon Blackley	Kawasaki
14	Jason Davis	Honda
15	Brett Sampson	Yamaha

RACE 2		
1	Steve Hislop	Ducati
2	John Reynolds	Ducati
3	Sean Emmett	Ducati
4	James Haydon	Yamaha
5	Michael Rutter	Kawasaki
6	Paul Brown	Ducati
7	Lee Jackson	Yamaha
8	Steve Plater	Yamaha
9	Jason Davis	Honda
10	Dean Ellison	Honda
11	John Crawford	Suzuki
12	Jamie Robinson	Yamaha
13	Mark Burr	Kawasaki
14	Paul Jones*	Honda
15	Steven Marks	Yamaha

STANDINGS

Hislop 389, Reynolds 369, Haydon 230, Emmett 206, Rutter 166, Brown 155

BRANDS HATCH INDY
ROUND 10 – SEPTEMBER 2

RACE 1		
1	Steve Hislop	Ducati
2	John Reynolds	Ducati
3	Sean Emmett	Ducati
4	James Haydon	Yamaha
5	Paul Brown	Ducati
6	John Crawford	Suzuki
7	Michael Rutter	Kawasaki
8	Shane Byrne	Suzuki
9	Jamie Robinson	Yamaha
10	Dean Ellison	Honda
11	Dave Wood	Kawasaki
12	Brett Sampson	Yamaha
13	Mark Burr	Kawasaki
14	Jason Davis	Honda
15	Steven Marks	Yamaha

RACE 2		
1	John Reynolds	Ducati
2	Steve Hislop	Ducati
3	Sean Emmett	Ducati
4	James Haydon	Yamaha
5	Paul Brown	Yamaha
6	Michael Rutter	Kawasaki
7	John Crawford	Suzuki
8	Shane Byrne	Suzuki
9	Jamie Robinson	Yamaha
10	Lee Jackson	Yamaha
11	Dean Ellison	Honda
12	Gordon Blackley	Kawasaki
13	Brett Sampson	Yamaha
14	Steven Marks	Yamaha
15	Nigel Nottingham	Yamaha

STANDINGS

Hislop 434, Reynolds 414, Haydon 256, Emmett 238, Rutter 185, Brown 178

MALLORY PARK
ROUND 11 – SEPTEMBER 16

RACE 1		
1	John Reynolds	Ducati
2	Sean Emmett	Ducati
3	Steve Hislop	Ducati
4	John Crawford	Suzuki
5	Paul Brown	Ducati
6	Steve Plater	Kawasaki
7	Jamie Robinson	Yamaha
8	Lee Jackson	Yamaha
9	Mark Burr	Kawasaki
10	Gordon Blackley	Kawasaki
11	Dean Ellison	Honda
12	Dave Wood	Kawasaki
13	Paul Jones*	Honda
14	Steven Marks	Yamaha
15	Peter Berwick	Honda

RACE 2		
1	Steve Hislop	Ducati
2	Paul Brown	Ducati
3	James Haydon	Yamaha
4	John Crawford	Suzuki
5	John Reynolds	Ducati
6	Steve Plater	Kawasaki
7	Shane Byrne	Suzuki
8	Sean Emmett	Ducati
9	Jamie Robinson	Yamaha
10	Lee Jackson	Yamaha
11	Mark Burr	Kawasaki
12	Jason Davis	Honda
13	Peter Berwick	Honda
14	Dave Wood	Kawasaki
15	Nigel Nottingham	Yamaha

STANDINGS

Hislop 475, Reynolds 450, Haydon 272, Emmett 268, Brown 208, Crawford 197

ROCKINGHAM
ROUND 12 – SEPTEMBER 30

RACE 1		
1	Sean Emmett	Ducati
2	Michael Rutter	Kawasaki
3	John Reynolds	Ducati
4	Paul Brown	Ducati
5	James Haydon	Yamaha
6	Lee Jackson	Yamaha
7	Dave Wood	Kawasaki
8	Nigel Nottingham	Yamaha
9	Dean Ellison	Honda
10	Steve Marks	Yamaha
11	Mark Burr	Kawasaki
12	John Crawford	Suzuki

RACE 2		
1	Michael Rutter	Kawasaki
2	John Reynolds	Ducati
3	Sean Emmett	Ducati
4	James Haydon	Yamaha
5	Shane Byrne	Suzuki
6	Paul Brown	Yamaha
7	Lee Jackson	Yamaha
8	Gordon Blackley	Kawasaki
9	Dean Ellison	Honda
10	Mark Burr	Kawasaki
11	Nigel Nottingham	Yamaha
12	Dave Wood	Kawasaki

STANDINGS

Reynolds 486, Hislop 475, Emmett 307, Haydon 296, Brown 231, Rutter 230

DONINGTON PARK NAT
ROUND 13 – OCTOBER 14

RACE 1		
1	John Reynolds	Ducati
2	Paul Brown	Ducati
3	Steve Plater	Yamaha
4	Sean Emmett	Ducati
5	John Crawford	Suzuki
6	Michael Rutter	Kawasaki
7	Shane Byrne	Suzuki
8	Jamie Robinson	Yamaha
9	Lee Jackson	Yamaha
10	Dean Ellison	Honda
11	Jason Davis	Honda
12	Gordon Blackley	Kawasaki
13	Nigel Nottingham	Yamaha
14	Mark Burr	Kawasaki
15	Paul Jones*	Honda

RACE 2		
1	John Reynolds	Ducati
2	James Haydon	Yamaha
3	Michael Rutter	Kawasaki
4	Paul Brown	Ducati
5	Steve Plater	Yamaha
6	John Crawford	Suzuki
7	Shane Byrne	Suzuki
8	Dean Ellison	Honda
9	Jamie Robinson	Yamaha
10	Sean Emmett	Ducati
11	Nigel Nottingham	Yamaha
12	Jason Davis	Honda
13	Paul Jones*	Honda
14	Mark Burr	Kawasaki

FINAL STANDINGS

Reynolds 536, Hislop 475, Emmett 326, Haydon 316, Brown 264, Rutter 256

2002 SEASON *MCN* BRITISH SUPERBIKE CHAMPIONSHIP

SILVERSTONE
ROUND 1 – APRIL 1

RACE 1

1	Sean Emmett	Ducati
2	Steve Hislop	Ducati
3	Steve Plater	Yamaha
4	John Reynolds	Suzuki
5	Shane Byrne	Ducati
6	Karl Harris	Suzuki
7	Michael Rutter	Ducati
8	Paul Brown	Ducati
9	Simon Crafar	Yamaha
10	Glen Richards	Kawasaki
11	Paul Jones	Yamaha
12	Jamie Morley	Suzuki
13	Dean Ellison	Ducati
14	Paul Young	Suzuki
15	Gary Mason	Honda

RACE 2

1	Steve Hislop	Ducati
2	John Reynolds	Suzuki
3	Sean Emmett	Ducati
4	Michael Rutter	Ducati
5	Paul Brown	Ducati
6	Steve Plater	Yamaha
7	Glen Richards	Kawasaki
8	Simon Crafar	Yamaha
9	Dean Thomas	Ducati
10	Dean Ellison	Ducati
11	Paul Jones*	Yamaha
12	Lee Jackson	Honda
13	Mark Burr	Kawasaki
14	Jamie Robinson	Honda
15	Shane Norval	Yamaha

STANDINGS

Hislop 45, Emmett 41, Reynolds 33, Plater 26, Rutter 22, Brown 19

BRANDS HATCH INDY
ROUND 2 – APRIL 14

RACE 1

1	Steve Hislop	Ducati
2	John Reynolds	Suzuki
3	Paul Brown	Ducati
4	Sean Emmett	Ducati
5	Shane Byrne	Ducati
6	Steve Plater	Yamaha
7	Michael Rutter	Ducati
8	Karl Harris	Suzuki
9	Simon Crafar	Yamaha
10	Gary Mason	Honda
11	Paul Jones*	Yamaha
12	Dean Ellison	Ducati
13	Dave Jefferies	Suzuki
14	Jamie Morley	Suzuki
15	Shane Norval	Yamaha

RACE 2

1	Steve Hislop	Ducati
2	Sean Emmett	Ducati
3	John Reynolds	Suzuki
4	Michael Rutter	Ducati
5	Paul Brown	Ducati
6	Steve Plater	Yamaha
7	Shane Byrne	Ducati
8	Dean Thomas	Ducati
9	Simon Crafar	Yamaha
10	Gary Mason	Honda
11	Dave Jefferies	Suzuki
12	Shane Norval	Yamaha
13	Lee Jackson	Honda
14	Phil Giles	Suzuki

STANDINGS

Hislop 95, Emmett 74, Reynolds 69, Brown & Plater 46, Rutter 44

DONINGTON PARK NAT
ROUND 3 – APRIL 28

RACE 1

1	Shane Byrne	Ducati
2	Steve Plater	Yamaha
3	Steve Hislop	Ducati
4	Michael Rutter	Ducati
5	Sean Emmett	Ducati
6	Glen Richards	Kawasaki
7	Dean Thomas	Ducati
8	Dean Ellison	Ducati
9	Paul Brown	Ducati
10	Paul Jones*	Yamaha
11	Jamie Robinson	Honda
12	Phil Giles	Suzuki
13	Shane Norval	Yamaha
14	Jason Davis	Suzuki
15	Marty Nutt	Suzuki

RACE 2

1	Michael Rutter	Ducati
2	Shane Byrne	Ducati
3	Simon Crafar	Yamaha
4	Sean Emmett	Ducati
5	Paul Brown	Ducati
6	Steve Hislop	Ducati
7	Steve Plater	Yamaha
8	Glen Richards	Kawasaki
9	Dean Thomas	Ducati
10	Dean Ellison	Ducati
11	Shane Norval	Yamaha
12	Karl Harris	Suzuki
13	Neil Faulkner	Suzuki
14	Marty Nutt	Suzuki
15	Gordon Blackley	Honda

STANDINGS

Hislop 121, Emmett 98, Rutter 82, Byrne 76, Plater 75, Reynolds 69

OULTON PARK
ROUND 4 – MAY 13

RACE 1

1	Steve Hislop	Ducati
2	Michael Rutter	Ducati
3	Sean Emmett	Ducati
4	Paul Brown	Ducati
5	John Reynolds	Suzuki
6	Steve Plater	Yamaha
7	Karl Harris	Suzuki
8	Shane Byrne	Ducati
9	Dean Ellison	Ducati
10	Glen Richards	Kawasaki
11	Simon Crafar	Yamaha
12	Gary Mason	Honda
13	Ross McCulloch	Ducati
14	Mark Burr	Kawasaki
15	Shane Norval	Yamaha

RACE 2

1	Michael Rutter	Ducati
2	Steve Hislop	Ducati
3	Sean Emmett	Ducati
4	Paul Brown	Ducati
5	John Reynolds	Suzuki
6	Karl Harris	Suzuki
7	Shane Byrne	Ducati
8	Dean Thomas	Ducati
9	Glen Richards	Kawasaki
10	Steve Plater	Yamaha
11	Dean Ellison	Ducati
12	Simon Crafar	Yamaha
13	Gary Mason	Honda
14	Shane Norval	Yamaha
15	Jason Davis	Suzuki

STANDINGS

Hislop 156, Emmett 122, Rutter 114.5, Byrne 88.5, Plater 88, Reynolds 85.5

SNETTERTON
ROUND 5 – JUNE 3

RACE 1

1	Sean Emmett	Ducati
2	John Reynolds	Suzuki
3	Steve Plater	Yamaha
4	Steve Hislop	Ducati
5	Paul Brown	Ducati
6	Simon Crafar	Yamaha
7	Giovanni Bussei	Suzuki
8	Dean Ellison	Ducati
9	Dean Thomas	Ducati
10	Adrian Coates	Suzuki
11	Mark Burr	Kawasaki
12	Jamie Robinson	Honda
13	Shane Norval	Yamaha
14	Marty Nutt	Suzuki
15	Jason Davis	Suzuki

RACE 2

1	Sean Emmett	Ducati
2	Steve Hislop	Ducati
3	Michael Rutter	Ducati
4	Steve Plater	Yamaha
5	Shane Byrne	Ducati
6	Paul Brown	Ducati
7	Simon Crafar	Yamaha
8	Glen Richards	Kawasaki
9	Dean Ellison	Ducati
10	Paul Jones*	Yamaha
11	Giovanni Bussei	Suzuki
12	Adrian Coates	Suzuki
13	Shane Norval	Yamaha
14	Jamie Robinson	Honda
15	Lee Jackson	Honda

STANDINGS

Hislop 189, Emmett 172, Rutter 130.5, Plater 117, Reynolds 105.5, Brown 104.5

BRANDS HATCH GP
ROUND 6 – JUNE 16

RACE 1

1	John Reynolds	Suzuki
2	Steve Plater	Yamaha
3	Michael Rutter	Ducati
4	Paul Brown	Ducati
5	Simon Crafar	Yamaha
6	Glen Richards	Kawasaki
7	Dean Ellison	Ducati
8	Giovanni Bussei	Suzuki
9	Shane Byrne	Ducati
10	Dean Thomas	Ducati
11	John Crawford	Suzuki
12	Steve Hislop	Ducati
13	Adrian Coates	Suzuki
14	Jamie Morley	Ducati
15	Mark Burr	Kawasaki

RACE 2

1	Sean Emmett	Ducati
2	Steve Hislop	Ducati
3	Michael Rutter	Ducati
4	John Reynolds	Suzuki
5	Shane Byrne	Ducati
6	Steve Plater	Yamaha
7	Paul Brown	Ducati
8	Giovanni Bussei	Suzuki
9	Simon Crafar	Yamaha
10	Dean Ellison	Ducati
11	Glen Richards	Kawasaki
12	Mark Burr	Kawasaki
13	Paul Jones*	Yamaha
14	Jamie Robinson	Honda
15	Shane Norval	Yamaha

STANDINGS

Hislop 213, Emmett 197, Rutter 162.5, Plater 147, Reynolds 143.5, Brown 126.5

ROCKINGHAM
ROUND 7 – JUNE 23

RACE 1

1	Michael Rutter	Ducati
2	Steve Hislop	Ducati
3	Sean Emmett	Ducati
4	Shane Byrne	Ducati
5	Dean Thomas	Ducati
6	John Reynolds	Suzuki
7	Glen Richards	Kawasaki
8	Jamie Morley	Ducati
9	Dave Jefferies	Suzuki
10	Dean Ellison	Ducati
11	Simon Crafar	Yamaha
12	Paul Young	Suzuki
13	Shane Norval	Yamaha
14	Paul Jones*	Yamaha
15	Gary Mason	Honda

RACE 2

1	Michael Rutter	Ducati
2	Sean Emmett	Ducati
3	Dean Thomas	Ducati
4	Steve Hislop	Ducati
5	Shane Byrne	Ducati
6	Glen Richards	Kawasaki
7	Jamie Morley	Ducati
8	Dave Jefferies	Suzuki
9	Mark Burr	Kawasaki
10	Dean Ellison	Ducati
11	Paul Young	Suzuki
12	Shane Norval	Yamaha
13	Jason Davis	Suzuki
14	Paul Jones*	Yamaha
15	Marty Nutt	Suzuki

STANDINGS

Hislop 246, Emmett 233, Rutter 212.5, Reynolds 153.5, Plater 147, Byrne 141.5

KNOCKHILL
ROUND 8 – JULY 7

RACE 1

1	Steve Hislop	Ducati
2	Sean Emmett	Ducati
3	Michael Rutter	Ducati
4	Paul Brown	Ducati
5	John Reynolds	Suzuki
6	Simon Crafar	Yamaha
7	Dave Jefferies	Suzuki
8	Glen Richards	Kawasaki
9	Paul Jones*	Yamaha
10	Dean Ellison	Ducati
11	Marty Nutt	Suzuki
12	Jon Kirkham	Suzuki
13	Jason Davis	Suzuki
14	Mark Burr	Kawasaki
15	Jamie Robinson	Honda

RACE 2

1	Shane Byrne	Ducati
2	Paul Brown	Ducati
3	Sean Emmett	Ducati
4	John Reynolds	Suzuki
5	Steve Plater	Yamaha
6	Glen Richards	Kawasaki
7	Steve Hislop	Ducati
8	Dean Thomas	Ducati
9	Simon Crafar	Yamaha
10	Dean Ellison	Ducati
11	Jamie Morley	Ducati
12	Paul Jones*	Yamaha
13	Mark Burr	Kawasaki
14	Paul Young	Suzuki
15	Jason Davis	Suzuki

STANDINGS

Hislop 280, Emmett 269, Rutter 228.5, Reynolds 177.5, Byrne 166.5, Brown 159.5

THRUXTON
ROUND 9 – AUGUST 11

RACE 1

1	Michael Rutter	Ducati
2	Steve Hislop	Ducati
3	Sean Emmett	Yamaha
4	John Reynolds	Suzuki
5	Simon Crafar	Yamaha
6	Shane Byrne	Ducati
7	Steve Plater	Yamaha
8	Glen Richards	Kawasaki
9	Dean Thomas	Ducati
10	John Crawford	Suzuki
11	John Crockford	Suzuki
12	Karl Harris	Suzuki
13	Gary Mason	Honda
14	Mark Burr	Kawasaki
15	Dean Ellison	Ducati

RACE 2

1	Shane Byrne	Ducati
2	Steve Hislop	Ducati
3	Sean Emmett	Yamaha
4	Steve Plater	Yamaha
5	Glen Richards	Kawasaki
6	Karl Harris	Suzuki
7	Simon Crafar	Yamaha
8	Dean Thomas	Ducati
9	John Crawford	Suzuki
10	Mark Burr	Kawasaki
11	Jason Davis	Yamaha
12	Shane Norval	Yamaha
13	Lee Jackson	Yamaha
14	Paul Young	Suzuki
15	Jamie Robinson	Honda

STANDINGS

Hislop 320, Emmett 301, Rutter 253.5, Byrne 201.5, Reynolds 190.5, Plater 180

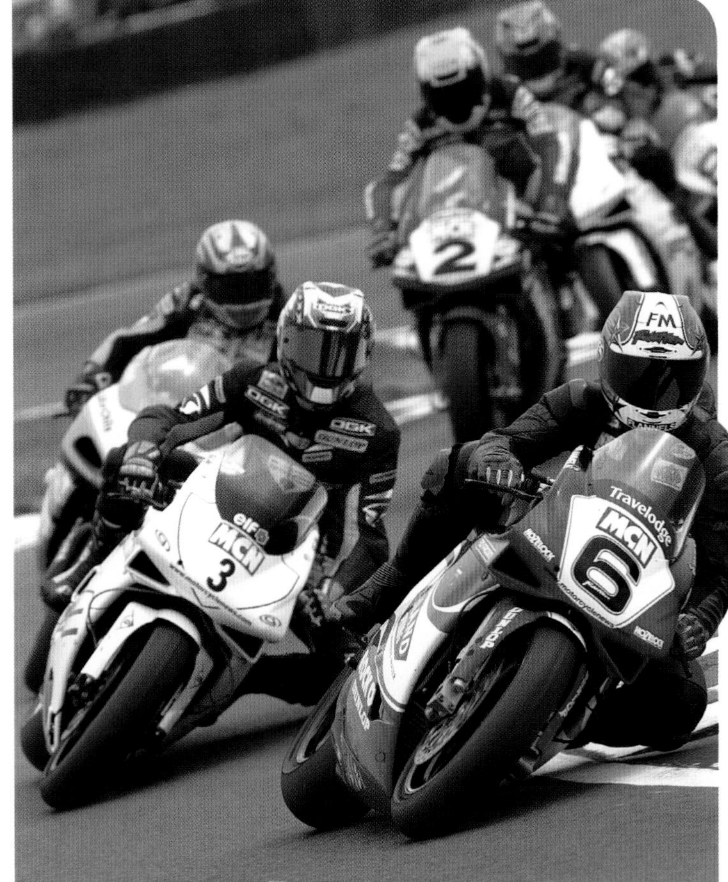

*Signifies Paul Jones of Liverpool, as opposed to Paul Jones of Cardiff

LEFT Rutter leads Emmett, Reynolds and Hislop through the Oulton Park chicane

CADWELL PARK
ROUND 10 – AUGUST 26

RACE 1

1	Steve Hislop	Ducati
2	Shane Byrne	Ducati
3	Michael Rutter	Ducati
4	John Reynolds	Suzuki
5	Sean Emmett	Yamaha
6	Simon Crafar	Yamaha
7	Glen Richards	Kawasaki
8	Karl Harris	Suzuki
9	Gary Mason	Honda
10	John Crawford	Suzuki
11	Mark Burr	Kawasaki
12	Dean Ellison	Ducati
13	Paul Young	Suzuki
14	Phil Giles	Suzuki
15	Paul Jones*	Yamaha

RACE 2

1	Steve Hislop	Ducati
2	Michael Rutter	Ducati
3	Shane Byrne	Ducati
4	John Reynolds	Suzuki
5	Steve Plater	Yamaha
6	Sean Emmett	Yamaha
7	Karl Harris	Suzuki
8	John Crawford	Suzuki
9	Mark Burr	Kawasaki
10	Dean Ellison	Ducati
11	Paul Young	Suzuki
12	Paul Jones*	Yamaha
13	Jason Davis	Yamaha
14	Phil Giles	Suzuki
15	Lee Jackson	Yamaha

STANDINGS

Hislop 370, Emmett 322, Rutter 289.5, Byrne 237.5, Reynolds 216.5, Plater 191

OULTON PARK
ROUND 11 – SEPTEMBER 1

RACE 1

1	Steve Hislop	Ducati
2	Shane Byrne	Ducati
3	Michael Rutter	Ducati
4	Steve Plater	Yamaha
5	Karl Harris	Suzuki
6	Glen Richards	Kawasaki
7	John Crawford	Suzuki
8	John Reynolds	Suzuki
9	Sean Emmett	Yamaha
10	Dean Thomas	Ducati
11	Paul Young	Suzuki
12	Adrian Coates	Suzuki
13	Dean Ellison	Ducati
14	Phil Giles	Suzuki
15	Jamie Robinson	Honda

RACE 2

1	Steve Plater	Yamaha
2	John Reynolds	Suzuki
3	Simon Crafar	Yamaha
4	Karl Harris	Suzuki
5	Michael Rutter	Ducati
6	Sean Emmett	Yamaha
7	John Crawford	Suzuki
8	Dean Thomas	Ducati
9	Paul Young	Suzuki
10	Gary Mason	Honda
11	Adrian Coates	Suzuki
12	Dean Ellison	Ducati
13	Phil Giles	Suzuki
14	Jamie Robinson	Honda
15	Lee Jackson	Yamaha

STANDINGS

Hislop 395, Emmett 339, Rutter 316.5, Byrne 275.5, Reynolds 244.5, Plater 229

MALLORY PARK
ROUND 12 – SEPTEMBER 15

RACE 1

1	Steve Plater	Yamaha
2	Sean Emmett	Yamaha
3	Michael Ruter	Ducati
4	Shane Byrne	Ducati
5	Glen Richards	Kawasaki
6	Steve Hislop	Ducati
7	Karl Harris	Suzuki
8	John Crawford	Suzuki
9	Simon Crafar	Yamaha
10	Dean Ellison	Ducati
11	Paul Young	Suzuki
12	Dean Thomas	Ducati
13	Gary Mason	Honda
14	Phil Giles	Suzuki
15	Adrian Coates	Suzuki

RACE 2

1	Michael Rutter	Ducati
2	Sean Emmett	Yamaha
3	Steve Plater	Yamaha
4	Shane Byrne	Ducati
5	Steve Hislop	Ducati
6	Glen Richards	Kawasaki
7	John Reynolds	Suzuki
8	Karl Harris	Suzuki
9	John Crawford	Suzki
10	Simon Crafar	Yamaha
11	Gary Mason	Honda
12	Paul Young	Suzuki
13	Adrian Coates	Suzuki
14	Dean Thomas	Ducati
15	Phil Giles	Suzuki

STANDINGS

Hislop 416, Emmett 379, Rutter 357.5, Byrne 283.5, Plater 270, Reynolds 253.5

DONINGTON PARK GP
ROUND 13 – SEPTEMBER 29

RACE 1

1	Michael Rutter	Ducati
2	John Reynolds	Suzuki
3	Steve Hislop	Ducati
4	Glen Richards	Kawasaki
5	Simon Crafar	Yamaha
6	John Crawford	Suzuki
7	Karl Harris	Suzuki
8	Dean Ellison	Ducati
9	Dean Thomas	Ducati
10	Gary Mason	Honda
11	Phil Giles	Suzuki
12	Lee Jackson	Yamaha
13	Jon Kirkham	Suzuki
14	Adrian Coates	Suzuki
15	Simon Smith	Suzuki

RACE 2

1	Michael Rutter	Ducati
2	Steve Hislop	Ducati
3	Steve Plater	Yamaha
4	Glen Richards	Kawasaki
5	Shane Byrne	Ducati
6	John Reynolds	Suzuki
7	Dean Ellison	Ducati
8	John Crawford	Suzuki
9	Gary Mason	Honda
10	Simon Crafar	Yamaha
11	Dean Thomas	Ducati
12	Paul Brown	Ducati
13	Phil Giles	Suzuki
14	Mark Burr	Kawasaki
15	Lee Jackson	Yamaha

FINAL STANDINGS

Hislop 452, Rutter 407.5, Emmett 379, Byrne 294.5, Plater 286, Reynolds 283.5

2003 SEASON BRITISH SUPERBIKE CHAMPIONSHIP POWERED BY HALLS

SILVERSTONE
ROUND 1 – MARCH 30

RACE 1

Pos	Rider	Make
1	Shane Byrne	Ducati
2	Yukio Kagayama	Suzuki
3	Glen Richards	Kawasaki
4	Michael Rutter	Ducati
5	Gary Mason	Yamaha
6	Scott Smart	Kawasaki
7	Dean Ellison	Ducati
8	Steve Hislop	Yamaha
9	Lee Jackson	Kawasaki
10	Dean Thomas	Yamaha
11	Paul Jones	Suzuki

RACE 2

Pos	Rider	Make
1	Michael Rutter	Ducati
2	Shane Byrne	Ducati
3	Glen Richards	Kawasaki
4	Yukio Kagayama	Suzuki
5	Steve Hislop	Yamaha
6	John Crawford	Ducati
7	Scott Smart	Kawasaki
8	Gary Mason	Yamaha
9	Dean Thomas	Yamaha
10	Steve Plater	Honda
11	Lee Jackson	Kawasaki
12	Paul Jones	Suzuki

STANDINGS
Byrne 45, Rutter 38, Kagayama 33, Richards 32, Hislop, Mason & Smart 19

SNETTERTON
ROUND 2 – APRIL 13

RACE 1

Pos	Rider	Make
1	Michael Rutter	Ducati
2	Shane Byrne	Ducati
3	John Reynolds	Suzuki
4	Steve Plater	Honda
5	Glen Richards	Kawasaki
6	John Crawford	Ducati
7	Paul Young	Yamaha
8	Gary Mason	Yamaha
9	Scott Smart	Kawasaki
10	Jon Kirkham	Yamaha
11	Lee Jackson	Kawasaki
12	Nick Medd	Ducati
13	Mike Walker	Yamaha
14	Paul Jones	Suzuki

RACE 2

Pos	Rider	Make
1	Shane Byrne	Ducati
2	Sean Emmett	Ducati
3	John Reynolds	Suzuki
4	Gary Mason	Yamaha
5	Yukio Kagayama	Suzuki
6	John Crawford	Ducati
7	Mark Heckles	Honda
8	Steve Plater	Honda
9	Paul Young	Yamaha
10	Scott Smart	Kawasaki
11	Jon Kirkham	Yamaha
12	Lee Jackson	Kawasaki
13	Nick Medd	Ducati
14	Paul Jones	Suzuki
15	Mike Walker	Yamaha

STANDINGS
Byrne 90, Rutter 63, Kagayama 44, Richards 43, Mason 40, Reynolds & Smart 32

THURXTON
ROUND 3 – APRIL 20

RACE 1

Pos	Rider	Make
1	Shane Byrne	Ducati
2	Steve Hislop	Yamaha
3	Michael Rutter	Ducati
4	Glen Richards	Kawasaki
5	Steve Plater	Honda
6	Sean Emmett	Ducati
7	Gary Mason	Yamaha
8	Mark Heckles	Honda
9	Yukio Kagayama	Suzuki
10	John Crawford	Ducati
11	Lee Jackson	Kawasaki
12	John Reynolds	Suzuki
13	Scott Smart	Kawasaki
14	Paul Young	Yamaha
15	Francis Williamson	Yamaha

RACE 2

Pos	Rider	Make
1	Shane Byrne	Ducati
2	Michael Rutter	Ducati
3	Glen Richards	Kawasaki
4	Steve Plater	Honda
5	Steve Hislop	Yamaha
6	Gary Mason	Yamaha
7	Sean Emmett	Ducati
8	Mark Heckles	Honda
9	Yukio Kagayama	Suzuki
10	Dean Ellison	Ducati
11	Scott Smart	Kawasaki
12	Lee Jackson	Kawasaki
13	John Crawford	Ducati
14	Francis Williamson	Yamaha
15	Paul Young	Yamaha

STANDINGS
Byrne 140, Rutter 99, Richards 72, Mason 59, Kagayama 58, Plater 51

OULTON PARK
ROUND 4 – MAY 5

RACE 1

Pos	Rider	Make
1	Shane Byrne	Ducati
2	Michael Rutter	Ducati
3	Steve Hislop	Yamaha
4	Steve Plater	Honda
5	Yukio Kagayama	Suzuki
6	John Crawford	Ducati
7	Gary Mason	Yamaha
8	John Reynolds	Suzuki
9	Glen Richards	Kawasaki
10	Mark Heckles	Honda
11	Jon Kirkham	Yamaha
12	Scott Smart	Kawasaki
13	Lee Jackson	Kawasaki
14	Paul Young	Yamaha
15	Nick Medd	Ducati

RACE 2

Pos	Rider	Make
1	Shane Byrne	Ducati
2	John Reynolds	Suzuki
3	Michael Rutter	Ducati
4	Yukio Kagayama	Suzuki
5	Steve Hislop	Yamaha
6	Mark Heckles	Honda
7	Dean Ellison	Ducati
8	Glen Richards	Kawasaki
9	Gary Mason	Yamaha
10	John Crawford	Ducati
11	Paul Young	Yamaha
12	Lee Jackson	Kawasaki
13	Scott Smart	Kawasaki
14	Dave Wood	Suzuki
15	Francis Williamson	Yamaha

STANDINGS
Byrne 190, Rutter 135, Richards 87, Kagayama 82, Hislop 77, Mason 75

RIGHT Shane Byrne went unbeaten in eight races in the first half of the season to establish a stranglehold on the 2003 championship

KNOCKHILL
ROUND 5 – MAY 18

RACE 1

1	Shane Byrne	Ducati
2	Paul Young	Yamaha
3	John Reynolds	Suzuki
4	Steve Plater	Honda
5	Sean Emmett	Ducati
6	Glen Richards	Kawasaki
7	Gary Mason	Yamaha
8	John McGuinness	Ducati
9	John Crawford	Ducati
10	Yukio Kagayama	Suzuki
11	Lee Jackson	Kawasaki
12	Scott Smart	Kawasaki
13	Steve Hislop	Yamaha
14	Dennis Hobbs	Suzuki
15	Francis Williamson	Yamaha

RACE 2

1	Shane Byrne	Ducati
2	John Reynolds	Suzuki
3	Steve Plater	Honda
4	Glen Richards	Kawasaki
5	Steve Hislop	Yamaha
6	Gary Mason	Yamaha
7	Yukio Kagayama	Suzuki
8	Sean Emmett	Ducati
9	Paul Young	Yamaha
10	John McGuinness	Ducati
11	Scott Smart	Kawasaki
12	Lee Jackson	Kawasaki
13	Jon Kirkham	Yamaha
14	Dave Wood	Suzuki
15	Dennis Hobbs	Suzuki

STANDINGS

Byrne 240, Rutter 136, Richards 110, Reynolds 100, Kagayama 97, Mason 94

BRANDS HATCH GP
ROUND 6 – JUNE 22

RACE 1

1	Shane Byrne	Ducati
2	John Reynolds	Suzuki
3	Steve Plater	Honda
4	Gary Mason	Yamaha
5	Steve Hislop	Yamaha
6	Glen Richards	Kawasaki
7	Scott Smart	Kawasaki
8	John McGuinness	Ducati
9	John Crawford	Ducati
10	Lee Jackson	Kawasaki
11	Nick Medd	Ducati
12	Dennis Hobbs	Suzuki
13	Francis Williamson	Yamaha
14	Jeremy Goodall	Yamaha
15	Adam Hitchcox	Suzuki

RACE 2

1	John Reynolds	Suzuki
2	Shane Byrne	Ducati
3	Michael Rutter	Ducati
4	Sean Emmett	Ducati
5	Glen Richards	Kawasaki
6	Gary Mason	Yamaha
7	Steve Hislop	Yamaha
8	Steve Plater	Honda
9	Scott Smart	Kawasaki
10	Yukio Kagayama	Suzuki
11	John Crawford	Ducati
12	John McGuinness	Ducati
13	Lee Jackson	Kawasaki
14	Nick Medd	Ducati
15	Dave Wood	Suzuki

STANDINGS

Byrne 285, Rutter 152, Reynolds 145, Richards 131, Mason & Plater 117

ROCKINGHAM
ROUND 7 – JULY 6

RACE 1

1	Yukio Kagayama	Suzuki
2	Shane Byrne	Ducati
3	Steve Plater	Honda
4	Michael Rutter	Ducati
5	John Reynolds	Suzuki
6	Glen Richards	Kawasaki
7	Sean Emmett	Ducati
8	Leon Haslam	Ducati
9	Scott Smart	Kawasaki
10	Steve Hislop	Yamaha
11	Jon Kirkham	Yamaha
12	Lee Jackson	Kawasaki
13	Jamie Morley	Suzuki
14	Dennis Hobbs	Suzuki
15	Dave Wood	Suzuki

RACE 2

1	Yukio Kagayama	Suzuki
2	Shane Byrne	Ducati
3	Michael Rutter	Ducati
4	Steve Plater	Honda
5	John Reynolds	Suzuki
6	Scott Smart	Kawasaki
7	Gary Mason	Yamaha
8	Sean Emmett	Ducati
9	Leon Haslam	Ducati
10	Mark Heckles	Honda
11	Steve Hislop	Yamaha
12	Paul Young	Yamaha
13	Lee Jackson	Kawasaki
14	Jamie Morley	Suzuki
15	Dennis Hobbs	Suzuki

STANDINGS

Byrne 325, Rutter 181, Reynolds 167, Kagayama 153, Plater 148, Richards 141

MONDELLO PARK
ROUND 8 – JULY 20

RACE 1

1	John Reynolds	Suzuki
2	Sean Emmett	Ducati
3	Yukio Kagayama	Suzuki
4	Glen Richards	Kawasaki
5	Michael Rutter	Ducati
6	Steve Plater	Honda
7	Gary Mason	Yamaha
8	Scott Smart	Kawasaki
9	Shane Byrne	Ducati
10	Leon Haslam	Ducati
11	Mark Heckles	Honda
12	Jon Kirkham	Yamaha
13	Dennis Hobbs	Suzuki
14	Lee Jackson	Kawasaki
15	Hilton Hincks	Honda

RACE 2

1	John Reynolds	Suzuki
2	Shane Byrne	Ducati
3	Glen Richards	Kawasaki
4	Gary Mason	Yamaha
5	Michael Rutter	Ducati
6	Steve Plater	Honda
7	Leon Haslam	Ducati
8	Sean Emmett	Ducati
9	Mark Heckles	Honda
10	Paul Young	Yamaha
11	Jon Kirkham	Yamaha
12	Lee Jackson	Kawasaki
13	Scott Smart	Kawasaki
14	Hilton Hincks	Honda
15	Dave Wood	Suzuki

STANDINGS

Byrne 352, Reynolds 217, Rutter 203, Richards 170, Kagayama 169, Plater 166

OULTON PARK
ROUND 9 – AUGUST 10

RACE 1

1	Steve Plater	Honda
2	Yukio Kagayama	Suzuki
3	Sean Emmett	Ducati
4	Michael Rutter	Ducati
5	Glen Richards	Kawasaki
6	Scott Smart	Kawasaki
7	Mark Heckles	Honda
8	Leon Haslam	Ducati
9	Dave Wood	Suzuki
10	Dean Ellison	Ducati
11	Paul Young	Yamaha
12	Lee Jackson	Kawasaki
13	Dennis Hobbs	Suzuki
14	Jason Vincent	Yamaha
15	Sam Corke	Suzuki

RACE 2

1	Yukio Kagayama	Suzuki
2	John Reynolds	Suzuki
3	Sean Emmett	Ducati
4	Shane Byrne	Ducati
5	Steve Plater	Honda
6	Michael Rutter	Ducati
7	Leon Haslam	Ducati
8	Glen Richards	Kawasaki
9	Mark Heckles	Honda
10	Scott Smart	Kawasaki
11	Dave Wood	Suzuki
12	Dean Ellison	Ducati
13	Paul Young	Yamaha
14	Jason Vincent	Yamaha
15	Lee Jackson	Kawasaki

STANDINGS

Byrne 365, Reynolds 237, Rutter 226, Kagayama 214, Plater 202, Richards 189

CADWELL PARK
ROUND 10 – AUGUST 25

RACE 1

1	Shane Byrne	Ducati
2	John Reynolds	Suzuki
3	Michael Rutter	Ducati
4	Gary Mason	Yamaha
5	Glen Richards	Kawasaki
6	Scott Smart	Kawasaki
7	Sean Emmett	Ducati
8	Dennis Hobbs	Suzuki
9	Lee Jackson	Kawasaki
10	Nick Medd	Ducati
11	Jeremy Goodall	Yamaha
12	Phil Giles	Suzuki
13	James Buckingham	Suzuki
14	Sam Corke	Suzuki
15	Gordon Blackley	Honda

RACE 2

1	Steve Plater	Honda
2	John Reynolds	Suzuki
3	Shane Byrne	Ducati
4	Leon Haslam	Ducati
5	Gary Mason	Yamaha
6	Glen Richards	Kawasaki
7	Sean Emmett	Ducati
8	Chris Burns	Yamaha
9	Lee Jackson	Kawasaki
10	Dean Ellison	Ducati
11	Jon Kirkham	Yamaha
12	Dennis Hobbs	Suzuki
13	Jeremy Goodall	Yamaha
14	Dave Wood	Suzuki
15	Nick Medd	Ducati

STANDINGS

Byrne 406, Reynolds 277, Rutter 243, Plater 227, Kagayama 214, Richards 210

BRANDS HATCH INDY
ROUND 11 – SEPTEMBER 14

RACE 1

1	John Reynolds	Suzuki
2	Sean Emmett	Ducati
3	Shane Byrne	Ducati
4	Michael Rutter	Ducati
5	Glen Richards	Kawasaki
6	Gary Mason	Yamaha
7	Steve Plater	Honda
8	Scott Smart	Kawasaki
9	Leon Haslam	Ducati
10	Chris Burns	Yamaha
11	Mark Heckles	Honda
12	Jon Kirkham	Yamaha
13	Lee Jackson	Kawasaki
14	Sam Corke	Suzuki
15	Dean Ellison	Ducati

RACE 2

1	Sean Emmett	Ducati
2	John Reynolds	Suzuki
3	Shane Byrne	Ducati
4	Glen Richards	Kawasaki
5	Leon Haslam	Ducati
6	Steve Plater	Honda
7	Gary Mason	Yamaha
8	Scott Smart	Kawasaki
9	Michael Rutter	Ducati
10	Mark Heckles	Honda
11	Jon Kirkham	Yamaha
12	Chris Burns	Yamaha
13	Dean Ellison	Ducati
14	Tom Sykes	Suzuki
15	Dave Wood	Suzuki

STANDINGS

Byrne 438, Reynolds 322, Rutter 263, Plater 246, Richards 234, Kagayama 214

DONINGTON PARK GP
ROUND 12 – SEPTEMBER 28

RACE 1

1	Shane Byrne	Ducati
2	Sean Emmett	Ducati
3	John Reynolds	Suzuki
4	Michael Rutter	Ducati
5	Glen Richards	Kawasaki
6	Scott Smart	Kawasaki
7	Leon Haslam	Ducati
8	Gary Mason	Yamaha
9	Dean Ellison	Ducati
10	Jon Kirkham	Yamaha
11	Mark Heckles	Honda
12	Dennis Hobbs	Suzuki
13	Lee Jackson	Kawasaki
14	Dave Wood	Suzuki
15	Sam Corke	Suzuki

RACE 2

1	Shane Byrne	Ducati
2	John Reynolds	Suzuki
3	Sean Emmett	Ducati
4	Michael Rutter	Ducati
5	Leon Haslam	Ducati
6	Glen Richards	Kawasaki
7	Gary Mason	Yamaha
8	Jon Kirkham	Yamaha
9	Mark Heckles	Honda
10	Dennis Hobbs	Suzuki
11	Phil Giles	Suzuki
12	James Buckingham	Suzuki
13	Sam Corke	Suzuki
14	Vince Whittle	Ducati
15	Gordon Blackley	Honda

FINAL STANDINGS

Byrne 488, Reynolds 358, Rutter 289, Richards 255, Emmett 247, Plater 246

2004 SEASON THINK! BRITISH SUPERBIKE CHAMPIONSHIP

SILVERSTONE
ROUND 1 – MARCH 28

RACE 1

1	Michael Rutter	Honda
2	Ryuichi Kiyonari	Honda
3	John Reynolds	Suzuki
4	Yukio Kagayama	Suzuki
5	Sean Emmett	Ducati
6	Marty Nutt	Yamaha
7	Scott Smart	Kawasaki
8	Dean Thomas	Ducati
9	Glen Richards	Kawasaki
10	Craig Coxhell	Honda
11	Stuart Easton	Ducati
12	James Ellison	Yamaha
13	Jon Kirkham	Suzuki
14	Tommy Hill	Yamaha
15	Sam Corke	Suzuki

RACE 2

1	John Reynolds	Suzuki
2	Ryuichi Kiyonari	Honda
3	Michael Rutter	Honda
4	Sean Emmett	Ducati
5	Scott Smart	Kawasaki
6	Dean Thomas	Ducati
7	Stuart Easton	Ducati
8	Gary Mason	Yamaha
9	Steve Plater	Yamaha
10	Tommy Hill	Yamaha
11	Jon Kirkham	Suzuki
12	Craig Coxhell	Honda
13	Dennis Hobbs	Suzuki
14	Dean Ellison	Ducati
15	James Ellison	Yamaha

STANDINGS

Reynolds & Rutter 41, Kyonari 40, Emmett 24, Smart 21, Thomas 19

BRANDS HATCH INDY
ROUND 2 – APRIL 12

RACE 1

1	John Reynolds	Suzuki
2	Michael Rutter	Honda
3	Yukio Kagayama	Suzuki
4	Scott Smart	Kawasaki
5	Gary Mason	Yamaha
6	Ryuichi Kiyonari	Honda
7	Sam Corke	Suzuki
8	Jon Kirkham	Suzuki
9	Tommy Hill	Yamaha
10	Kieran Clarke	Yamaha
11	Steve Plater	Yamaha
12	Dennis Hobbs	Suzuki
13	Malcolm Ashley	Ducati
14	James Ellison	Yamaha
15	James Buckingham	Suzuki

RACE 2

1	Sean Emmett	Ducati
2	Michael Rutter	Honda
3	John Reynolds	Suzuki
4	Scott Smart	Kawasaki
5	Yukio Kagayama	Suzuki
6	Ryuichi Kiyonari	Honda
7	Glen Richards	Kawasaki
8	Dean Thomas	Ducati
9	Gary Mason	Yamaha
10	Tommy Hill	Yamaha
11	Jon Kirkham	Suzuki
12	Steve Plater	Yamaha
13	Kieran Clarke	Yamaha
14	Dennis Hobbs	Suzuki
15	James Buckingham	Suzuki

STANDINGS

Reynolds 82, Rutter 81,Kiyonari 60, Emmett 49, Smart 47, Kagayama 40

SNETTERTON
ROUND 3 – APRIL 25

RACE 1

1	Yukio Kagayama	Suzuki
2	John Reynolds	Suzuki
3	Michael Rutter	Honda
4	Sean Emmett	Ducati
5	Scott Smart	Kawasaki
6	Dean Thomas	Ducati
7	Ryuichi Kiyonari	Honda
8	Tommy Hill	Yamaha
9	Glen Richards	Kawasaki
10	James Haydon	Ducati
11	James Ellison	Yamaha
12	Dennis Hobbs	Suzuki
13	Sam Corke	Suzuki
14	James Buckingham	Suzuki
15	Chris Martin	Suzuki

RACE 2

1	John Reynolds	Suzuki
2	Michael Rutter	Honda
3	Sean Emmett	Ducati
4	Yukio Kagayama	Suzuki
5	Dean Thomas	Ducati
6	Scott Smart	Kawasaki
7	Glen Richards	Kawasaki
8	Steve Plater	Yamaha
9	Ryuichi Kiyonari	Honda
10	Tommy Hill	Yamaha
11	Gary Mason	Yamaha
12	James Ellison	Yamaha
13	Craig Coxhell	Honda
14	James Haydon	Ducati
15	Kieran Clarke	Yamaha

STANDINGS

Reynolds 127, Rutter 117, Emmett & Kagayama 78, Kiyonari 76, Smart 68

OULTON PARK
ROUND 4 – MAY 3

RACE 1

1	Yukio Kagayama	Suzuki
2	John Reynolds	Suzuki
3	Michael Rutter	Honda
4	Dean Thomas	Ducati
5	Scott Smart	Kawasaki
6	Glen Richards	Kawasaki
7	Gary Mason	Yamaha
8	Sean Emmett	Ducati
9	Tommy Hill	Yamaha
10	James Ellison	Yamaha
11	Craig Coxhell	Honda
12	Dennis Hobbs	Suzuki
13	Sam Corke	Suzuki
14	Jon Kirkham	Suzuki
15	James Buckingham	Suzuki

RACE 2

1	Yukio Kagayama	Suzuki
2	John Reynolds	Suzuki
3	Michael Rutter	Honda
4	Dean Thomas	Ducati
5	Scott Smart	Kawasaki
6	Leon Haslam	Ducati
7	Gary Mason	Yamaha
8	James Ellison	Yamaha
9	Glen Richards	Kawasaki
10	Noriyuki Haga	Ducati
11	Craig Coxhell	Honda
12	Jon Kirkham	Suzuki
13	Kieran Clarke	Yamaha
14	Tommy Hill	Yamaha
15	James Buckingham	Suzuki

STANDINGS

Reynolds 167, Rutter 149, Kagayama 128, Smart 89, Emmett 86, Kiyonari 76

MONDELLO PARK
ROUND 5 – MAY 23

RACE 1

1	Scott Smart	Kawasaki
2	John Reynolds	Suzuki
3	Glen Richards	Kawasaki
4	Yukio Kagayama	Suzuki
5	Dean Thomas	Ducati
6	Sean Emmett	Ducati
7	James Buckingham	Suzuki
8	Craig Coxhell	Honda
9	James Haydon	Yamaha
10	Kieran Clarke	Yamaha
11	Jon Kirkham	Suzuki
12	Dennis Hobbs	Suzuki
13	James Ellison	Yamaha
14	Sam Corke	Suzuki
15	Derek Shiels	Suzuki

RACE 2

1	Michael Rutter	Honda
2	John Reynolds	Suzuki
3	Scott Smart	Kawasaki
4	Glen Richards	Kawasaki
5	Yukio Kagayama	Suzuki
6	Tommy Hill	Yamaha
7	Sean Emmett	Ducati
8	Kieran Clarke	Yamaha
9	Craig Coxhell	Honda
10	James Buckingham	Suzuki
11	Dennis Hobbs	Suzuki
12	James Haydon	Yamaha
13	Jon Kirkham	Suzuki
14	Stuart Easton	Ducati
15	Cameron Donald	Suzuki

STANDINGS

Reynolds 207, Rutter 174, Kagayama 152, Smart 130, Emmett 105, Thomas 84

THRUXTON
ROUND 6 – JUNE 6

RACE 1

1	Michael Rutter	Honda
2	John Reynolds	Suzuki
3	Sean Emmett	Ducati
4	Gregorio Lavilla	Suzuki
5	Dean Thomas	Ducati
6	Scott Smart	Kawasaki
7	Gary Mason	Yamaha
8	James Ellison	Yamaha
9	Tommy Hill	Yamaha
10	Kieran Clarke	Yamaha
11	Craig Coxhell	Honda
12	James Buckingham	Suzuki
13	Ryuichi Kiyonari	Honda
14	Jonn Kirkham	Suzuki
15	Stuart Easton	Ducati

RACE 2

1	Sean Emmett	Ducati
2	Michael Rutter	Honda
3	Gregorio Lavilla	Suzuki
4	Scott Smart	Kawasaki
5	James Ellison	Yamaha
6	Tommy Hill	Yamaha
7	Kieran Clarke	Yamaha
8	Ryuichi Kiyonari	Honda
9	Craig Coxhell	Honda
10	James Buckingham	Suzuki
11	Jon Kirkham	Suzuki
12	Stuart Easton	Ducati
13	Dennis Hobbs	Suzuki
14	Sam Corke	Suzuki
15	Cameron Donald	Suzuki

STANDINGS

Reynolds 227, Rutter 219, Smart 153, Kagayama 152, Emmett 146, Thomas 95

BRANDS HATCH GP
ROUND 7 – JUNE 20

RACE 1

1	John Reynolds	Suzuki
2	Sean Emmett	Ducati
3	John McGuinness	Kawasaki
4	Yukio Kagayama	Suzuki
5	Michael Rutter	Honda
6	James Haydon	Yamaha
7	Tommy Hill	Yamaha
8	Leon Haslam	Ducati
9	Sam Corke	Suzuki
10	Dean Thomas	Ducati
11	Dennis Hobbs	Suzuki
12	Chris Platt	Kawasaki
13	Jon Kirkham	Suzuki
14	Craig Coxhell	Honda
15	James Ellison	Yamaha

RACE 2

1	Leon Haslam	Ducati
2	Sean Emmett	Ducati
3	Yukio Kagayama	Suzuki
4	James Haydon	Yamaha
5	Scott Smart	Kawasaki
6	John McGuinness	Kawasaki
7	John Reynolds	Suzuki
8	Tommy Hill	Yamaha
9	Craig Coxhell	Honda
10	Gary Mason	Yamaha
11	Steve Brogan	Yamaha
12	Sam Corke	Suzuki
13	James Ellison	Yamaha
14	Michael Rutter	Honda
15	Dennis Hobbs	Suzuki

STANDINGS

Reynolds 261, Rutter 232, Emmett 186, Kagayama 181, Smart 164, Thomas 101

KNOCKHILL
ROUND 8 – JULY 4

RACE 1

1	Scott Smart	Kawasaki
2	James Haydon	Yamaha
3	Yukio Kagayama	Suzuki
4	John Reynolds	Suzuki
5	Jon Kirkham	Suzuki
6	Gary Mason	Yamaha
7	James Ellison	Yamaha
8	Iain MacPherson	Ducati
9	Michael Rutter	Honda
10	Ryuichi Kiyonari	Honda
11	Chris Platt	Kawasaki
12	Kieran Clarke	Yamaha
13	Chris Martin	Suzuki
14	Dennis Hobbs	Suzuki
15	Craig Coxhell	Honda

RACE 2

1	James Haydon	Yamaha
2	Sean Emmett	Ducati
3	John Reynolds	Suzuki
4	Michael Rutter	Honda
5	Yukio Kagayama	Suzuki
6	Scott Smart	Kawasaki
7	John McGuinness	Kawasaki
8	Craig Coxhell	Honda
9	Dean Thomas	Ducati
10	James Ellison	Yamaha
11	Jon Kirkham	Yamaha
12	Kieran Clarke	Yamaha
13	Sam Corke	Suzuki
14	Ryuichi Kiyonari	Honda
15	Dennis Hobbs	Suzuki

STANDINGS

Reynolds 290, Rutter 252, Kagayama 208, Emmett 206, Smart 199, Thomas 108

MALLORY PARK
ROUND 9 – JULY 17

RACE 1

1	John Reynolds	Suzuki
2	Yukio Kagayama	Suzuki
3	Scott Smart	Kawasaki
4	Ryuichi Kiyonari	Honda
5	James Haydon	Yamaha
6	Michael Rutter	Honda
7	Sean Emmett	Ducati
8	Dean Thomas	Ducati
9	John McGuinness	Kawasaki
10	Dennis Hobbs	Suzuki
11	Steve Plater	Yamaha
12	Kieran Clarke	Yamaha
13	Iain MacPherson	Ducati
14	Gary Mason	Yamaha
15	James Ellison	Yamaha

RACE 2

1	Scott Smart	Kawasaki
2	John Reynolds	Suzuki
3	Ryuichi Kiyonari	Honda
4	James Haydon	Yamaha
5	Sean Emmett	Ducati
6	Tommy Hill	Yamaha
7	Gary Mason	Yamaha
8	Dean Thomas	Ducati
9	John McGuinness	Kawasaki
10	Steve Plater	Yamaha
11	Craig Coxhell	Honda
12	Dennis Hobbs	Suzuki
13	James Ellison	Yamaha
14	Iain MacPherson	Ducati
15	Yukio Kagayama	Suzuki

STANDINGS

Reynolds 335, Rutter 262, Smart 240, Kagayama 229, Emmett 226, Kiyonari & Thomas 124

CROFT
ROUND 10 – AUGUST 15

RACE 1

1	Michael Rutter	Honda
2	Yukio Kagayama	Suzuki
3	Scott Smart	Kawasaki
4	Ryuichi Kiyonari	Honda
5	John Reynolds	Suzuki
6	James Haydon	Yamaha
7	Sean Emmett	Ducati
8	Dean Thomas	Ducati
9	Tommy Hill	Yamaha
10	John McGuinness	Kawasaki
11	James Ellison	Yamaha
12	Paul Brown	Ducati
13	Craig Coxhell	Honda
14	Dennis Hobbs	Suzuki
15	Jon Kirkham	Suzuki

RACE 2

1	Michael Rutter	Honda
2	Scott Smart	Kawasaki
3	John Reynolds	Suzuki
4	Ryuichi Kiyonari	Honda
5	James Haydon	Yamaha
6	Gary Mason	Yamaha
7	John McGuinness	Kawasaki
8	Craig Coxhell	Honda
9	James Ellison	Yamaha
10	Steve Plater	Yamaha
11	Sean Emmett	Ducati
12	Paul Brown	Ducati
13	Jon Kirkham	Suzuki
14	Dennis Hobbs	Suzuki
15	James Buckingham	Suzuki

STANDINGS

Reynolds 362, Rutter 312, Smart 276, Kagayama 249, Emmett 240, Kiyonari 150

CADWELL PARK
ROUND 11 – AUGUST 30

RACE 1

1	Michael Rutter	Honda
2	Ryuichi Kiyonari	Honda
3	Yukio Kagayama	Suzuki
4	James Haydon	Yamaha
5	Tommy Hill	Yamaha
6	Dean Thomas	Ducati
7	Glen Richards	Kawasaki
8	Kieran Clarke	Yamaha
9	John McGuinness	Kawasaki
10	Sean Emmett	Ducati
11	Gary Mason	Yamaha
12	Jon Kirkham	Suzuki
13	Paul Brown	Ducati
14	James Ellison	Yamaha
15	Chris Martin	Suzuki

RACE 2

1	Yukio Kagayama	Suzuki
2	Scott Smart	Kawasaki
3	Sean Emmett	Ducati
4	Dean Thomas	Ducati
5	Glen Richards	Kawasaki
6	James Haydon	Yamaha
7	Kieran Clarke	Yamaha
8	John Reynolds	Suzuki
9	John McGuinness	Kawasaki
10	James Ellison	Yamaha
11	Sam Corke	Suzuki
12	Gus Scott	Suzuki
13	Craig Coxhell	Honda
14	Jon Kirkham	Suzuki
15	Michael Pensavalle	Ducati

STANDINGS

Reynolds 370, Rutter 337, Smart 296, Kagayama 290, Emmett 262, Kiyonari 170

OULTON PARK
ROUND 12 – SEPTEMBER 11

RACE 1

1	John Reynolds	Suzuki
2	Michael Rutter	Honda
3	Yukio Kagayama	Suzuki
4	Sean Emmett	Ducati
5	Steve Plater	Yamaha
6	Glen Richards	Kawasaki
7	Dean Thomas	Ducati
8	Scott Smart	Kawasaki
9	Tommy Hill	Yamaha
10	Paul Brown	Ducati
11	Gary Mason	Yamaha
12	Ryuichi Kiyonari	Honda
13	John McGuinness	Kawasaki
14	James Haydon	Yamaha
15	James Ellison	Yamaha

RACE 2

1	John Reynolds	Suzuki
2	Michael Rutter	Honda
3	Yukio Kagayama	Suzuki
4	Sean Emmett	Ducati
5	Dean Thomas	Ducati
6	Ryuichi Kiyonari	Honda
7	Steve Plater	Yamaha
8	James Haydon	Yamaha
9	Glen Richard	Kawasaki
10	Tommy Hill	Yamaha
11	Kieran Clarke	Yamaha
12	Craig Coxhell	Honda
13	James Ellison	Yamaha
14	Jon Kirkham	Suzuki
15	James Buckingham	Suzuki

STANDINGS

Reynolds 420, Rutter 377, Kagayama 322, Smart 304, Emmett 288, Kiyonari 184

DONINGTON PARK
ROUND 13 – SEPTEMBER 19

RACE 1

1	Ryuichi Kiyonari	Honda
2	Michael Rutter	Honda
3	John Reynolds	Suzuki
4	Scott Smart	Kawasaki
5	Sean Emmett	Ducati
6	Glen Richards	Kawasaki
7	Dean Thomas	Ducati
8	James Haydon	Yamaha
9	Gary Mason	Yamaha
10	Tommy Hill	Yamaha
11	James Ellison	Yamaha
12	Jon Kirkham	Suzuki
13	Chris Martin	Suzuki
14	Yukio Kagayama	Suzuki
15	James Buckingham	Suzuki

RACE 2

1	Ryuichi Kiyonari	Honda
2	Michael Rutter	Honda
3	Sean Emmett	Ducati
4	Scott Smart	Kawasaki
5	Yukio Kagayama	Suzuki
6	John Reynolds	Suzuki
7	Dean Thomas	Ducati
8	James Haydon	Yamaha
9	James Ellison	Yamaha
10	Steve Plater	Yamaha
11	John McGuinness	Kawasaki
12	Gary Mason	Yamaha
13	Paul Brown	Ducati
14	Tommy Hill	Yamaha
15	Craig Coxhell	Honda

FINAL STANDINGS

Reynolds 446, Rutter 417, Kagayama 335, Smart 330, Emmett 315, Kiyonari 234

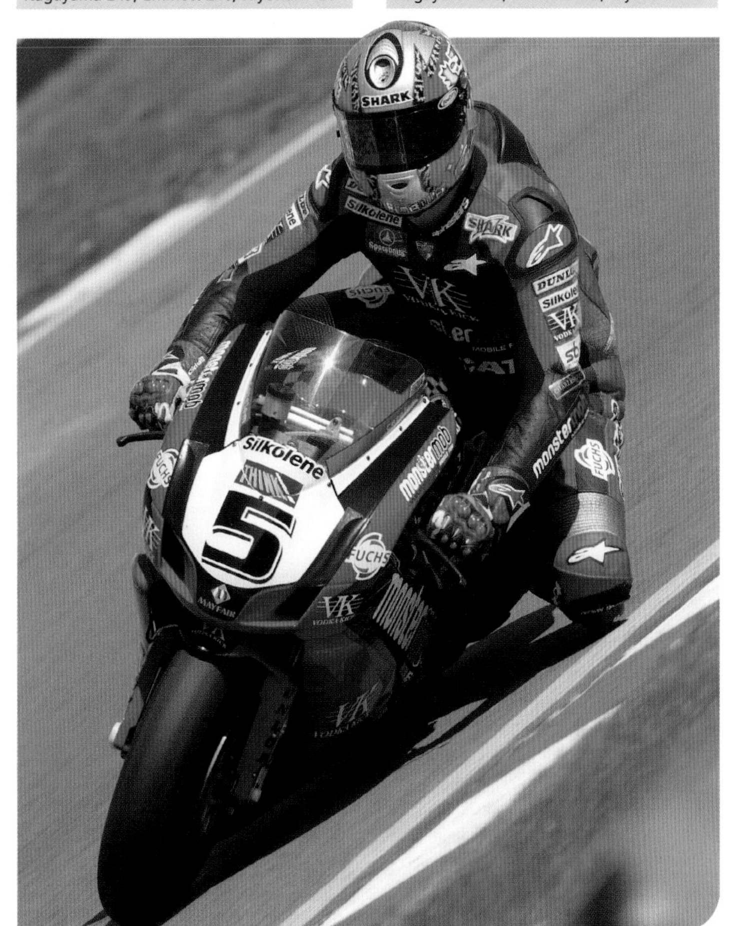

LEFT Sean Emmett complained bitterly about the Ducati 999's inability to change direction and hold a line, but he still won races at Brands and Thruxton

2005 SEASON BENNETTS BRITISH SUPERBIKE CHAMPIONSHIP

BRANDS HATCH INDY
ROUND 1 – MARCH 28

RACE 1

1	Ryuichi Kiyonari	Honda
2	Gregorio Lavilla	Ducati
3	Glen Richards	Kawasaki
4	Michael Rutter	Honda
5	Sean Emmett	Yamaha
6	Karl Harris	Honda
7	Jeremy McWilliams	Honda
8	Dean Thomas	Kawasaki
9	John Reynolds	Suzuki
10	Tommy Hill	Yamaha
11	Ben Wilson	Kawasaki
12	Danny Beaumont	Honda
13	Jonathan Rea	Honda
14	Tristan Palmer	Kawasaki
15	Michael Laverty	Honda

RACE 2

1	Ryuichi Kiyonari	Honda
2	Michael Rutter	Honda
3	Gregorio Lavilla	Ducati
4	Leon Haslam	Ducati
5	Sean Emmett	Yamaha
6	Karl Harris	Honda
7	Glen Richards	Kawasaki
8	Scott Smart	Suzuki
9	John Reynolds	Suzuki
10	Gary Mason	Honda
11	Dean Thomas	Kawasaki
12	Tommy Hill	Yamaha
13	Ben Wilson	Kawasaki
14	John McGuinness	Yamaha
15	Michael Laverty	Honda

STANDINGS

Kiyonari 50, Lavilla 36, Rutter 33, Richards 25, Emmett 22, Harris 20

THRUXTON
ROUND 2 – APRIL 10

RACE 1

1	Ryuichi Kiyonari	Honda
2	Michael Rutter	Honda
3	Gregorio Lavilla	Ducati
4	Leon Haslam	Ducati
5	Sean Emmett	Yamaha
6	Karl Harris	Honda
7	Scott Smart	Suzuki
8	Dean Thomas	Kawasaki
9	Glen Richards	Kawasaki
10	Tommy Hill	Yamaha
11	James Buckingham	Suzuki
12	Gary Mason	Honda
13	Steve Plater	Kawasaki
14	John Reynolds	Suzuki
15	Michael Laverty	Honda

RACE 2

1	Ryuichi Kiyonari	Honda
2	Gregorio Lavilla	Ducati
3	Michael Rutter	Honda
4	Sean Emmett	Yamaha
5	Glen Richards	Kawasaki
6	Dean Thomas	Kawasaki
7	Leon Haslam	Ducati
8	Karl Harris	Honda
9	Jeremy McWilliams	Honda
10	Steve Plater	Kawasaki
11	Kieran Clarke	Honda
12	Jonathan Rea	Honda
13	Gary Mason	Honda
14	Steve Brogan	Honda
15	Ben Wilson	Kawasaki

STANDINGS

Kiyonari 100, Lavilla 72, Rutter 69, Emmett 46, Richards 43, Harris 38

MALLORY PARK
ROUND 3 – APRIL 24

RACE 1

1	Michael Rutter	Honda
2	Glen Richards	Kawasaki
3	Leon Haslam	Ducati
4	Sean Emmett	Yamaha
5	Scott Smart	Suzuki
6	Dean Thomas	Kawasaki
7	Michael Laverty	Honda
8	Gary Mason	Honda
9	Danny Beaumont	Honda
10	Steve Brogan	Honda
11	John McGuinness	Yamaha
12	Dennis Hobbs	Yamaha
13	Tristan Palmer	Kawasaki
14	Jonathan Rea	Honda
15	James Buckingham	Suzuki

RACE 2

1	Michael Rutter	Honda
2	Glen Richards	Kawasaki
3	Gregorio Lavilla	Ducati
4	Dean Thomas	Kawasaki
5	Leon Haslam	Ducati
6	Karl Harris	Honda
7	Gary Mason	Honda
8	Scott Smart	Suzuki
9	Michael Laverty	Honda
10	Sean Emmett	Yamaha
11	Ben Wilson	Kawasaki
12	John McGuinness	Yamaha
13	Tristan Palmer	Kawasaki
14	Jonathan Rea	Honda
15	Kieran Clarke	Honda

STANDINGS

Rutter 119, Kiyonari 100, Lavilla 88, Richards 83, Emmett 65, Haslam 62

OULTON PARK
ROUND 4 – MAY 2

RACE 1

1	Michael Rutter	Honda
2	Gregorio Lavilla	Ducati
3	Karl Harris	Honda
4	Leon Haslam	Ducati
5	Glen Richards	Kawasaki
6	Dean Thomas	Kawasaki
7	Gary Mason	Honda
8	James Haydon	Suzuki
9	Scott Smart	Suzuki
10	Kieran Clarke	Honda
11	Steve Plater	Kawasaki
12	Jonathan Rea	Honda
13	Michael Laverty	Honda
14	John Laverty	Honda
15	Ben Wilson	Kawasaki

RACE 2

1	Leon Haslam	Ducati
2	Michael Rutter	Honda
3	Karl Harris	Honda
4	James Haydon	Suzuki
5	Julian da Costa	Kawasaki
6	Glen Richards	Kawasaki
7	Steve Plater	Kawasaki
8	Kieran Clarke	Honda
9	Jonathan Rea	Honda
10	Michael Laverty	Honda
11	Sean Emmett	Yamaha
12	Jon Kirkham	Kawasaki
13	Tristan Palmer	Kawasaki
14	Ben Wilson	Kawasaki
15	Dean Thomas	Kawasaki

STANDINGS

Rutter 164, Lavilla 108, Richards 104, Kiyonari & Haslam100, Harris 80

MONDELLO PARK
ROUND 5 – MAY 15

RACE 1

1	Ryuichi Kiyonari	Honda
2	Michael Rutter	Honda
3	Gregorio Lavilla	Ducati
4	Karl Harris	Honda
5	Scott Smart	Suzuki
6	Michael Laverty	Honda
7	Sean Emmett	Yamaha
8	Gary Mason	Honda
9	Jeremy McWilliams	Honda
10	James Haydon	Suzuki
11	Kieran Clarke	Honda
12	Jon Kirkham	Kawasaki
13	Ben Wilson	Kawasaki
14	Steve Plater	Kawasaki
15	Dean Thomas	Kawasaki

RACE 2

1	Gregorio Lavilla	Ducati
2	Leon Haslam	Ducati
3	Ryuichi Kiyonari	Honda
4	Michael Laverty	Honda
5	Michael Rutter	Honda
6	Glen Richards	Kawasaki
7	Karl Harris	Honda
8	Scott Smart	Suzuki
9	Gary Mason	Honda
10	Jeremy McWilliams	Hond
11	Steve Plater	Kawasaki
12	Jon Kirkham	Kawasaki
13	Dean Thomas	Kawasaki
14	Tommy Hill	Yamaha
15	Ben Wilson	Kawasaki

STANDINGS

Rutter 195, Lavilla 149, Kiyonari 141, Haslam 120, Richards 114, Harris 102

CROFT
ROUND 6 – JUNE 4

RACE 1

1	Ryuichi Kiyonari	Honda
2	Michael Rutter	Honda
3	Gregorio Lavilla	Ducati
4	Michael Laverty	Honda
5	Glen Richards	Kawasaki
6	Leon Haslam	Ducati
7	Jonathan Rea	Honda
8	James Haydon	Yamaha
9	Gary Mason	Honda
10	Dean Thomas	Kawasaki
11	Steve Plater	Kawasaki
12	Ben Wilson	Kawasaki
13	Scott Smart	Suzuki
14	Marty Nutt	Honda
15	Steve Brogan	Honda

RACE 2

1	Gregorio Lavilla	Ducati
2	Michael Rutter	Honda
3	Ryuichi Kiyonari	Honda
4	Glen Richards	Kawasaki
5	Gary Mason	Honda
6	Dean Thomas	Kawasaki
7	Steve Plater	Kawasaki
8	Kieran Clarke	Honda
9	Steve Brogan	Honda
10	John Laverty	Honda
11	Chris Martin	Suzuki
12	John Reynolds	Suzuki
13	Scott Smart	Suzuki
14	James Buckingham	Suzuki
15	Tristan Palmer	Kawasaki

STANDINGS

Rutter 235, Lavilla 190, Kiyonari 182, Richards 138, Haslam 130, Harris 102

KNOCKHILL
ROUND 7 – JUNE 26

RACE 1

1	Ryuichi Kiyonari	Honda
2	Michael Rutter	Honda
3	Michael Laverty	Honda
4	Glen Richards	Kawasaki
5	Leon Haslam	Ducati
6	Gregorio Lavilla	Ducati
7	John Reynolds	Suzuki
8	Karl Harris	Honda
9	Gary Mason	Honda
10	Dean Thomas	Kawasaki
11	James Buckingham	Suzuki
12	Scott Smart	Kawasaki
13	Tristan Palmer	Kawasaki
14	Ben Wilson	Kawasaki
15	Tommy Hill	Yamaha

RACE 2

1	Ryuichi Kiyonari	Honda
2	Michael Rutter	Honda
3	Gregorio Lavilla	Ducati
4	Michael Laverty	Honda
5	Leon Haslam	Ducati
6	John Reynolds	Suzuki
7	Glen Richards	Kawasaki
8	James Haydon	Suzuki
9	Jonathan Rea	Honda
10	Dean Thomas	Kawasaki
11	Karl Harris	Honda
12	Tommy Hill	Yamaha
13	Gary Mason	Honda
14	Kieran Clarke	Honda
15	Tristan Palmer	Kawasaki

STANDINGS

Rutter 275, Kiyonari 232, Lavilla 216, Richards 160, Haslam 152, Harris 115

SNETTERTON
ROUND 8 – JULY 10

RACE 1

1	Ryuichi Kiyonari	Honda
2	Leon Haslam	Ducati
3	John Reynolds	Suzuki
4	James Haydon	Suzuki
5	Michael Rutter	Honda
6	Karl Harris	Honda
7	Steve Plater	Honda
8	Gary Mason	Honda
9	Ben Wilson	Kawasaki
10	Tommy Hill	Yamaha
11	Dean Thomas	Ducati
12	Richard Wren	Yamaha
13	Tristan Palmer	Kawasaki
14	Scott Smart	Kawasaki
15	Dennis Hobbs	Yamaha

RACE 2

1	Gregorio Lavilla	Ducati
2	Michael Laverty	Honda
3	Michael Rutter	Honda
4	John Reynolds	Suzuki
5	Steve Plater	Honda
6	Ben Wilson	Kawasaki
7	Tommy Hill	Yamaha
8	Gary Mason	Honda
9	Dean Thomas	Kawasaki
10	Chris Burns	Yamaha
11	Danny Beaumont	Honda
12	Richard Wren	Yamaha
13	Lee Jackson	Kawasaki
14	Scott Smart	Kawasaki
15	Steve Brogan	Honda

STANDINGS

Rutter 302, Kiyonari 257, Lavilla 241, Haslam 172, Richards 160, Harris 125

SILVERSTONE
ROUND 9 – AUGUST 21

RACE 1

1	Gregorio Lavilla	Ducati
2	Leon Haslam	Ducati
3	John Reynolds	Suzuki
4	Karl Harris	Honda
5	Glen Richards	Kawasaki
6	Dean Thomas	Kawasaki
7	Gary Mason	Honda
8	Ryuichi Kiyonari	Honda
9	Tommy Hill	Yamaha
10	James Haydon	Suzuki
11	Steve Plater	Honda
12	Jonathan Rea	Honda
13	Dennis Hobbs	Yamaha
14	Tristan Palmer	Kawasaki
15	Michael Rutter	Honda

RACE 2

1	Ryuichi Kiyonari	Honda
2	Gregorio Lavilla	Ducati
3	Leon Haslam	Ducati
4	Michael Rutter	Honda
5	Glen Richards	Kawasaki
6	Dean Thomas	Kawasaki
7	Gary Mason	Honda
8	James Haydon	Suzuki
9	Karl Harris	Honda
10	Tommy Hill	Yamaha
11	Jonathan Rea	Honda
12	James Buckingham	Suzuki
13	Dennis Hobbs	Yamaha
14	Tristan Palmer	Kawasaki
15	Kieran Clarke	Honda

STANDINGS

Rutter 316, Kiyonari 290, Lavilla 286, Haslam 208, Richards 182, Harris 145

LEFT Rutter won races early in the year but his title challenge faded later in the season

CADWELL PARK
ROUND 10 – AUGUST 29

RACE 1

1	Tommy Hill	Yamaha
2	Gregorio Lavilla	Ducati
3	Glen Richards	Kawasaki
4	Karl Harris	Honda
5	Ryuichi Kiyonari	Honda
6	Leon Haslam	Ducati
7	James Haydon	Suzuki
8	Michael Rutter	Honda
9	Dean Thomas	Kawasaki
10	James Buckingham	Suzuki
11	Gary Mason	Honda
12	John Reynolds	Suzuki
13	Sean Emmett	Yamaha
14	Ben Wilson	Kawasaki
15	Danny Beaumont	Honda

RACE 2

1	Leon Haslam	Ducati
2	Gregorio Lavilla	Ducati
3	Ryuichi Kiyonari	Honda
4	Tommy Hill	Yamaha
5	Karl Harris	Honda
6	James Haydon	Suzuki
7	Dean Thomas	Kawasaki
8	John Reynolds	Suzuki
9	Steve Plater	Honda
10	Gary Mason	Honda
11	James Buckingham	Suzuki
12	Tristan Palmer	Kawasaki
13	Kieran Clarke	Honda
14	Chris Martin	Suzuki
15	Glen Richards	Kawasaki

STANDINGS

Lavilla 326, Rutter 324, Kiyonari 317, Haslam 243, Richards 199, Harris 169

OULTON PARK
ROUND 11 – SEPTEMBER 11

RACE 1

1	Ryuichi Kiyonari	Honda
2	Gregorio Lavilla	Ducati
3	John Reynolds	Suzuki
4	Leon Haslam	Ducati
5	Glen Richards	Kawasaki
6	James Haydon	Suzuki
7	Tommy Hill	Yamaha
8	Karl Harris	Honda
9	Gary Mason	Honda
10	Michael Rutter	Honda
11	Dean Thomas	Kawasaki
12	James Buckingham	Suzuki
13	Sean Emmett	Yamaha
14	Ben Wilson	Kawasaki
15	Tristan Palmer	Kawasaki

RACE 2

1	Ryuichi Kiyonari	Honda
2	Gregorio Lavilla	Ducati
3	John Reynolds	Suzuki
4	Leon Haslam	Ducati
5	Karl Harris	Honda
6	Tommy Hill	Yamaha
7	Dean Thomas	Kawasaki
8	Glen Richards	Kawasaki
9	Gary Mason	Honda
10	Steve Plater	Honda
11	Sean Emmett	Yamaha
12	James Buckingham	Suzuki
13	Richard Wren	Yamaha
14	Steve Brogan	Honda
15	John McGuinness	Honda

STANDINGS

Kiyonari 367, Lavilla 366, Rutter 330, Haslam 289, Richards 218, Harris 188

DONINGTON PARK
ROUND 12 – SEPTEMBER 25

RACE 1

1	Gregorio Lavilla	Ducati
2	Ryuichi Kiyonari	Honda
3	Leon Haslam	Ducati
4	Glen Richards	Kawasaki
5	John Reynolds	Suzuki
6	Michael Rutter	Honda
7	Scott Smart	Kawasaki
8	Tommy Hill	Yamaha
9	Dean Thomas	Ducati
10	Gary Mason	Honda
11	Steve Plater	Honda
12	Ben Wilson	Kawasaki
13	Sean Emmett	Yamaha
14	Julien da Costa	Kawasaki
15	James Buckingham	Suzuki

RACE 2

1	Gregorio Lavilla	Ducati
2	Leon Haslam	Ducati
3	Ryuichi Kiyonari	Honda
4	Michael Rutter	Honda
5	James Haydon	Suzuki
6	Dean Thomas	Kawasaki
7	Gary Mason	Honda
8	Scott Smart	Kawasaki
9	Karl Harris	Honda
10	Michael Laverty	Honda
11	Jonathan Rea	Honda
12	Dean Ellison	Honda
13	Ben Wilson	Kawasaki
14	Marty Nutt	Honda
15	Luke Quigley	Yamaha

STANDINGS

Lavilla 416, Kiyonari 403, Rutter 353, Haslam 305, Richards 231, Harris 195

BRANDS HATCH
ROUND 13 – OCTOBER 9

RACE 1

1	Gregorio Lavilla	Ducati
2	Leon Haslam	Ducati
3	James Haydon	Suzuki
4	Ryuichi Kiyonari	Honda
5	Dean Thomas	Kawasaki
6	Michael Rutter	Honda
7	Gary Mason	Honda
8	Steve Plater	Honda
9	Jeremy McWilliams	Honda
10	Jonathan Rea	Honda
11	Michael Laverty	Honda
12	Scott Smart	Kawasaki
13	Ben Wilson	Kawasaki
14	Kieran Clarke	Honda
15	David Johnson	Kawasaki

RACE 2

1	Leon Haslam	Ducati
2	Gregorio Lavilla	Ducati
3	Steve Plater	Honda
4	Ryuichi Kiyonari	Honda
5	Dean Thomas	Kawasaki
6	Glen Richards	Kawasaki
7	Gary Mason	Honda
8	Michael Rutter	Honda
9	Tommy Hill	Yamaha
10	Jonathan Rea	Honda
11	Michael Laverty	Honda
12	Ben Wilson	Kawasaki
13	Danny Beaumont	Honda
14	James Buckingham	Suzuki
15	Sean Emmett	Yamaha

FINAL STANDINGS

Lavilla 461, Kiyonari 429, Rutter 371, Haslam 360, Richards 241, Thomas 198

INDEX

PERSONALITIES